THE TASTE OF BEER

THE TASTE OF BEER

ROGER PROTZ

SEVEN
DIALS

Pro bono cerevisiam

First published in the United Kingdom in 1998 by
Weidenfeld & Nicolson

This paperback edition first published in 2000 by
Seven Dials, Cassell & Co
Wellington House, 125 Strand
London, WC2R 0BB

Distributed in the United States of America by
Sterling Publishing Co., Inc.
387 Park Avenue South,
New York, NY 10016-8810

A CIP catalogue record for this book is available
from the British Library

ISBN 1 84188 066 3

Styled by Nigel Soper
Designed by KingfisherDesign
Copy edited by Anthony Lambert
Printed in Italy

CONTENTS

ACKNOWLEDGEMENTS

First and foremost to my friend, colleague and fellow beer writer Ted Bruning who had the idea and generously passed on the light bulb.

IN GREAT BRITAIN
Caroline and Lynne Zilkha of BB Supplies and Denis Cox of Ryan & Cox for help with Budweiser Budvar; Chris Varley and Jacqui Bright of Serenus International for help with Pilsner Urquell; Rupert Ponsonby of R&R Teamwork/National Hop Association of England; Nicholas Redman of the Whitbread Archive; Richard Wheeler of Tuckers Maltings; Sarah Bennett and James Murray of Brewing Research International; Barrie Bremner of McMullen & Sons; James Merrington of Scottish & Newcastle Breweries; Russell Sharp of the Caledonian Brewing Company; Michael Hardman of Young & Co; Frances Brace of Greene King; Tony Millns; Giles Dennis of J W Lees; Paul Bayley of Marston's; Dr Keith Thomas of Brewlab; Catherine Maxwell Stuart of Traquair House; Ken and Ingrid Brooker of Harviestoun Brewery; Lesley Allman of Bass Brewers for help with Staropramen; John Emerson of Emerson & Co; Richard Horton for help with Kaltenberg; Arthur Taylor for help with Northern France; Robin Appel Associates; Stephen Benton of Bitburger UK.

IN THE REPUBLIC OF IRELAND
David Twomey, past-president of the International Brewers' Guild; Diarmuid O Drisceoil of Murphy's; Ed Hinchy of Beamish & Crawford; Peter Walsh of the Guinness Museum.

IN GERMANY
HRH Crown Prince Luitpold of Kaltenberg; Regina Gerschermann of Spaten-Franziskaner-Bräu; Niclas Müller-Klönne of Holsten AG.

IN AUSTRIA
Conrad Seidl.

IN DENMARK
Henrik Mølstrøm of Carlsberg.

IN THE CZECH REPUBLIC
Vladimir Sraier of Agentura Triumf; Jaroslav Pomp of Pilsner Urquell; Peter Zizkovsky, director of the Pilsen Brewing Museum; Steve Denny, Bass micro-biologist, working at Prague Breweries/Staropramen.

IN BELGIUM
Jan de Brabanter of the Belgian Confederation of Brewers; François De Harenne of Abbaye de Notre-Dame d'Orval; Olav Blancquaerts of Moortgat; Jacques De Keersmaecker of Brasserie Belle-Vue; Jean-Pierre Van Roy of Brasserie Cantillon.

IN THE NETHERLANDS
Pieter Pieters of Brouwerij Schaapskooi, Abdij Koningshoeven; Guy Thornton.

IN THE UNITED STATES
Rob Haiber; Alan Eames; Charles Finkel of Pike Place/Merchant du Vin, Seattle; Tony Forder of *Ale Street News*; Julie Johnson Bradford and Daniel Bradford of *All About Beer Magazine*; Benjamin Myers; Fritz Maytag and Mark Carpenter of Anchor Brewing, San Francisco; John Hickenlooper of Wynkoop Brewing, Denver, Colorado; Ray Daniels and Steve Hamburg of the Craft Beer Institute, Chicago; Garrett Oliver and Steve Hindy of the Brooklyn Brewery, New York City; Dave Grinnell, head brewer, Boston Beer Company.

IN CANADA
John Hadfield at Spinnakers and Michael Hughes of Swans Hotel, both in Victoria, BC.

And, as always, my love and thanks to my wife Diana and sons Adam and Matthew.

Pro Bono Cerevisiam (For Good Beer) is used by the Campaign for Real Ale in conjunction with the annual Great British Beer Festival, and is reproduced by kind permission.

INTRODUCTION

This is the age of beer and *The Taste of Beer* celebrates the world's most popular alcoholic drink. In many wine-producing countries, drinkers are turning to beer with great enthusiasm, and while consumption of beer in many of the beer-producing nations is falling, there has never been greater interest in the product. The speciality beers of Belgium are in great demand. Northern France has emerged as the home of superb members of the ale family known as bières de garde. Britain is revered throughout the world as the last country to produce substantial volumes of ale in cask-conditioned form, beers that reach maturity in the pub cellar. The United States is witnessing a beer revolution: the hegemony of giant brewers and their insipid lagers are being challenged by small craft brewers who are restoring a great beer culture destroyed by Prohibition and Depression.

The Taste of Beer is a voyage round the world's great beer styles. Here you will find pale ales and Pilsners, brown ales and Bocks, mild ales and March beers, sour beer and stouts. You will find the stories behind the styles, unravel the truth about the origins of Pilsner and discover the genuine Budweiser. Readers can revel in the aromas and palates of each style by using the unique flavour wheel for each section. The wheels give an indication of what to expect from each style, but within styles, beers will vary according to the malts, hops and yeast strains that are used. The wheels are designed to encourage a greater understanding of styles by allowing the reader to savour the aromas, palates and aftertastes of all beers.

Beer at its best is more than a quick refresher. It is a drink with a depth and complexity to rival that of wine, and one with a fascinating history dating from the dawn of civilization. Drink deep and enjoy.

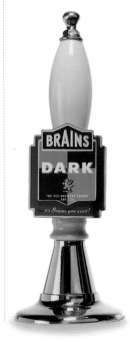

Bibendum! Roger Protz

1

IN THE
BEGINNING

Beer is as old as civilization. In the Ancient World people shifted away from a nomadic way of life into a more settled existence in order to grow grain and make beer. At a time when water was insanitary, the healthy nature of beer and the pleasure it gave to drinkers were important contributing factors in the gradual development of settled communities. This move toward settled agricultural life allowed the creation of industries to produce this life-enhancing drink on a considerable scale. Production of beer has survived political, cultural and religious upheavals down the ages and around the globe; as a result, beer has become the world's most popular alcoholic drink.

THE HISTORY AND THE MYSTERY

In July 1996 one of London's most famous department stores, Harrods of Knightsbridge, was the unlikely setting for the launch of a new beer. But this was no ordinary beer. Brewers and scientists had combined their skills to recreate an ale from Ancient Egypt, and Harrods, owned by the Egyptian al-Fayed brothers, was the ideal setting in which to present this remarkable link with the Old World. Against a backdrop of Egyptian artefacts and with Mr Mohammed al-Fayed dressed in a fetching Pharoah's head-dress, the world's media converged on Dr Delwen Samuel as she presented them with bottles of Tutankhamun's Ale. It is not often that someone engaged in the rare field of archaeo-botany appears on the main television news or the pages of the tabloid press, but Dr Samuel, a Canadian from Montreal carrying out research at Cambridge University, was talking about a topic dear to journalists' hearts: beer.

Tutankhamun's Ale was the result of years of painstaking work by archaeologists, archaeo-botanists, Egyptologists and brewers. The end result not only gave us a glimpse of what beer from the Old World may have tasted like but it also deepened

The cup that cheers: a wall-painting of Ancient Egypt showing beer being drunk.

our knowledge of life in those days, the importance of beer to those societies and its role in turning nomadic people into settled communities. Until Dr Samuel and her colleagues from the Egypt Exploration Society at Cambridge University presented their recreation of Egyptian ale, the received wisdom of historians was that beer had been a by-product of bread making in the Old World. Now history was turned on its head. It was beer, not bread, that came first and it was alcohol that had convinced the ancients to stop wandering the fertile valleys of the Nile and the Euphrates, and settle down to grow grain.

Brewing was a far more sophisticated skill than previous surveys had found. It became a major industry in Ancient Egypt, Babylonia, the Levant and Mesopotamia, regions that today encompass Egypt, Israel, Palestine, Iraq and Iran. Earlier research suggested that beer making was a rudimentary process using unmalted grain, but Delwen Samuel believes that malting may date from the earliest recorded times: it is only when barley and other cereals are malted that their

Tutankhamun's beer was a re-creation of an Ancient Egyptian ale based on research into the original ingredients.

starches can be turned into fermentable sugars. 'Sprouting grain is easy,' Dr Samuel says. 'The Ancient Egyptians probably laid the grain out in the sun to dry. They may have heated it, but there is no evidence of that. They would have controlled the level of drying in the sun or in ovens for darker or paler beers – there were many different styles of beer in the Old World.'

Brewing the ancient beer was the result of six years' research that had begun with the discovery of a massive kitchen complex at Tell el Armarna, the birthplace of Tutankhamun and the site of Queen Nefertiti's Sun Temple, built for her by the Pharoah Akhenaten during the period known as the New Kingdom that lasted

from 1550 to 1100 BC. Because the kingdom lasted for such a short period it has allowed archaeologists to date relics more precisely than in other periods.

Dr Delwen Samuel, who specializes in analysing ancient forms of food and drink, was called in to analyse beer-making vessels in the palace kitchen as well as the dregs and starchy residues found in the remains of clay brewing pots. Floors were swept to find seeds and grains used in brewing. Using an electron microscope, Dr Samuel was able to detect the composition of the dregs on the shards of pottery. She said, 'The microscope can show starch granules in ancient bread crumbs and beer dregs. The structure of these granules preserves a record of the processes they were exposed to during preparation, so it is possible to reconstruct the baking and brewing methods. Yeast cells in beer dregs can also be seen. They are beautifully preserved cells that actively grew and budded as the residues dried out.'

Dr Samuel doubts whether the ancients would have used a cultured yeast; they would probably have kept back some yeasty deposits from one brew to the next. Yeast would also have stuck to the fabric of the brewing pots while other natural micro-flora would have helped fermentation. Previous research had shown that both barley and a type of wheat called emmer were grown in Ancient Egypt. From the residues studied by Dr Samuel, she was able to determine that emmer had been used to make beer in the pots found at Tell el Armarna. Some well-preserved spikelets of emmer were found when the floors of the temple kitchen were swept and analysed. Three years after the Egypt Exploration Society started its work, the major British brewing group Scottish & Newcastle Breweries offered its experience to recreate a beer from the time of Tutankhamun. Led by James Merrington,

S&N's Director of Corporate Affairs, the company sent a team to Egypt to study the ingredients unearthed by Dr Samuel and her colleagues. Before anything could be brewed, emmer wheat had to be grown. This variety of cereal had not been seen for centuries in Britain but it is still grown in Turkey. Some 4 kilos (8 pounds) of emmer wheat were brought to England from Turkey and the seeds were used to grow 350 kilos (850 pounds) at the National Institute of Agricultural Botany in Cambridge. The wheat was malted in Scotland at Moray Firth Maltings.

Now Peter Bolt, a senior brewer with S&N, had the raw material to begin brewing beer. Water in the desert wells was analysed so the correct 'liquor' would be used. The water is free from phosphates and agri-business chemicals and only a small amount of gypsum was added

A model in the Glypothèque in Copenhagen showing grain being prepared for brewing in the Old World.

Xingu Black Beer, an attempt to recreate an ancient beer style from the Amazon.

to harden it. A modern yeast strain was used as it would have taken several further years of DNA research to reveal the exact type of yeast used in Ancient Egypt. The brewery chose an ale-type yeast that works at a comparatively high temperature because it would have been warm in the New Kingdom. While hops are known to have been grown in Babylonia, they were not used in brewing in the Old World. Other plants and herbs were used to balance the sweetness of the malted grain. Dr Delwen Samuel acknowledges that many experts believe dates were used in brewing, as some

contemporary recipes often referred to the use of the 'sweet thing'. But she found no evidence of dates in her research and she suggests that the 'sweet thing' may have been a reference to the malt itself.

'The flavourings in the beer brewed by Scottish & Newcastle are an educated guess,' she admits. 'We used coriander because we know it grew widely in Ancient Egypt and was also used in baking.' Juniper was also used and both plants were added in small amounts in the boiling copper in place of hops. Emmer wheat, unlike modern cereals used in brewing, has a thick husk. Grinding was done, slowly and arduously, in a pestle and mortar using dampened grain, the method used in Ancient Egypt in the New Kingdom. Dr Samuel's work indicates that the 'mash', the porridge that results from mixing grain with water, was made solely for brewing rather than being made from bread. The mash was squeezed or strained to produce a sugary liquid, and the grains left behind were then dried to make bread.

In spite of the thick husk, emmer in other respects was similar to modern brewing grain. It has a slight lactic flavour, which is similar to the variety of cereal used to make German wheat beers. It produced a good 'extract' or sugary solution after mashing, though the level of natural enzymes is lower than in modern malts. Mashing and boiling took place in conventional modern brewing

Dr Delwen Samuel whose research into malt and other ingredients in the Old World led to Tutankhamun's Ale being brewed in 1996.

vessels but, in order to be true to style, fermentation was carried out in a gallon jar and lasted for three days. It was impossible for Dr Samuel and her team to measure the strength of beer in the Old World but, as it was an important element of the people's diet, they assumed it would have been strong by modern standards. As a result, Tutankhamun's Ale was brewed to 6 per cent alcohol by volume. A thousand bottles were made and went on sale in Harrods at £50 ($80) a bottle. The beer was promoted as the most expensive in the world and the proceeds went to further research in Egypt.

The beer was a pale, hazy gold colour and had a delicately fruity, toffeeish and spicy aroma, with more spices and fruit in the mouth, and a dry and pleasingly quenching finish. For a drink made without barley malt or hops, it was definably a beer, though much of its character came from the modern yeast. It was nevertheless a remarkable achievement that gave an insight into brewing in the cradle of civilization.

Dr Samuel and her Cambridge colleagues did not work in the dark. Similar research undertaken in the United States in the 1980s had also concluded that beer, not bread, had been the motive force that led the people of North Africa and the Middle East to settle down and grow grain. The long-held view that bread cakes had been made for eating and some had been set aside for brewing was now contested. The modern theory was that bread cakes were made for brewing. Although during the period of the New Kingdom in Ancient Egypt, emmer wheat was the preferred grain for beer making, in other parts of the Old World barley malt was the chosen cereal. By trial and error, the ancients had discovered that while barley did not make good bread it made a drink which, in the words of Professor Solomon Katz of the University of Pennsylvania, made them feel 'exhilarated, wonderful and blissful'. Beer contained some vitamins and proteins that helped keep people of the Old World healthy at a time when water was insanitary. The American anthropologist and beer writer Alan Eames says: 'Protected by alcohol, beer had a palatability lasting far longer than any other food stuff. A vitamin-rich porridge, daily beer drinking increased both health and longevity, reducing disease and malnutrition. Additionally, the self-medicating properties of alcohol-rich beer eased the daily stresses and tensions of day-to-day life in a hostile world. As time passed, those who drank deeply and daily thrived and the search for new sources of grain from which to make beer continued. It was this appetite for beer-making material that led to crop cultivation, permanent settlement and agriculture. Ten thousand years ago, barley was domesticated and worshipped as a god in the highlands of the southern Levant. Thus was beer the driving force that led nomadic mankind into village life. With the creation of writing – stylus on wet tablet – beer, its history and mystery, became a part of ancient man's literary repertoire.'

Babylonia, Mesopotamia and other areas of North Africa and the Middle East may seem unlikely places to find the origins of brewing. But they were much warmer and wetter regions than they are today. Following the last Ice Age, there was a wide-spread rise in world temperature. Between 4000 and 2000 BC the world was two to three degrees Celsius warmer than now and it rained a great deal. A profoundly important agricultural revolution around 6000 BC led to the domestication of cereals. Cereals such as barley and wheat are developments of tall grass, and now their seeds could be hus-banded and used systematically for sowing and harvesting. The next important step was to malt the cereals. Malting, which involves

A beer dedicated to Ninkasi, the goddess of beer in Ancient Babylon, was brewed in San Francisco in the 1980s and used bappir loaves and dates.

germinating the grain and then drying and curing it, allows its starches to be trans-formed into sugars in the form of glucose and dextrin. This rich store of natural sugar not only allows a powerful fermentation to take place but also produces vitamins and proteins essential for a healthy diet.

A German study of brewing in Babylon and Egypt published in 1926 showed the Babylonians using raw, unmalted emmer and malted barley. Beer bread was made into cakes and baked either light or dark brown, depending on the colour of the beer required. Heated water was poured over the cakes to make a mash, which was filtered and left to ferment spontaneously. It was then transferred to smaller vessels that were half buried in cool cellars where a second fermentation took place. The Egyptians used more varieties of barley and emmer than the Babylonians and they malted both cereals. They baked their malt cakes a dark brown and made no light-coloured beers. Plants,

including mandrake with its powerful leek-like flavour, and salt were added to the sugary solution.

There is evidence that in such a vast region different methods were used to brew beer. The methods would also have changed as a result of improvements in technology. While the beer created in Britain by Dr Samuel and Scottish & Newcastle Breweries used a wort made by straining cereal mash, the older method of using bread cakes was still widely used. It was the accumulated writings about brewing in the Old World and the research by Dr Solomon Katz that encouraged Fritz Maytag, owner of the Anchor Brewery in San Francisco, to try to recreate in the 1980s a Sumerian beer from southern Babylon, dedicated to Ninkasi (or Ninkasis or Ninkaasis), the goddess of beer.

Maytag and his team from the Anchor Brewery rented a bakery during the day, as bakers work at night. The brewers moved in and made five thousand small loaves.

Anchor Steam Brewery made a faithful re-creation of Sumerian ale.

Maytag recalls the process: 'They are called bappir loaves, and we made them as if we were brewing in 3000 BC. In the bread there was raw barley flour, for barley was overwhelmingly the grain of the ancient world. There was a little bit of roasted barley because the husk on the barley is difficult to get off and we know from the ancient Sumerian records that roasted barley was common. We used a little bit of malted barley because we knew the Sumerians had malted barley. We made a thousand big thick pies in the oven in the bakery. We let them cool and cut them into strips and about an hour later we baked them again. By the end of the day we had a little over five thousand of these little loaves. A few days later we put them into the mash tun in our brewery along with some malted barley, which we needed for the enzymes to make the sugar and we made a beer with no hops because we knew from the experts that there were no hops in Sumeria.'

Dates were added to the brew because Maytag knew that they grew in Sumeria and that a song dating from 1800 BC referred to brewers using a 'sweet material'. The song, 'Hymn to Ninkasi', the Goddess of Brewing, refers to her adding sweetness twice to beer. 'We knew the Sumerians had honey as well as dates,' Maytag says, 'so we put honey in the bread and we put dates in the beer because we thought that might give the beer a little flavour, not quite like hops but a spicy flavour. It wasn't a wonderful beer but it was an interesting beer and one of its qualities was a slightly aromatic bouquet of dates. We put the bappir bread in the mash tun and we started cooking it and I can tell you it was a very eerie feeling, as though we were rubbing the magic lamp. We were calling up the ancient words of brewing.'

When Fritz Maytag gave me a bottle of Ninkasi Beer, I cooled it in a refrigerator, then decanted some into a glass jug and drank it through a straw. The beer was 5 per cent alcohol and was a cloudy, orange-red colour. It had a powerful aroma of honey and dates. The palate, despite the use of the 'sweet things', was surprisingly quenching and the finish was dry. As the beer warmed up, the sweetness of the honey and dates became more apparent but it remained deeply refreshing despite the lack of hops. As with Tutankhamun's Ale, the drink was surprisingly beery but once again a modern brewer's yeast strain had been used. These re-creations are fascinating interpretations of beer from the Old World, but the true aromas and flavours of beer from across the great divide of time will be captured only when DNA research can recreate a yeast strain from three thousand years ago.

The Arabs put an abrupt end to brewing in North Africa in the eighth century. But the art of brewing had spread. The great sea traders, the Phoenicians, had carried shipments of cereals to other countries, and brewing was soon established in northern Europe, beginning in Bavaria and Bohemia and working its way up to the Baltic region and across to the British Isles. Further

climatic changes saw the grape flourish in the Mediterranean lands while barley and wheat grew in abundance in the harsher climes of Germany, northern Spain, France, the British Isles and Scandinavia. Beer, along with cider and mead, became part of the people's staple diet. As the Romans marched north they came across beer for the first time. Tacitus reported that the German tribes drank a liquor made from barley or wheat while Pliny wrote: 'The nations of the west have their own intoxicant from grain soaked in water; there are many ways of making it in Gaul or Spain and under different names, though the principle is the same. The Spanish have taught us that these liquors keep well.'

Following the fall of the Roman empire and the withdrawal of its garrisons from northern Europe, the brewing of ale became deeply rooted in the societies fashioned by the waves of Germanic and Scandinavian peoples who overran much of the lands previously occupied by the Romans. By the time of the Norman conquest of Britain, the new rulers found that brewing was so ingrained in the indigenous people that it was impossible to wean them on to wine. Before the spread of Christianity, brewing had been a largely domestic affair: the women of the house made ale at the same time as they made bread. Gradually those women who made the best ale in a village set up shop to become commercial 'ale wives' or brewsters. Monks began to brew, too, to satisfy the needs of their brothers, to offer sustenance to pilgrims, and to corner and control a burgeoning market. Monastic brewhouses were vast. The malthouse at Fountains Abbey in Yorkshire measured 5.5 square metres (60 square feet) and the brewhouse produced 60 barrels of strong ale every ten days. According to the Domesday Book, the monks of St Paul's Cathedral in London brewed 67,814 gallons (3082 hecto-litres) of ale a year, – 1884 barrels. They used barley, wheat and oats. In the early Middle Ages there were about 500 monasteries brewing in Germany. An Irish Benedictine monk named St Gall brought the art of brewing to the region that is now Switzerland in the seventh century. The abbey he founded at St Gallen was heavily involved in brewing: plans from the ninth century show a malthouse, kiln, mill room for grinding the malt, three brewhouses and storage cellars. The maltings was large enough to allow four separate 'couches' of grain to be processed at a time.

Ale was made without hops. In England such plants as bog myrtle, rosemary and yarrow were added to balance the sweetness of the malt. In Germany, the Low Countries and Scandinavia, bags of mixed herbs and plants called gruit were placed, like bouquet garni, in the brewing vessel when the mash was boiled. Yeast had not yet been cultured scientifically. In England it was called 'God-is-good' and brewers watched in awe as the frothy liquid they kept from one brew to the next magically turned the malt sugars into alcohol, the result of intervention by the Almighty. It was the custom then to make several brews from one mash. The grain would be washed two or three times with brewing liquor, producing first a strong ale, then a moderately strong one and finally a weak brew drunk by women and children, the 'small beer' made famous by Shakespeare. As late as the seventeenth century, the staff of the Civic Orphanage in Amsterdam gave young inmates a pint each of small beer a day: milk was considered unhealthy as it gave children tuberculosis and 'spongy brains'.

Brewing was a seasonal activity. It was confined to late autumn, winter and early spring as the high temperatures during the rest of the year made beer sour and pro-moted infection by wild yeasts. But the keeping quality of beer was helped immea-surably when brewers began to use the hop plant as both a bittering agent and as a preservative. Hops were grown in Babylon around AD 200, the Romans ate them as a delicacy like asparagus, and there are records of the plant being used in brewing from the eighth century.

Hops were probably used at first as just another plant, herb or spice to balance the sweetness of the malt. But brewers soon dis-covered the special properties of the hop that made it superior to other plants. The hop has resins, acids and tannins that give delightful aromas and a deep, refreshing bit-terness to beer, and also prevent bacterial infection. Boiling the sweet wort with hops at a time when water was insanitary marked a giant step forward in brewing technology. Knowledge of the hop's role in brewing was taken to the Caucasus and into parts of Germany by the Slavs during the great migration of people that followed the collapse of the Roman empire.

Hop gardens were recorded in the Hallertau region of Bavaria in AD 736. In 1079 the Abbess Hildegarde of St Ruprechtsberg near Bingen referred to the use of hops in beer. Hop cultivation was also reported in Prague, already emerging as a major brewing centre. The church, which had cornered the market in gruit, fiercely resisted the use of the hop. In Cologne, for example, the archbishop controlled gruit through a decree called the Grutrecht and he attempted to outlaw the hop. In Holland in the fourteenth century the Dutch devel-oped a craving for hopped beer from Hamburg and rejected local ales brewed with gruit. When the Dutch began to brew hopped beer themselves, the controllers of the gruit market imposed strict punitive taxes on hopped beer, taxes that helped build the city of Amsterdam on marshland. Hops reigned supreme when agreements were reached throughout Europe with gruit suppliers, who agreed to accept royalties and tithes in lieu of giving up their rights to sup-ply the herb mixture.

The hop plant arrived late in England. It was brought to Kent during the fifteenth century by Flemish weavers who preferred hopped beer to the local ale. Use of the 'wicked and pernicious weed' was prohib-ited in Shrewsbury in 1519 and it was also banned in Norwich, even though East Anglia was home to many people of Flemish origin. King Henry VIII, who had rudely ended the church's grip on brewing by dissolving the monasteries, instructed his court brewer to make ale and to ignore the hop. In spite of powerful opposition, the hop started to establish itself in England. Dutch merchants introduced hop cultivation to Kent and Sussex. The first hop gardens were laid out in Kent in 1520. The hop made headway because it made better beer and greatly improved the profits of new commercial or 'common' brewers.

The hop transformed brewing, and the better keeping qualities of hopped beer encouraged entrepreneurs. In Hamburg, according to Professor J.R. Hale, brewers were among the wealthiest men in the city. Dutch brewers and coopers also became enormously powerful. In 1618 in Haarlem, 21 of the 24 city councillors were brewers. By the mid-sixteenth century there were twenty-six 'common' brewers in London, most in Southwark close to the hop market supplied by growers in Kent. And it was the common brewers of London who were to change the face of beer in the eighteenth century with a new style of ale called porter.

CALLING UP THE PAST

Several brewers have 'rubbed the lamp' – to use Fritz Maytag's phrase – in an attempt to recreate old beer styles. Unlike the Egyptian and Sumerian beers, the re-creations are now widely available commercially and allow a large cross-section of drinkers the opportunity to sample them and compare them with modern ales and lagers.

The oldest style now on sale in both Britain and the United States comes from Scotland and is a fascinating interpretation of heather ale, brewed by the oldest inhabitants of the country, the Picts, from around 200 BC. Its fame spread far beyond Scotland.

In 1993, Bruce Williams in Glasgow produced a version of heather ale after years of research. A recipe for the beer had been discovered on the Western Isles and translated there from Gaelic. Williams called his first brew *Leann Fraoch*, Gaelic for heather ale. The cask-conditioned beer was 3.6 per cent alcohol by volume and was made from bell and ling varieties of heather, as well as roid (bog myrtle), honey, barley malt, water and conventional top-fermenting ale yeast. It had a delicate but decided perfume from the heather but was otherwise rather refreshing if thin flavoured. Since then, Williams has refined the recipe several times. The beer is now just called Fraoch (pronounced 'frook') and comes in two versions: 4 per cent alcohol on draught and 5 per cent in bottle. Williams uses Scotch ale malt (90 per cent), carapils (a well-cured lager malt, 5 per cent), and wheat malt (5 per cent), with 200 grams (7 ounces) per barrel of hops, 100 grams (3.5 ounces) of fresh ginger root, and 12 litres (2.5 gallons) per barrel of heather flowers. The heather makes up a quarter of the volume of the 'grist' or fermentable ingredients. Half the heather is put in the copper with hops and ginger and is boiled for an hour and a half. The remainder of the heather lines the hop back, a receiving vessel for the hopped wort, the boiled sugary extract. Froach is brewed for Williams by Maclay of Alloa and now has an earthy aroma of heather and herbs with a hint of licorice, a dry herbal palate with orange fruit, and a finish that becomes dry and minty. The heather flowers

used come from organic wild heather and are picked only during a six-week period when millions of acres of 'purple glow' cover Scotland's hills and glens. The organic nature of the plants means there are some flavour variations of the beer from brew to brew. Dr Keith Thomas, who runs the Brewers Laboratory or Brewlab, an organization that teaches both professional and home brewers the skills of making better beer, at Sunderland University in north-east England has discovered that heather contains a white powder known as fog made from a series of micro-organisms. Heather that grows on wet uplands, as in Scotland, has a high level of micro-flora and wild yeasts that would have fermented spontaneously when the heather was brewed.

Dr Keith Thomas was involved in a brilliant piece of detective work that recreated a nineteenth-century porter. Thomas's Flag Porter, brewed by Elgood of Wisbech in Cambridgeshire and sold in Britain and the US, can lay claim to having a genuine taste as it uses a yeast from that century. In 1988 deep-sea divers investigating the wreck of a ship that had sunk in the English Channel in 1825 near the Sussex town of Littlehampton brought several bottles of porter up to the surface. The bottles were

Bruce Williams brews a Heather Ale using a Gaelic recipe handed down from the earliest settlers in Scotland.

handed to Thomas. He found that the beer was contaminated with sea water but he was able to isolate a few living yeast cells in one bottle. He cultured them in a laboratory and produced a strain with which he could brew. He went to Whitbread, one of the great porter brewers of London in the eighteenth and nineteenth centuries, and used a porter recipe from 1850 to fashion his 5 per cent Flag Porter. The beer is brewed from pale, brown, crystal and black malts with Fuggles hops. It has a dark ruby-red colour, and a tangy, slightly smoky and nutty aroma underpinned by earthy Fuggles. In the mouth there is a distinctive bitter fruitiness reminiscent of blood oranges, and the finish is rich in fruit, hops and bitter chocolate, finally becoming intensely dry with a herbal hint from the yeast. In spite of its complexity, it is a wonderfully refreshing beer and its appeal to London porters keen to slake their thirsts is obvious.

Dr Ian Hornsey, a micro-biologist who brews at the Nethergate Brewery in Clare, Suffolk, has recreated a mid-eighteenth-century

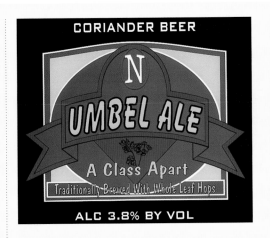

Umbel Ale is based on a nineteenth-century porter recipe that used coriander and bog myrtle as flavourings.

beer called Old Growler, named after his dog. It is based on a 1750s London strong dark recipe. It is brewed from pale malt, wheat flour, crystal

Right: Xingu Black Beer from the Amazon region is based on a recipe that included cassava roots.

Below: Jopen is an old name for a Dutch beer cask and was given to a beer based on a sixteenth-century recipe that used oats.

malt and black malt, with Challenger hops. It has a fine peppery hop aroma with a powerful hint of licorice. It is intensely bitter and fruity and the finish is hoppy with dark chocolate from the malt. Old Growler was a considerable success in both cask-conditioned and bottled forms, and the success encouraged Dr Hornsey to look more closely at the original recipe for the beer. It included coriander and bog myrtle as well as hops as bittering agents. Hornsey decided to brew a beer using coriander: he was unable to locate any bog myrtle. Ground coriander seeds were added with the hops during the copper boil. The finished beer has a powerful herbal and medicinal aroma. It is ferociously dry in the mouth and the finish is hoppy with more herbs and spices. The beer is called Umbel Ale from the old English for coriander and is 3.8 per cent alcohol.

In the Netherlands, the Haarlems Jopenbier Brewery has revived beers from the time when the town of Haarlem was a major brewing centre. The first beer, Jopen Hoppenbier, was brewed with barley malt, wheat, oats and hops. The use of oats in brewing, with a few exceptions, had disappeared centuries ago. Jopen was based on a 1501 recipe and is thought to be the first beer brewed in Haarlem with hops. It has a pale colour, a superb aroma of sherry-like fruit with spicy hops and a creamy oats note in the mouth. The finish becomes dry with a good balance of malt and hops. The brewery's second beer is called Koyt and is based on an

even earlier recipe dating from 1407 which used the mixture of herbs and spices known as 'gruit'. The modern brewery had to use some hops as Dutch law forbids the sale of beer brewed without them. Oats were again used in the recipe and the gruit was composed principally of myrica. The beer has a cloudy russet colour and has a chocolate and spices aroma. The palate is tart, bitter and spicy followed by a long finish with more chocolate, spices, herbs and a touch of lactic sourness.

American beer writer and historian Alan Eames undertook a hazardous journey in search of an old beer style, the black beer of the Amazon. Voyager Hans Staden wrote the first Western account of native beer brewing in the Amazon region in 1557, which described how women cooked manioc (cassava) roots and roasted barley over open fires to give it a dark colour and then chewed the grain to start fermentation: their saliva turned malt starches into sugar. More than four hundred years later, Eames travelled by plane and boat to the Xingu River that flows into the Amazon and found the natives still brewing black beer in the same way. Having determined the flavour, strength and consistency of the beer, Eames had to find a Brazilian brewery willing to make it on a commercial basis. Most breweries in the country make only light lagers but he found a tiny brewery called Cacador in the state of Santa Catarina. Cacador had been built in 1936 to supply just the surrounding area. The owners were willing to attempt to brew Black Beer. The intense roasting of the grain was done by open-fire malting. The only significant departure from Indian brewing was the exclusion of manioc. The first consignment of Xingu Black Beer was sent to the United States in 1987 and it is now on sale throughout the country. The *New York Times* commented on the 'unique, slightly smoky aftertaste' and called it 'one of the newest and most surprising light, mild yet complex tastes found in this potent brown-headed black brew'.

THE AGE OF PORTER

Porter has such a pivotal role to play in the history of brewing that it is remarkable that, until recently, so little was known about it. It refashioned the brewing industry in both Britain and Ireland, and was exported to the British colonies, the Baltic states and the court of the Russian Tsars. It was the favourite beer of George Washington, who had supplies sent to him from London until the War of Independence, when he switched to local brewers. Porter was so popular in the American colonies and the young United States that specialist taverns called Porter Houses sprang up to serve it. They developed a cut of meat, the Porterhouse Steak, that was consumed with tankards of the ale. At the end of the war with Britain,

Washington gave a farewell dinner to his officers at Fraunces Tavern, a celebrated porter house built in 1762 and still standing in Pearl Street, New York City.

The origins of porter lie in London at the turn of the eighteenth century. Drinkers at the time demanded a mixture called 'three threads', a blend of pale, brown and 'stale' or old ale. Both pale ale and stale ale were supplied to the London trade by country brewers at considerable cost and profit. The country brewers were able to make pale malt from coal-fired kilns as they were outside the jurisdiction of London. They had also cornered the market in stale beer. They made this by buying fresh brown ale from London brewers and storing it in large oak vats for a year or more. During this long

maturation, the beer was attacked by wild yeasts and micro-flora which gave the beer a sour, lactic acid character that was much appreciated by the drinkers of the time. Brewers in London, based either in taverns or in small, cramped premises, did not have the space to store beer in large vats.

The country brewers made vast profits from the supply of both pale and stale ales. London brewers were determined to break

Pomp and porter. . .Sam Whitbread's brewery in London's Barbican was one of the wonders of the early Industrial Revolution. It turned brewing into a major commercial activity that rapidly sent ale-house brewing into terminal decline.

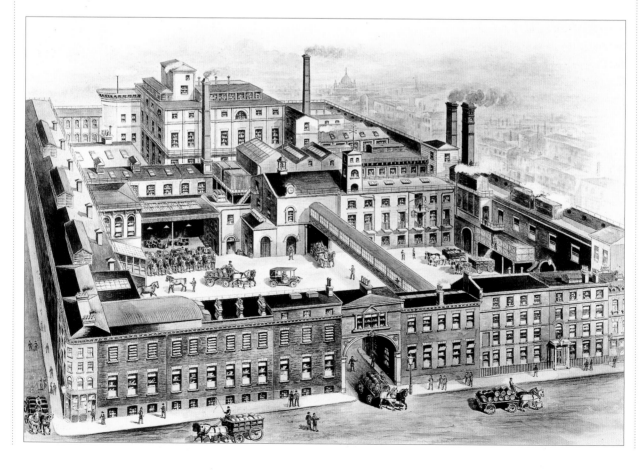

this stranglehold. The first attempt, an unblended brown beer, was a failure because of its rough flavours. Drinkers blended it with pale ale made by country brewers and sold through 'ale drapers' shops in London.

The turning point for London brewers came in 1722 when a commercial brewer named Ralph Harwood successfully made a beer he called 'entire butt' at his Bell Brewhouse in Byde's Place, Shoreditch. Harwood supplied pubs in East London with beer that was served from just one cask or butt. At a stroke, publicans were spared the back-breaking work of mixing three beers in their cellars. Harwood's entire butt attempted to replicate the taste of three threads and clearly did so with some success. The ease of handling entire butt and its cheapness had an immediate attraction for London tavern owners. Just four years after Harwood first brewed entire butt, César de Saussure, a French visitor to London, wrote home: '26 November 1726: Would you believe it, although water is to be had in abundance in London and of fairly good quality, absolutely none is drunk? The lower classes, even the paupers, do not know what it is to quench their thirst with water. In this country nothing but beer is drunk and it is made in several qualities. Small [weak] beer is what everyone drinks when thirsty; it is used in even the best houses and costs only a penny a pot. Another kind of beer is called porter. . .because the greater quantity of this beer is consumed by the working classes. It is a thick and strong beverage, and the effect it produces if drunk in excess is the same as that of wine; this porter costs threepence the pot. In London there are a number of ale houses where nothing but this sort of beer is sold.' Pale ale, on the other hand, cost between one shilling and one shilling and six pence a bottle, according to de Saussure,

putting it well beyond the reach of the impoverished working class.

Porter was the nickname given to the new dark beer of London, whether it was entire butt or a blended version. Demand for the beer from a fast-growing industrial working class outstripped the ability of both tavern-owners and even small brewers such as Ralph Harwood. They were replaced by entrepreneurs with the capital to invest in new breweries dedicated to making porter with cast-iron mash tuns, copper kettles,

Vast wooden tuns used by Whitbread to store and 'stale' their porters and stouts to give them the bitter, lactic character demanded by London drinkers.

steam engines, mechanical pumps, powered rakes for stirring the mash, saccharometers for measuring the sugar content of brews and thermometers for testing temperatures. Samuel Whitbread, the first and greatest of the porter brewers, opened a modest plant in Old Street in 1742 and within three years had built a new site in the Barbican that was called one of the wonders of the new industrial age. By 1812 Sam Whitbread II was brewing 122,000 barrels of porter a year, compared to the modest 21,000 barrels of Ralph Harwood less than a century earlier. Barclay Perkins brewed 270,000 barrels a year, Meux Reid 180,000 and Truman Hanbury 150,000. Brewing was no longer a cottage industry but was a major commerce, fuelled by the new technologies and scientific advances of the Industrial Revolution.

At first Sam Whitbread I rented 54 buildings in London to store his beer. According to contemporary sources, London porter was vatted for four to five months. From 1760, maturation was transferred to huge underground cisterns below Whitbread's Barbican brewery. Each one contained 4000 barrels of beer and they were cooled by internal copper pipes through which cold water was pumped. Brewing was no longer seasonal but continued during the summer. Maturing porter in bulk speeded up the production, allowing Whitbread and his competitors to reduce their costs.

Porter in the eighteenth century was a dark brown beer brewed from pale and brown malts. It was heavily hopped to balance the sweetness of the malts: the early porters were not fully attenuated, which means malt sugars were left in the beer to restore energy to drinkers engaged in hard manual labour. The strength of alcohol was not measured, but from brewing books it seems that the average strength of porter was around 6 per cent alcohol by volume. Stronger versions were known as 'stout porters'. At the time the strongest beer in a brewery, regardless of colour, was called 'stout beer'. In the fullness of time, as porter went into decline in both Britain and Ireland, the strongest versions remained, and stout as a rich, dark, roasty and bitter

Founder of a dynasty, founder of a style: Arthur Guinness opened a small brewery in Dublin in 1759, moved into porter brewing in 1787 and helped to create a style – Dry Irish Stout – that went on to conquer the world.

beer became a style in its own right.

Major changes in porter and stout production took place at the turn of the nineteenth century. The lifting of tax on coal encouraged brewers to make far greater use of pale malt, with its higher levels of fermentable sugar than wood-cured brown malt. But pale malt had to be blended with colouring matter to achieve the colour and consistency expected by brewers. The colour and character of porter and stout changed dramatically in 1817 when Daniel Wheeler introduced his New or Improved Method of Drying and Preparation of Malt. Daniel Wheeler took the principle of the iron coffee-roasting machine and used it to kiln malt to high temperatures of around 210°C/450°F. The deep brown or black malts

produced by this method contained little or no fermentable sugars. But small amounts added colour to the beer as well as flavours reminiscent of bitter chocolate and coffee with hints of the smokiness associated with wood-curing.

Patent malts, as the new roasted grain was called, revolutionized porter and stout brewing. Whitbread grasped its potential in the year it was invented. The specialist dark maltsters French & Jupp's, still in business today, built a patent malt factory next to Whitbread's brewery in the Barbican in order to supply the brewery on a daily basis. Barclay Perkins moved from colouring agents to dark malt by 1820. By the middle of the century porter and stout had moved from being beers of varying colours and flavours, as a result of blending, to ruby-black ones made from one mash, well-matured and with a bitter, hoppy and dark malt character from the use of roasted grain and large amounts of hops.

Porter brewing was such big business that it spread beyond London. A Bristol Porter Brewery opened in the great sea-going city in 1730s. When the company was bought by Philip George he began to export porter to Cork and Waterford in Ireland and also to Liverpool. In Scotland, the Anderston Brewery and John Struthers, both in Glasgow, and Robert Meiklejohn of Alloa hired London brewers to teach them how to make porter. William Younger and Archibald Campbell Younger merged their business in order to concentrate on porter and dominate the Scottish market.

The London porter brewers, having fashioned the market for dark beer, began to export to all parts of the world. In 1796, Thrale's brewery supplied porter 'that would keep seven years' to the Empress of Russia. Thales was bought by Barclay Perkins in 1781, and Barclay's Imperial Russian Stout was so popular in Russia and the Baltic that a brewery was built in Estonia to help meet demand. The beer is still brewed by Barclay Perkins' successor, Courage, which also bought George's of Bristol.

Porter brewing took off at a rapid pace in Ireland as brewers attempted to stem the flood of London, and Bristol-brewed beer coming in through Cork and Dublin. Arthur Guinness had bought a small brewery in County Kildare in 1756. Three years later he moved to Dublin where he took a lease on a derelict brewery at St James's Gate. By 1787 Guinness was brewing porter as well as ale and in 1799 he took the momentous decision to phase out ale in order to concentrate on porter. In Cork, two farmers, William

Beamish and William Crawford from Belfast, had gone south to sell beef and butter. When they found that 60,000 barrels of English porter were coming through Cork every year, they decided to start brewing and bought a site in 1792. So successful were both Beamish & Crawford and Guinness that by the early nineteenth century they were the two biggest breweries in the United Kingdom of Great Britain and Ireland: Beamish brewed 100,000 barrels a year, Guinness 66,000.

The recession that followed the Napoleonic Wars and the Irish famine of 1845–9 destroyed the economy and both brewers lost half their trade. Beamish never regained its dominant position but Guinness rebuilt its business by skilful use of the canal system, the new railway and a vigorous export policy to Britain and its colonies. As Ireland started the long and painful process of industrialization, Guinness was able to meet the demand for porter and stout from a new urban working class. He opened up the rural market by setting up agents and local bottling stores throughout the country. Casks of freshly brewed porter would be packed on to barges and would reach maturity on the voyage, ready to be drunk on draught or bottled by the company's agents. Guinness's two main beers were marked or blessed with crosses on their casks. Single X was porter, known as 'plain', and drunk mainly in Ireland and among the Irish community in Liverpool. XX Stout Porter, also known as Double Stout, was reserved for export.

Arthur Guinness's son, Arthur II, expanded his father's business and tinkered with the recipes of the beers. Tax in the early nineteenth century was paid on malt, not on alcoholic strength. As the Irish disliked paying taxes to the London government, Guinness started to blend some unmalted

and untaxed roasted barley with his malt to lower his duty bill. The acrid flavour of the charred barley added a distinctive roasted and bitter fruit character to the beers. The style known as 'dry Irish stout' had been born and other Irish brewers followed in Guinness's footsteps. As the term porter fell into disuse, Guinness Double Stout was seen as a quite distinct type of beer to British-brewed dark beers. Arthur Guinness II also developed a strong and heavily hopped beer for the colonial market that was known as Foreign Extra Porter Stout and later just Foreign Extra Stout.

The Guinness company grew rapidly. In the twenty-one years from 1885, production increased from 116,425 to 778,597 barrels. The brewery had to be rebuilt in the 1870s to meet demand. By the end of the century Guinness was the biggest brewery in Europe. By the end of World War I it achieved the remarkable feat for a country of just five million people of becoming the biggest brewery in the world. It was later overtaken by the new European and American lager brewers but it has remained a potent force in world brewing.

During World War I the British government imposed severe restrictions on brewing. Alcoholic strengths were reduced and brewers were not allowed to use heavily kilned dark malts, as coke and gas were needed for the munitions industry. Porter, already in decline as a result of the rise of pale ale, went into free fall. With Ireland on the brink of Home Rule, the British dare not impose such draconian restrictions on brewers there. Strength was reduced but much less so than in Britain, and barley and malt continued to be used in both pale and dark versions. Irish stout flourished and came to be seen as both a definitive style in its own right and as potent symbol of Ireland's nationhood.

THE PALE ALE REVOLUTION

If porter and stout were compromises between the old and the new technologies of brewing, pale ale marked a decisive leap forward and a significant break with the past. As ale brewing on a large scale is now confined to the British Isles, it is easy to forget that pale ale for most of the nineteenth century was the world's dominant style. It predated commercial lager brewing and outshone it for decades until the arrival of Pilsner beer caused another tumultuous change in brewing practice. But the great innovators of Munich, Pilsen and Vienna looked to Britain and to Burton-on-Trent in particular for their inspiration.

Pale ale was made possible by the new technology. Scientists had unravelled the mysteries of enzymes in malt and the action of yeast during fermentation. Thermometers and hydrometers measured temperatures and the levels of sugar in wort. Cast-iron mash tuns retained heat better than wooden vessels and held vast quantities of liquid. The mash was stirred by steam-driven rakes. Coppers, fired by coal or coke fires, were turned from open pans into domed vessels that avoided heat loss and retained the vital aromas of the hops. Scottish brewers developed the method known as 'sparging', from the French *asperger*, to sprinkle. At the end of the mashing cycle, the grains in the mash tun were sprayed or sparged with hot liquor to wash out any remaining sugars. This marked the end of making three or four beers from the same mash. The mash tun could be used more effectively and prof-itably by pushing a new brew through every couple of hours. Open coolers were replaced by closed heat-exchange units, with cold water running through pipes to reduce the temperature of the wort before fermentation. The wort was no longer open to the atmosphere and attack by wild yeasts. Ice-making machines, invented in the latter half of the nineteenth century, were embraced with as much enthusiasm in Britain and Ireland as they were in Bavaria and Bohemia.

When coke replaced coal, the production of pale malt free from noxious gases became possible on a vast commercial scale, with the advantage that it contained much higher levels of enzymes and potential sugar than wood-kilned brown malt. When the

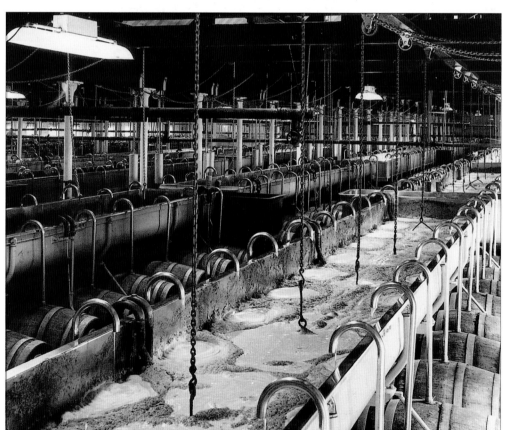

Our strength is in our unions. . .the union sets at Bass, developed in the nineteenth century to cleanse the new Burton pale ales of yeast. Fermenting beer rises from oak casks, up swan-necked pipes into troughs that retain the yeast. Bass no longer uses unions.

A re-creation of a nineteenth-century brewery laboratory, seen in the Bass Museum in Burton-on-Trent. Encouraged by Louis Pasteur, who visited several British breweries, brewers created laboratories and installed microscopes to ensure their ales were free from infection.

tax on glass was removed in the middle of the century and drinkers were offered glass rather than pewter tankards in most public houses, the clarity and sparkle of pale ale over dark and often murky brown and black beers added to the attraction of the new style. Brewers developed methods of fermentation that cleansed beer of yeast to give it the crystal-clear appearance in glass or bottle now expected by drinkers.

In Burton-on-Trent the system known as 'union set' became synonymous with pale ale brewing. Large oak casks contained the fermenting wort. Fermentation drove liquid and yeast out of the casks and up pipes into troughs above. The wort returned to the casks, leaving the yeast behind. The name 'union' came from the fact that the casks were linked or 'held in union' by pipes and troughs. In Yorkshire, two-storey ferment-

ing vessels acted in a similar fashion, with wort and yeast rising through a manhole into the top storey, where the yeast was retained. Other brewers used a more rudimentary but equally effective method known as the 'dropping system': fermenting wort was dropped from the bases of one set of vessels into a second bank below, leaving behind spent yeast and other detritus.

The development of pale ale goes hand-in-hand with the East Midlands town of Burton-on-Trent. It had been an important brewing centre since the eleventh century when monks found that the water bubbling up from countless wells in the valley of the River Trent produced ale with a fine taste and good keeping qualities. Centuries later, when it was possible to analyse Burton water, it was found to contain high levels of salts, especially calcium sulphate (gypsum)

and magnesium. The salts encouraged a powerful fermentation, drew the best from hops and gave the finished beer a tempting sparkle and refreshing flavour. London, on the other hand, had water high in calcium carbonate that was better suited to brewing soft, dark ales. Burton ales enjoyed a fine reputation, aided by the spread of a canal system that linked the Midlands with such great ports as Hull, London and Liverpool.

The Burton brewers were great exporters. Burton ale was popular in the Baltic states and Russia, but old technologies and the seasonal nature of brewing were fetters to increased production. Benjamin Wilson, who founded a brewery that was later to become the renowned Samuel Allsopp's, railed against his inability to brew before the start of winter and told potential customers in Germany in 1791 that even a

The success of Burton pale ales encouraged brewers to invest in modern methods of transport. Hensons used a steam-powered dray for pub deliveries.

mild winter could force him to suspend brewing as he could not control his mashing and fermenting temperatures. He was equally frustrated by his inability to produce an ale of standard colour and strength. In a further letter to customers in the Baltic, also written in 1791, he said: 'I have committed one fault in the brewing of my ale last winter, and that is, in making it too strong – if I had made it weaker it certainly would have been lighter coloured and would have pleased better at first sight.' Customers were clearly asking for a paler and more refreshing beer. Wilson was anxious to supply them but at that stage he could not meet the demand.

Burton was plunged into recession when the Baltic trade collapsed as a result of the wars between Britain and France that last-

ed, on and off, from 1793 to the defeat of Napoleon at Waterloo in 1815. The French closed port after port to the British. The effect in Burton was calamitous. Between 1780 and the mid-1820s, the number of breweries in the town fell from thirteen to five. The surviving brewers, including Wilson (now joined by his nephew Allsopp), William Bass, William Worthington and Thomas Salt, desperately searched for new markets and turned to the colonies for survival. Britain had first colonized India in 1722 and brewers had been supplying the subcontinent with ale from the earliest days. But brown ales and porters were not the best thirst-quenchers in that torrid climate. They tended to arrive sour and flat after a sea journey that lasted from three to five months with wild fluctuations of temperature.

By a quirk of history, the brewer who first made a special beer for the India trade that could withstand the arduous journey was based in London not Burton. George

Hodgson of Abbot & Hodgson's Bow Brewery in East London started to brew for the export trade because of his proximity to the East and West India Docks where great sailing ships set sail for the subcontinent. Rates for cargo on the outward journeys were low. Hodgson had heard from ship owners that soldiers and civilians in India were dissatisfied with the ales sent to them and he thought he could make a substantial profit by supplying the India market with a lighter and more refreshing beer.

No records survive of this small brewery and nobody knows what Hodgson's 'India Ale' was like. It must have been genuinely pale, for when the Burton brewers rushed to emulate Hodgson, they brewed pale ales based on his style. As an experienced brewer, Hodgson knew that the best defences against spoilage on the journey to India would be alcohol and hops. It is therefore likely that he brewed a strong ale of at least 6 per cent alcohol and with twice the hops used in conventional beers. Additional hops may have been added to the casks when they left the brewery as a further step against infection. Priming sugar in the casks would have encouraged a slow second fermentation that would also have kept the yeast active and helped ward off spoilage. Mark Hodgson expanded his father's business when he took over: at one stage the Bow Brewery was responsible for the bulk of the 9000 barrels exported annually to India.

Hodgson had a virtual monopoly of the India trade but he was ruffling colonial feathers. He didn't pay his agents in Bombay and Calcutta, and his prices fluctuated wildly. The directors of the powerful East India Company, which handled Hodgson's beer, were determined to break his domination. Over dinner in 1821 a director of the company named Marjoribanks told Samuel

Allsopp that India offered 'a trade that can never be lost: for the climate is too hot for brewing. We are now dependent upon Hodgson who has given offence to most of the merchants of India. But your Burton ale, so strong and sweet, will not suit our market.' Marjoribanks' butler gave Allsopp a bottle of Hodgson's beer. Allsopp took it back to Burton where he handed it to his head brewer and maltster, Job Goodhead. Goodhead said he could make a beer of that colour by kilning his malt at a lower temperature. According to legend, Goodhead brewed a tiny amount of pale ale, using a teapot as his mash tun. In a small town such as Burton with its brewery bush telegraph,

other brewers soon learned of Allsopp's experiments and they attempted to make pale ales. At first the Burton brewers struggled to replace Hodgson in popularity. But within ten years Allsopp and Bass accounted for more than half the beer shipped to Calcutta. Throughout the 1830s the two breweries sent some 6,000 barrels of pale ale a year to India and their success eclipsed Hodgson, whose company went into decline and eventual closure.

The success of Burton pale ales stemmed from the yeast strain developed by the union set method of fermentation and the hard spring water. Burton yeast is described as 'greedy'. It attacks the sugars in the wort

with great ferocity, producing dry, fully attenuated beers. The use of brewing sugar in the copper, which, unlike malt sugars, is almost completely fermentable, would have added to the dryness and high alcohol of the finished beer. The active yeast left in the casks would have fought infection during the sea voyage. Burton brewing liquor played an equally important role in the flavour and keeping qualities of pale ale. According to Paul Bayley, head brewer at Marstons, the last Burton brewery to use the union set system, 'calcium reduces sugar and helps produce more alcohol. It keeps the yeast active, reduces haze, decreases beer colour and improves hop utilization. The

Steam breweries – the Burton brewers not only used the new railways to send their ales to all parts of Britain, but also built their own networks to move beer and ingredients around their plants. A measure of the traffic is reflected in Bass alone handing over 113,825 wagons of beer to the main-line railways in 1900.

result is a more bitter beer. Magnesium acts in a similar fashion and sulphate gives a drier flavour and enhances bitterness.' Archivists at Bass claim that export ales brewed until the 1970s were based on recipes dating from the 1850s. This means that a Bass pale ale brewed for the India trade would have had an original gravity of around 1060°, which is approximately 6 per cent alcohol. This is not exceptionally strong for the time, but assuming the casks were primed with sugar and a vigorous second fermentation took place, the final alcohol would have been higher. The ales were heavily hopped in the copper at between 1.3–1.8 kilos (3–4 pounds) per barrel. Dry hops were added in the casks at around 170 grams (6 ounces) per barrel. Although the units of bitterness could not be measured at the time, it is thought they would have reached 70 or 80, almost twice as high as in a modern bitter beer, but the bitterness would have softened considerably during the voyage. Bass used Fuggles and Goldings hop varieties from Worcestershire and Kent.

The development of India Pale Ales or IPA for short, marked the beginning of the end of vatted beers. As IPAs were brewed for long voyages, vatting before racking into casks was unnecessary. Some beer went to India, Australasia, the Caribbean, the United States and even Latin America in bottle as well as cask. But for all its importance in changing the face of British brewing, the hey-day of India Pale Ale was brief – not more than thirty years. By the 1880s exports were falling fast. The British brewers could not match the zeal of the German lager brewers, who not only supplied their African colonies but even set up bridgeheads in British colonies and settlements. Two German brewers founded the Gambrinus brewery in Melbourne in 1885. In 1900 a Swiss brewer named Conrad

A beer fit for a king . . .Bass's head brewer Cornelius O'Sullivan examining the clarity of the King's Ale brewed in 1902 for the coronation of Edward VII. O'Sullivan's research and development helped to turn brewing from a seasonal activity into a continuous commercial one.

Breutsch was invited to New Zealand specifically to brew lager. Ironically he used the site of the Captain Cook Brewery in Auckland, named in honour of the Yorkshire sea captain who had brewed a rough beer there to cure his crew of scurvy when he landed in New Zealand. A colonial critic of the British brewers complained that their beers had 'too much alcohol, too much sediment, too much hops and too little gas'. The brewers, however, were not prepared to change their methods. They had invested massively in their breweries. As members of the greatest empire the world have ever seen, they had no intention of using the cold fermentation methods of their deadly rivals, the Germans.

And they now had a home market to satisfy. Brewing historian Richard Wilson has described pale ale as 'the fashion beer of

the railway age'. The new lower middle class wanted no truck with the dark beers favoured by the working class. They embraced pale ale, especially when it became possible to have the beer delivered in bottles to their homes. IPA had begun to challenge the domination of porter as early as 1827 when a ship carrying three hundred hogsheads of the beer was wrecked in the Irish Sea. The beer was sold by the underwriters in pubs in and around Liverpool and its reputation spread. But sales did not become national until the railway system allowed the Burton brewers to send supplies via the Derby to Birmingham line and then into the national network. When St Pancras station was built in London its cellars were designed to accommodate giant hogsheads of Burton beer. During the 1840s the output of Burton's brewers increased from 70,000 to 300,000 barrels a year. By 1851 there were fifteen breweries in the town, with Allsopp and Bass responsible for 70 per cent of the total output. Between 1850 and 1880 Burton brewing trebled in size every ten years. Bass forged ahead of Allsopp and by 1874, with an annual output of 900,000 barrels, it had become the largest brewing company in the world. It entered the twentieth century with an annual production of over one and half million barrels.

Once it became possible to treat brewing water with salts to replicate the gypsum and magnesium-rich spring waters of Burton, brewers throughout Britain began to produce pale ales. They were anxious to maximize profits by brewing beer in the most efficient way possible. Louis Pasteur's work *Études sur la Bière* had a profound effect. Pasteur visited several British breweries and so impressed Whitbread in London on the need for absolute cleanliness to avoid infections that the directors immediately ordered the purchase of a microscope in order to study their brewing yeast. It was now possible to isolate pure strains of yeast and prevent spoiled beer. In 1895 the *Journal of the Institute of Brewing* said that the modern brewer should be 'essentially a chemist, as brewing is practically the conversion of certain substances into certain chemically different substances by what is more or less a chemical process.' Even before Pasteur had published his findings in 1876, Allsopp had taken on a German chemist, Dr Heinrich Böttinger, as the company's scientific adviser. Bass appointed John Matthews as its 'chemist and principal brewer'. He was joined by the legendary Cornelius O'Sullivan in 1865. O'Sullivan's work won him many awards and in 1885 he was appointed a Fellow of the Royal Society. It was his pioneering research that enabled brewers to move from seasonal brewing to

A special beer was brewed in London in 1995 to mark the 100th anniversary of Louis Pasteur's death and honour his contribution to good brewing. Lectures were given in the Whitbread brewery.

all-year-round production. O'Sullivan was paid £3500 a year by Bass, an enormous salary for the time. Far-reaching research was carried out by Dr Horace Tabberer Brown at Worthington on barley germination, yeast nutrition and microbiology.

The nature of the beer brewed by Bass and its competitors was changing. India Pale Ale had been developed for export, to replace the trade lost to the Baltic. IPAs, by necessity, had been high in alcohol and heavily hopped. By the 1880s drinkers at home, the middle-class consumers of pale ale in particular, were demanding weaker

and less bitter beers. Pale Ale, as distinct from IPA, was a somewhat modified version of the original, which was lower in alcohol, less heavily hopped and brewed quickly for a fast turnover. Brewers were not prepared to lock up large quantities of costly liquid for months by vatting them and then waiting for months or years for the money to be paid to them. Many of the bigger breweries were now public companies with shareholders keen to receive their dividends. The brewers were also investing heavily in pubs in order to have controlled outlets for their products.

The new breed of pale ales, known as 'running beers' in the trade, were the result of scientific research. All brewers could now 'Burtonise' their liquors by adding gypsum and magnesium. Treated with sulphates, brewing liquor contributed to the better extraction of malt sugars, improved hop utilization and cleaner fermentations. Malting had been greatly improved and the move to pale malt meant that more extract could be produced from smaller amounts of grain. Better understanding of yeast was also an important aid in brewing pale ales. Pure strains meant that fermentation could be better controlled. Yeast packed down and cleared in casks within a few days, enabling beer to 'drop bright' within a day or two of arriving in pub cellars.

By the turn of the twentieth century, India Pale Ale, for all its epoch-making importance, was largely dead and buried, replaced by weaker bottled pale ales and draught 'running beers' that became popularly known as Bitter. Those beers labelled IPA today are, in the main, pastiches of the original. But the survival of the term honours the great contribution which the style made to the development of brewing and the continuing devotion to top-fermented ales among British beer drinkers.

LAGER AND THE GOLDEN TRIANGLE

Lager beer, in common with pale ale, was a product of the Industrial Revolution. But unlike pale ale, its impact has endured on a world scale. Today around 90 per cent of all beer is made by the lager method. Outside Britain and Ireland, there are only small pockets of ale brewing in a few countries. The style developed and perfected in central Europe in the last century in the 'golden triangle' of Munich, Pilsen and Vienna has conquered the world.

Lager is a German word meaning 'to store'. Many centuries ago, monks in Bavaria who brewed in hill-top monasteries dug cellars deep in the Alps to store their beer, as part of the Benedictine requirement for self-sufficiency. As in other countries, beer could not be brewed in the summer months. A sixteenth-century decree by the electoral prince of Bavaria banned brewing during the period from 23 April to 29 September. The last beers brewed in March or early April were then stored for consumption during the summer and early autumn. The monks found that, kept at low temperatures in ice-filled caves, their beers fermented

slowly and the yeast sank to the bottom of the vessels. Protected by cold and alcohol, the beers were largely free from bacterial infection and the off-flavours of wild, airborne yeasts. Empirically, the monastic brewers were developing the method known as cold or bottom fermentation.

The Bavarian capital Munich is called München in German, a corruption of Mönchen, meaning 'the monks' place'. Several of the great Munich brewers, such as Augustiner, Franziskaner and Paulaner were founded by monks. Weihenstephan on the outskirts of the city started life as the Bendictine monastery of Sacred Stephan and has had a brewery since 1040. Today it is a world-famous brewing school and makes small amounts of commercial beer. The early brewers from the city of the monks took their strong March or Märzen beers to the surrounding Alps and stored their beers in caves packed with ice from rivers and lakes. 'Cold fermented beer' was mentioned in a report of Munich town council in 1420.

But cold fermentation was sporadic and often unsuccessful. There was no scientific

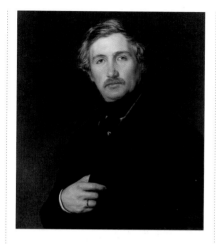

Gabriel Sedlmayr, the driving force behind the new lager brewing method.

understanding of yeast at the time and no distinction between baker's and brewer's yeast: in many households the same yeast would be used for making bread and beer. The first microscope was invented by the Dutchman Anton van Leeuwenhoek in the seventeenth century, but a true understanding of yeast did not come until the nineteenth century with the work of Louis Pasteur in France and Emil Christian Hansen in the Carlsberg laboratory in Copenhagen. As late as 1831 there were 16,000 breweries in Prussia producing warm-fermenting ale-style beers. It was from that date, with the Industrial Revolution in full swing, that cold fermentation started to dominate. By 1839 the number of Prussian brewers using warm fermentation had fallen to 12,000 and to 7400 by 1865.

The brewery at the heart of the lager revolution was in Bavaria, not Prussia. The Spaten Brewery dates from 1397, when it was attached to a tavern in Munich. The name means 'spade' and its logo today is a

DIE BIERE DER SPATEN-BRAUEREI·
IN DER BRAUEREI AUF FLASCHEN ABGEFÜLLT MÜNCHEN · FERNSPRECHER: 52530 und 57102

Spaten of Münich, where cold fermentation of beer was first developed.

malt shovel. In 1807 the brewery was bought by the Sedlmayr family, whose relatives also owned the Franziskaner Brewery in the city. Gabriel Sedlmayr the Elder had been the brewer for the Bavarian royal family before setting up on his own. He and his son, Gabriel Sedlmayr the Younger, embraced the new technologies of the time. It was the advent of steam power as much as cold fermentation that enabled the Munich brewers to grow. As in London and Burton-on-Trent, steam locomotives allowed raw ingredients to be moved in bulk around breweries, while steam engines stirred the mash, heated the coppers, and pumped beer and water from floor to floor. Brewing was suddenly possible on a vast commercial scale and the canals and railway network carried beer long distances to new markets.

At the royal court brewery, Sedlmayr had brewed a warm-fermenting beer, probably the wheat beer most preferred by the nobility. In his own brewery he switched to cold fermentation. He built chambers deep beneath his brewery and cooled them by packing cellars above with ice. Beer was stored in oak casks in the chambers for a number of months and underwent a slow secondary fermentation at temperatures close to freezing point. 'Bottom working' yeasts were the result of natural selection and careful storage from one brew to the next. Long before the term 'lager beer' came into vogue, Europe and Scandinavia began to hear about and then clamour for the new 'Bavarian beer'. The beer's taste was the result not only of cold fermentation but of other methods developed by Sedlmayr and the Munich brewers, who often shared supplies of yeast. They employed what was then called the 'thick mash' or decoction system. Instead of the British infusion mash, with the grain and liquor heated in one vessel, the Bavarians boiled the mash several times

Anton Dreher (left) and Sedlmayr in the centre seen with a friend as young men. The two pioneers of lager went on an extensive tour of Europe and Britain to study the methods of other brewing companies.

at increasingly higher temperatures in linked vessels in order to ensure saccharification. Long storage or lagering produced beer with a rich vinous character and saturated with naturally produced carbon dioxide, making the beer resistant to acidification. This enabled the Munich brewers to use fewer hops than English brewers as there was less risk of their beer going sour. The chemist E.A. Scharling, who toured Bavaria in 1845, believed that the character of beer from the region owed a great deal to the brewers' method of preparing their casks. In order to stop the carbonic gas from penetrating the wood, they lined the inside of the casks once a year with a layer of resin. This gave the casks a 'piquant tang'.

The first cold-fermented Bavarian beers were made from wood-cured malts and were said to be a translucent brown in colour as

a result of long storage. They are likely to have been smoky in flavour with coffee and chocolate notes from the malt and with a delicate and gentle hoppiness. These are certainly the characteristics of the 'Gamle' (Old) Bavarian-style brown lager still brewed at the Carlsberg Brewery in Copenhagen, which was powerfully influenced by Sedlmayr in its early days.

Once the railways made travel easier, it became the custom of the new commercial breweries of the nineteenth century to send sons of the owners on long visits to other great brewing centres to study the methods of competitors. At Spaten, Gabriel Sedlmayr the Younger, accompanied by another aspiring brewer, Anton Dreher of Vienna, embarked on a six-year grand tour of Prussia, the Rhineland, Belgium, the Netherlands and Britain. They were espe-

Carl Jacobsen's New Carlsberg brewery is called 'the Cathedral of Brewing'.

cially impressed by the technical and scientific advances made by the British brewers. Bass in Burton-on-Trent presented Sedlmayr with a saccharometer so that he could measure the fermentable sugars in wort. In spite of this generosity, the young Bavarian and Dreher engaged in subterfuges that would be called 'industrial espionage' today in order to gain a better understanding of British brewing methods. They used thermometers surreptitiously to measure brewing temperatures and they had hollowed-out walking sticks with hidden valves in which they kept samples of beer and wort for later analysis. They wrote home that even though they had been warmly welcomed in one brewery 'we still stole as much as we could'. 'It always surprises me that we can get away with these thefts without being beaten up,' Sedlmayr added.

Sedlmayr returned to Munich and took over the running of the Spaten Brewery in 1836 following the death of his father. He busily developed the use of steam power and later embraced the invention of the ice-

making machine by Carl von Linde. It was von Linde's machine, from which refrigerators developed, that was finally to transform lager brewing into a great industrial enterprise. Breweries were no longer dependent on supplies of ice cut from rivers and lakes, and could now brew all the year round. But the Bavarian beers were still dark. While Sedlmayr had been impressed by the new kilning methods used in Belgium and Britain, with malt cured more gently and thoroughly by indirect coke fires rather than coming into direct contact with the fierce flames from wood, he still brewed brown lagers. According to records at Spaten, the brewery's beers actually became darker after 1830. This was due to consumer demand, especially from drinkers in working-class areas: dark or 'Dunkel' Bavarian lagers, in common with English dark mild ales, were more popular than pale beers until the 1950s and the beginning of the decline of heavy industry. Coal was expensive to

Carlsberg still brews dark lagers in the Bavarian style.

J.C. Jacobsen perfected cold-fermented beers with yeast brought from Munich.

mine in Germany and was also heavily taxed, facts that would have encouraged brewers to remain faithful to wood. In 1843 the increased use of wood by the new commercial brewers caused a severe shortage and a sharp increase in price. They looked for new sources of energy and in 1845 Spaten first used peat, which must have given an intriguing new aroma and flavour to its beers. It was not until 1867 that Spaten used coal to fire its malt kilns.

In Vienna Anton Dreher had also put his travels to good use. Working closely with Sedlmayr, he developed lagering techniques at his brewery at Schwechat in the Viennese suburbs. He also built breweries at Michelob in Bohemia, at Trieste and in Budapest. The deep lagering cellars dug from the limestone in the Hungarian capital still exist and were used by resistance fighters as hiding places in World War II. Dreher developed a style known as Vienna Red, an amber-brown lager that was a half-way house between the

Dunkel lagers of Munich and the golden Pilsner that was soon to burst upon the scene from Bohemia. Dreher used a more lightly kilned malt and must have adopted the kilning processes he had seen in Belgium and Britain. Writing in the journal *Brauwelt* (*Brew World*) in 1961, Ottomar Menzel recalled the days of his studies in Vienna in 1900 and the beer he drank: 'The Viennese beers with their reddish colour formed a style of their own which has unfortunately become extinct by now. They had strengths of nine, ten and twelve degrees: the Schwechater [Dreher's beer] was even stronger. The weak form of it was called

and characterized as "Fensterschwitz".' Fensterschwitz is an Austrian dialect word meaning the condensed water on the inside of a window on a cold day. A description of Viennese brewing in 1910 said the beer was a three-mash decoction brew, with each mash boiled for 15–30 minutes.

The onslaught of Pilsner beer sent Dreher's style into rapid decline. Today Austrian brewers concentrate on pale lagers, though one Viennese brewpub, the Siebenstern-Bräu, has introduced a Märzen that is true to the Dreher style. Curiously amber lagers survive in Mexico as a result of the country briefly being part of the

Austrian empire. Such beers as Negra Modelo, Negra Léon and Dos Equis are heavily influenced by the Austrian style.

But Dreher's biggest influence was in Munich. In 1871, Sedlmayr's brother Josef, who owned the Franziskaner Brewery, produced an amber lager in the Dreher fashion. It proved popular and went into regular production the following year. It was called Märzen as it was brewed in March and

The magnificent Elephants Gate entrance to the New Carlsberg brewery in Copenhagen is modelled on the Minerva Square Obelisk in Rome.

32

Emil Christian Hansen seen in his laboratory in the Carlsberg Brewery in Copenhagen where he isolated the first pure strain of lager yeast.

stored until autumn, when it was ceremonially tapped at the opening of the Oktoberfest. Today true March beers are hard to find in Munich. Most of the brewers have abandoned them in favour of paler Oktoberfest beers lagered for much shorter periods. At the time Josef Sedlmayr's Märzen was a revelation and encouraged the growth of other paler beers, such as the strong Bock and Doppelbock lagers brewed for Lent and the rich Fasching beers that herald the arrival of spring. But despite the impact of Pilsner beers, Spaten did not produce a true pale lager known as 'Hell' (meaning light) until 1894. Samples of the beer were sent to Dresden and Hamburg and it went on sale for the first time in Munich on 20 June 1895. It was soon followed by a stronger Pilsner, but pale lagers accounted for only a small proportion of the output of the Munich brewers.

Steam power and refrigeration made it possible for brewers to move away from seasonal production. One obstacle stood in their way: yeast. The brewers may have moved to cold fermentation but their yeasts were still unreliable and never more so when they attempted to brew in the summer months. The obstacle was removed not in Munich but in the far north, in Copenhagen. What has become a great brewing and cultural

dynasty known as Carlsberg began life as a modest little brewery in the Danish capital. Christian Jacobsen, a farmer-brewer, arrived in Copenhagen from rural Jutland in 1801. Within ten years he had saved sufficient money to rent a brewery where he made warm-fermenting wheat beers. When his son, Jacob Christian Jacobsen, heard of the experiments in Munich and the development of 'Bavarian beer', he was determined to attempt to make a beer that was more stable and reliable than his father's ales. He experimented with small batches of beer made in his mother's wash tub and two small malt vats. The results were not completely satisfactory as he had access only to his father's warm-fermenting yeast. Jacobsen felt that Bavarian beer would have a major impact in Denmark and it was vital that Danish brewers should control the market.

Jacobsen made two visits to Bavaria and Bohemia to study the new brewing processes. On the second trip in 1845 he went to see Sedlmayr and was given two quarts of Spaten yeast. He kept the yeast in a special tin inside his hat box and he doused the tin with water at every stop on the long coach journey back to Copenhagen. The yeast survived and Jacobsen had the means to brew a true Bavarian beer. When his mother died, he used her small fortune to build a new

brewery at Valby outside the city where there was a supply of fresh spring water and where he could dig lagering cellars that would hold 5,000 barrels of beer. The first brew appeared on 10 November 1847. The brewery was on a hill or a 'berg' and Jacobsen called it Carlsberg after his son, Carl. The original or Gamle (Old) Carlsberg brewery had three cellars: the fermention cellar, the winter cellar for storage and the malt cellar where the steeping and germination of barley took place.

Jacobsen's Bavarian beer, brown in colour at first, was an enormous success. The brewery was constantly enlarged, its vessels replaced with more modern ones and the lager cellars developed to store more beer. A second brewery, Ny or New Carlsberg, was built on an adjacent site and was run by Carl Jacobsen. The New Brewery, still in operation (the Old is now a museum) is one of the finest in the world and is known as the 'cathedral of beer'. It has burnished copper brewing vessels inside while the exterior has a model of Thor, the God of Thunder, riding his chariot on the roof.

Hansen's equipment used to produce a single-strain, bottom-working yeast.

J.C. had other problems to contend with. As great industrial cities sprang up all over Europe and Scandinavia, brewers were under great pressure to supply more beer on a regular basis to a rapidly expanding population dominated by thirsty industrial workers. But summer brewing led to difficulties. Beer went sour and had to be poured away, to the consternation of drinkers and at great loss to the brewers. The epidemic was as serious for brewers as phylloxera was to wine makers. In the spring of 1882 the beer at Tuborg in Copenhagen went sour. In spite of the intense rivalry between the two companies, Tuborg appealed to J.C. Jacobsen for help. He sent supplies of his yeast three times a week to Tuborg until it was able to brew good beer again. Jacobsen boasted that his yeast, unaltered since he had bought the first supply from Sedlmayr, was the finest available. Imagine his horror when his own beer developed a most unpleasant taste and a disagreeable smell the following autumn. His brewing scientist Emil Christian Hansen used a powerful microscope to find that the yeast was made up of several competing strains, including some wild strains that were responsible for making the beer sour in warm weather.

Hansen, who had come from a poor background in Jutland, won a scholarship to study in Copenhagen and specialized in the physiology of fermentation. He went to work in the laboratory at Old Carlsberg in 1878 and was awarded a doctor's degree a year later. Hansen's problem at Carlsberg was that his employer Jacobsen was a great admirer of Louis Pasteur and some of Hansen's research brought him into conflict with the French scientist. Pasteur had preached cleanliness in breweries and had recommended that yeast should be purified with the use of tartaric acid. When Hansen read Pasteur's *Études sur la Bière*, he noted in the margin of the chapter on pure yeast and the tartaric acid method: 'It is possible that the question is more complicated and that it is a matter not of a single yeast but of several strains of yeast surviving the treatment in question.' Pasteur's purification method was capable of improving a yeast culture in the short term as bacteria were killed, but it did not produce a pure culture of yeast, whether it was 'top' or 'bottom' brewing yeast or wine yeast. Hansen's work went further. He showed that yeast is not a homogeneous substance but can be broken down into a number of strains of which only a few are usable in brewing. Using a special yeast culture chamber and leaves of gelatine, he was eventually able to isolate a pure strain of brewing yeast and then to clone it and reproduce it.

On 12 November 1883, Hansen's new single strain yeast was used for the first time at Old Carlsberg. A supply was given to New Carlsberg and then to other Danish breweries. The impact of Hansen's yeast was profound. Within a few years it was in use in lager breweries throughout the world and it was eventually given the scientific name of *Saccharomyces carlsbergenis* (literally, Carlsberg sugar fungus).

When Louis Pasteur came to Copenhagen in 1884, he appeared to snub Hansen by refusing to remove his hat when he visited the Carlsberg laboratory, considered a terrible slight in polite society. But a year later Pasteur invited Hansen to Paris and showed him all the laboratories in the city and the work he was doing on rabies. The two men were not rivals. Their research had coalesced, enabling lager brewing to rid itself of infections and become the world's dominant beer style.

The Old or Gamle Brewery founded by J.C. Jacobsen. It is now a museum.

2

THE INGREDIENTS

Beer is a highly complex alcoholic drink. The journey that ends with the finished product starts in the barley fields. Unlike a grape, if you crush an ear of barley, nothing happens. It takes the enormous skill of the maltster to turn the starch within each ear of grain into fermentable sugars. It is the task of the maltster to cure or kiln the 'green' malt to produce the correct colour needed by the brewer. Once the brewer has produced a sweet sugary extract, he has to add hops to give beer its second taste characteristic: the tangy, piny, citric bitterness that balances the biscuity flavours of malt.

BARLEY AND OTHER INGREDIENTS

Without barley there can be no beer. Brewers need hops and water and yeast as well. But malt is their springboard and their building block: they call it 'the soul of beer'. The way in which barley becomes malt is one of the great mysteries of the brewing process. It is rarely seen, locked away from view in maltings that are often far removed from breweries. Most modern maltings are mechanized and automated, the cereal grains hidden inside vast steel drums. There are a few surviving traditional 'floor maltings', so called because the grain is spread over large floors and turned by hand. At Tuckers of Newton Abbot in Devon in the West Country, you can not only watch the whole fascinating process but also finish the tour with a pint of the end product.

Edwin Tucker's maltings were built at a cost of £5000 in 1900 alongside the railway line so that both barley and Welsh anthracite coal for firing the kilns could be unloaded straight from wagons. In those days the main product was mild ale malt, but today Tuckers concentrates on pale ale varieties. It takes 12 tonnes of barley to make 9 tonnes of malt. Managing director Richard Wheeler chooses only the best barley, 80 per cent from farmers in Devon and some in Hampshire and Wiltshire. Tuckers is both a maltings and a working museum. Visitors can see the malting process interspersed with glimpses of Victorian working life.

The curious aspect of malting is that a grain of barley looks scarcely different from a grain of malt. Yet the steps taken to change one from the other trigger natural chemical reactions that make it possible for brewers to unlock the sugars in the grain and begin to make beer. When barley arrives at Tuckers, it is dried, 10 tonnes at a time, in a drum like a giant tumble dryer. Barley destined for brewing has not only to be of

Heart and soul . . .barley is a hardy cereal that developed from tall grass and which contains the vital starches and enzymes needed for brewing.

high quality but also must have a low level of nitrogen: too much nitrogen and you end up with hazy beer. Drying reduces the water content of the grain. Like every step in the malting process, this has to be judged carefully to stop the grain germinating while it is stored for up to 12 months in large bins. When it is needed for malting it is carried

by elevators to the screening area where a belt-driven sieve removes dirt, stones and 'chaff' (dead husks and stalks).

Now the serious business begins. The clean barley goes into four troughs called

Raking the grain at Tuckers' maltings to aerate the germinating barley.

steeping tanks, 5.25 tonnes per tank. The grain is soaked with water for 60 hours. After the first 12 hours, the water is drained, the grain is left for a day, and then more water is pumped in. Steeping washes the grain and also kills bacteria and wild yeasts that would impede both germination and, later, fermentation. But steeping also increases the water content of the grain from around 12 per cent to 40 per cent, vital to encourage germination. The soaked grain is dropped through hatches to the germination floors into barrows from which workers tip it in heaps on the ground. There is a curious, slightly rancid smell on the floors, a blend of sweet biscuits and a dog caught in a downpour. Workers shovel the grain into a smooth carpet or 'couch' across the floors. It is raked several times a day for four to five days as the grain starts to germinate: turning not only aerates the grain and stops the build up of heat (the floor is kept at 15°C/60°F) but stops the roots intertwining.

This stage demands careful and delicate analysis by Richard and his staff. Amazing biochemical changes take place inside the grain as it germinates: the starch in the grain becomes soluble, enabling it to turn into malt sugar, the key to fermentation in the brewery. The obvious sign of germination is the rootlet breaking through the husk.

Meanwhile, hidden from sight, the plant's embryo, the main root or acrospire, starts to grow, triggering a change that turns proteins into enzymes that will convert soluble starch into sugar during mashing in the brewery. Only partial germination takes place. If the grain were allowed to germinate fully, it would start to consume its own sugars. This is the great skill of the maltster: to judge when partial germination has gone far enough. He does this by chewing some grain. If it is soft and friable in the mouth,

Rootlets break through the husk of the barley as it germinates, triggering biochemical changes that make the grain soluble.

then 'modification' – the growth of the embryo and the solubility of the starch – has progressed successfully.

Germination is stopped by heating the grain in two kilns, large rooms with steeply pitched roofs. The floors are made of 'wedge wire' or slotted metal. Heat comes blasting up from below, provided by gas fires. The damp 'green' malt stays in the kilns for 48 hours. Tuckers produces only pale malts (stewed malts such as crystal and roasted malts need different techniques) with the temperature rising from 65°C to 75°C (149°F to 167°F) and then to 90°C (194°F) for the last eight hours.

Richard Wheeler poured some malt into

Bobey barrows used to move the grain from the washing troughs to the germination floors in a traditional maltings.

my cupped hands for me to chew. It was sweet, biscuity and delicious. If you've ever eaten raw Ovaltine, Bournvita or similar bedtime drinks, you will know the taste of pale malt. Tuckers makes malt from several varieties of barley. Halcyon, Pipkin, Puffin and Maris Otter are winter barleys, sown in the autumn and hardy enough to withstand the frosts and snows of winter. Alexis and Chariot are spring varieties, more delicate and favoured by lager brewers. The maltings also experiment with such new varieties as Gleam, Fanfare and Regina. They will be on trial for several years and will become regulars only if protracted brewing trials are satisfactory.

There are many reasons why a brewer will stick with a favoured variety of barley. There is price, the quality of the sugar-rich 'extract' in the mash tun, and the way in which the house yeast reacts with the malt sugars in the fermenters. But, Richard Wheeler admitted, it is the seed merchants who drive the business, endlessly developing new varieties of barley that have a higher yield with more tonnes per acre.

A tour of Tuckers' Maltings sees malt meet its destiny. The Teignworthy craft brewery, run by John Lawton, is housed at one end of the maltings. John uses Maris Otter and Pipkin malts which he brings in a barrow from the malting area. Richard Wood also encourages John to make trial brews with new malting varieties such as Regina. Teignworthy's main beer is Reel Ale (4 per cent), brewed with pale malt, a touch of wheat malt and 8 per cent crystal malt, made by specialist dark and stewed malt makers French and Jupp's in Hertfordshire. The hops are Challenger and Goldings. It has a pale copper colour and a rich malt aroma with a hint of toffee and an earthy blackcurrant fruitiness from the hops. Juicy malt and tart hops combine in the mouth and the

finish is dry with citric fruit, sweet malt and spicy, bitter hops. Teignworthy also makes bottle-conditioned ales for Tuckers' on-site shop, including Edwin Tucker's Maris Otter Premium Ale (5.5 per cent). With its burnished copper colour and rich biscuity malt and hops aroma and flavours, the beer is a superb example of both the maltster's and the brewer's art, made under one roof by craftsmen dedicated to traditional methods.

Barley lies in fourth position behind wheat, rice and maize (corn) in the world production of cereals. Barley, a tall grass of the family Hordeum, especially *Hordeum vulgare*, comes in many forms that enable it to withstand extreme climatic conditions in all parts of the world. The main areas of cultivation are, in descending order, Europe, followed by the region that formed the former Soviet Union (where the Ukraine is a major producer), North America and Asia. Africa does not provide a good climate or soil for barley growing and produces less in total than Australia and New Zealand. In Africa, local cereals such as sorghum are augmented with imported barley to make beer: African barley is grown on the north coast, in the hills of Ethiopia and, to a lesser extent, around the Cape. South American barley production is limited to the foothills of the Andes in Colombia, Ecuador, Peru, Bolivia and Chile. Further south there are smaller areas in the sub-tropical highlands of Brazil that extend to the lowlands of Uruguay and into the Argentinian pampas. The big barley-producing countries usually have an annual surplus of grain that is sold to brewers in Africa, Latin America and Asia. China has a burgeoning demand for malting barley as it begins to emerge as a major brewing nation.

Only a fraction of world barley production is suitable for brewing and distilling. Most barley and malted barley are used as

cattle feed, for cooking and for non-alcoholic drinks and confectionery. A brewer needs malt that is low in nitrogen: during mashing, nitrogen is converted into protein, which can cause haze in the finished beer. Protein haze is tasteless and harmless but in an age where clarity is equated with quality, brewers aim for crystal-clear beer. The preferred type of malt used by brewers comes from two-row maritime barley: the rows indicate the number of grains within each ear of barley. As you would expect, two-row maritime varieties are grown in countries with seaboards but the coarser six-row barley tends to dominate in vast areas such as the Midwest of the United States. It is the high level of natural enzymes in six-row barley varieties that enabled American brewers to use large amounts of 'adjuncts' such as rice and corn (maize) in their beers as the malt enzymes also convert the starch in adjuncts into fermentable sugar. Some beers brewed in the Americas have an adjunct level as high as 60 per cent of the total cereal grist. As six-row barley is high in nitrogen, the adjuncts help reduce haze.

Barley varieties suitable for brewing fall into two categories: spring and winter. Winter barleys are actually sown in the autumn and have to be hardy to withstand cold, frost and snow. Ale brewers favour winter barleys, such as Maris Otter and Pipkin, for their robust nutty, biscuity flavours. Lager brewers consider that spring barleys, such as Alexis, sown in kinder weather, have a gentler, sweeter character. Continental barley malt destined for lager brewing tends to be less 'modified' (ie its starches are less fully developed to turn to sugar) than malt used in traditional ale brewing. It is to continue modification that lager brewers use the exhaustive decoction mashing method described in the section on how lager is brewed.

TYPES OF MALT

Malt comes in three forms: enzymic malt, kilned or cured to keep the natural enzymes alive in order to convert starch into sugar (such malts are said to have diastatic power); stewed malts such as crystal and carapils which come with their starches turned into sugar by the maltster; and roasted malts cured at such high temperatures that the enzymes are destroyed. Roasted malts have no diastatic power and are used for colour and flavour. A colour chart gives ratings to malts in units known as EBCs, which stands for European Brewing Convention.

Pilsner or lager malt (2.5–4 EBC) is the palest malt available, kilned at a comparatively low temperature of 85°C (185°F) to preserve enzymes and allow brewers to make an exceptionally pale gold beer of the Pilsner type. High nitrogen and poor modification mean that lager malts can exhibit two characteristics that brewers are anxious to remove. One is diacetyl, a natural chemical compound that gives a toffee and butterscotch aroma and flavour to the finished beer. It is caused by oxidization of the malt and poor or short lagering techniques. The second problem is DMS, which stands for dimethyl sulphide. It imparts a sulphury element and a powerful hint of cornflour on the aroma. Both these characteristics are countered by decoction mashing with 'diacetyl rest' periods and by secondary fermentation and a long lagering period. Beers that exhibit diacetyl and DMS have probably been conditioned for a short period.

Pale malt (4–7.5 EBC) is the basis of ale brewing and is used predominantly in Britain. It is kilned at 100–105°C (212°F–221°F). It must be low nitrogen and well modified so it can be used in an infusion mash system.

Mild Ale malt (7 EBC), as the name

David Jupp of specialist maltsters French & Jupps with the range of special coloured malts made by his company.

Tanks at French & Jupps' maltings in Hertfordshire, where the barley germinates and becomes green malt prior to the kilning process. Stewed malts made by French & Jupps range from carapils to roasted black malt.

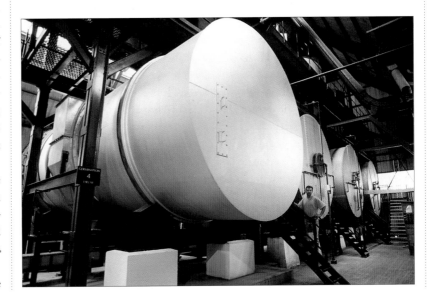

indicates, is used by British brewers to make Mild Ale. It is darker than pale malt as the result of higher kilning temperatures and can be made from barley higher in nitrogen as any haze will be masked by the colour of the finished beer and will be diluted by the use of brewing sugar and cereal adjuncts. As a result of the diminishing demand for Mild Ale, many brewers today use pale malt and add either darker malts or adjuncts such as caramel for colour.

Vienna malt (7 EBC) is similar in colour to Mild Ale malt and was used in Austria by Anton Dreher to make his amber lager in the nineteenth century. It is made from continental barley and will have a high nitrogen content.

Munich malt (14 EBC) is the classic type used by brewers in Bavaria to make their bronze-coloured lager beers. Munich dark malt (25 EBC) is a well-kilned version of standard Munich malt and is used in Dunkel (dark) lagers.

Amber malt (40–60 EBC) is a now rare type of British malt, well kilned to produce the colour. As it has little or no diastatic power, it must be used in small amounts with pale or mild ale malts.

Crystal malt (100–300 EBC) is a stewed malt that gives both colour and 'body' to classic English pale ales. After germination in specialist maltings, the green malt is loaded into a sealed kiln so the moisture cannot escape. The temperature is raised to 45°C/113°F, which matches the mashing temperature in a brewery. The enzymes inside each kernel of grain convert some of the starches into sugar. Vents in the kiln are opened and the temperature is increased so that the sugar crystallizes. It is a similar process to making toffee. Not all the sugar is converted and much of it is dextrin rather than maltose: as dextrin cannot be converted into alcohol by brewer's yeast, the

sugar remains in the beer, giving a fullness of palate and a pleasing nutty flavour. Brown malt, rarely used these days, is also a stewed malt kilned at a lower temperature.

Carapils (30 EBC) is the continental equivalent of crystal malt, kilned at a lower temperature to avoid deepening the colour of the finished beer.

Chocolate malt (1000 EBC) is cured at high temperatures until the grains look like coffee beans. The malt is used primarily to add colour and a luscious chocolate-coffee character to dark milds, porter and stouts.

Roasted barley (1000–1500 EBC) is unmalted and roasted until black. It gives a dry and burnt aroma and flavour to stouts, in particular the style known as 'dry Irish stout'. It also helps create a dense collar of foam on beer, another distinguishing characteristic of Irish stout.

Black malt (1250–1500 EBC) gives a tart, slightly astringent character to dark beers and an acrid bitterness. It imparts a flavour similar to that of espresso coffee and must be used sparingly to avoid unbalancing the flavour of beer. Scottish brewers often add a minute amount of black malt to their ales for both colour and flavour.

Wheat malt (5 EBC) is a major constituent of Bavarian wheat beers and is also popular among British ale brewers, as a small amount helps to create a good head on finished beer. It is an important consideration where cask-conditioned beer is concerned: the style is low in carbonation and needs some help to produce the foam that most modern drinkers expect.

ADJUNCTS

Cereal adjuncts and brewing sugars are a controversial subject. Many people ask why other countries do not have 'Pure Beer Laws' similar to Germany, which permits only malted barley and wheat to be used as

brewing cereals. But Germany's cold-fermented beers enjoy a lengthy lagering that removes such problems as protein haze and off-flavours. With the exception of 12° beers in the Czech Republic, few other lager-producing countries have such protracted periods of secondary fermentation and cold conditioning. Even warm-fermented beers in Germany are mashed with a decoction system and are usually cold conditioned after fermentation, methods that again counter problems of clarity and flavour caused by poorly modified malt. Conventional ale brewers in other countries have to use the brewing equipment available, which will mean an infusion mash, a maximum seven-day primary fermentation and a short period of conditioning either in the brewery or in cask. The main adjuncts used are wheat flour, flaked (gelatinized) grains or torrefied (scorched) grains: torrefied grain is similar to popcorn. Brewing sugar, either in the form of candy sugar (sucrose), which is popular with Belgian ale brewers, or invert sugar (glucose and fructose) widely used in Britain, encourage fermentation, reduce haze and add subtle colour and flavour. As sugar is highly fermentable, more so than malt which contains some unfermentable dextrins, it counters sweetness in strong ales and encourages a dry aftertaste.

The levels of adjuncts and sugars used in ales are tiny. The main problem lies with international lager brands that are heavily diluted with adjuncts. There is a world of difference between a brilliant ale with a small and carefully chosen amount of adjuncts and a 'lite' lager in which unmalted cereals, usually rice or corn (maize) account for as much as 60 per cent of the mash.

HOPS

The main function of the hop is to add bitterness to beer but this astonishing plant

The hop adds bitterness and complex aromas and flavours to beer.

contributes far more than that. The hop imparts aromas and flavours that are spicy, herbal, citric, resinous, peppery and perfumy. It gives added dimensions and depth to beer. It balances the biscuity sweetness of the malt's juices. It is an amazing plant that makes beer, in all its infinite variety and diversity, the world's greatest drinking experience. An English Fuggle or Golding, a Czech Zatec, a German Hersbrucker or Perle, or an American Cascade or Chinook will give tasteprints to beer as distinctive as those of the world's great grape varieties.

The cultivated hop plant is called *Humulus lupulus*, 'the wolf plant', so called because of its voracious growing and climbing abilities. It is a member of the *Cannabidaceae* hemp family, which includes cannabis and the order of nettle plants, *Urticaceae*. The hop plant is dioecious, meaning the male and female plants grow separately. With the exception of English and some Belgian and American varieties, hops are not fertilized. Only the female hop is used in brewing, and most brewers demand seedless hops, as they feel the more pungent and resinous character of fertilized hops does not marry well with the delicate flavours of lager

beer. Ale brewers, on the other hand, consider that the qualities of seeded hops better balance the more robust and fruity nature of their beers. As a result, English hop varieties are in great demand in North

After picking, the hops are dried in oast houses by warm air to reduce their moisture content. The rotating cowls on top of the oast house chimneys ensure the warm air is evenly spread.

America from the new generation of craft brewers as well as among ale brewers in Belgium and the Netherlands.

Like the grape, the hop needs the right soil conditions in order to flourish. It thrives in well-drained loamy or sandy soil. In some regions, such as the American Pacific Northwest, the soil has to be irrigated. The plants need warmth as well as moisture and long hours of sunlight: in the classic hop-growing regions of Bavaria, England and Zatec, there are more than 18 hours of sunlight during the summer months. The hop is propagated by cutting. The plant above ground is cut off at harvest time, leaving behind the rootstock, from which new shoots grow in the spring. The rootstock stores the reserves that allow the plant to grow: its most important function is to supply water. In spring shoots appear above ground. They are covered with hooked hairs that give the stems or bines a good grip as they climb the wires of the trellises on which they flourish. Bines can grow by as much as 35 centimetres (12 inches) in a single day, though 10 centimetres (4 inches) is more usual. By mid-June the plants have grown halfway up their trellises and new shoots known as laterals appear. The development of the laterals is keenly watched by farmers as the hop cones grow on them. By early July the hops will reach the tops of the trellises, about 4.8 metres (16 feet) in height in conventional plants, and will start to flower for three to four weeks, allowing the cones to form and mature. The cones will be ready to be picked in late August and mid-September.

Until the 1950s, hop picking was traditionally done by hand but manual labour has been replaced by machines. Special tractors with arms and rakes drive along the avenues of hops: the bines are gripped at the bottom and the hops are torn from the stalks at the top and fall into trailers drawn by the tractors. The hops go through a picking machine that cleans them and removes stalks, leaves and earth. They must be dried quickly or they will start to rot within a few hours. The water content has to be reduced from 80 per cent to around 10 to 12 per cent. The hops are laid out on perforated floors in buildings known as hop houses in Germany or oast houses in England. Underfloor heating from kilns dries the hops, with the temperature held at 60°C/140°F for about 10 hours. In oast houses, with their distinctive cowled roofs, a steady draft of warm air is maintained by rotating the cowl, which sits on top of a chimney and creates suction. In modern buildings, the hops are placed on conveyors that carry them through a dryer. At the end of the kilning process the dried hops are packed into sacks and are stored until bought by breweries.

The cones of the hop hold a fine yellow powder called lupulin. Lupulin contains the essential oils and bitter compounds needed by the brewer. The compounds break down into humulone and lupulone: the former creates the alpha acids that give bitterness to beer while lupulone helps to stabilize the wort during brewing. The oils in the cone give distinctive flavours to beer. Tannins also play a part in adding flavour and helping to prevent infection during the brewing process. Hops divide into two main groups: bittering hops and aroma hops. Bittering hops are high in alpha acid while aroma hops have low rates of acid and are used mainly for the delightful bouquet they give to beer. Traditionally brewers would blend aroma and bittering hops (in Britain the classic blend is the Fuggle for bitterness and the Golding for aroma), but the rise of large national and international brewing groups

Walk tall…American hop pickers once used stilts to move around between the high rows of hops. Today hop picking is mechanized and no longer provides jobs for the urban poor or migrant workers.

led to a demand for new 'high alpha' hops that combined both attributes within one variety. The English Target and the German Hüller and Perle are high alpha varieties. The trend today is away from high alphas, which can give a harsh note to the finish of beer. The heightened interest in hop character among beer drinkers has encouraged brewers to experiment with new blends or to brew 'single varietal beers' using just one hop variety. In England, the National Hop Association organizes an annual Beauty of Hops competition for brewers who produce 'single varietal beers' made from just one hop. It is fascinating to sample beers brewed with just one variety to appreciate their particular attributes. The citric attack of a Challenger, the plum jam flavour of a Bramling and the resinous punch of a Target come into their own in single varietal beers.

When hops reach the brewery they are added in stages during the copper boil. A proportion is added to the wort at the start of the boil in order to extract the oils and bittering compounds. But most of the aroma is evaporated during the boil and there are further additions during the boil followed by a 'late hop' addition just a few minutes before the boil ends. The final addition is purely to extract aroma, and a brewer may select a special low-alpha variety such as a Golding for this stage. Ale brewers often add a handful of hops to their casks of beer before they leave the brewery to add further aroma and to minimize the risk of infection. This is known as 'dry hopping'. Breweries with traditional coppers, which have slotted bases to separate hopped wort from spent hops, use the whole hop flower. Modern plants that use two vessels for the boiling stage, a brew kettle followed by a hop whirlpool or separator, will use pelletized hops. Pellets are made by crushing the hops into small tablets; they take up less space in a brewery.

The thick clusters of hops, rising to some 4.8 metres (16 feet), are called curtains. Trained to climb up poles that are criss-crossed by wires, the hops reach up for sun, air and rain.

HOP-PRODUCING COUNTRIES

Hop growing is restricted to parts of the world where the right soil and climatic conditions exist and the hours of daylight are long enough to allow the plants to photosynthesize – to draw in food from the air and sunlight. Hops, cultivated in 30 countries today, grow between the 35th and 55th parallels of latitude in the northern and southern hemispheres. Below the 35th parallel it is necessary to use artificial lighting to extend the day. The most northerly hop-growing region is Mari and Chuvash in Russia, the most southerly is the Australian island of Tasmania. Burma and Zimbabwe are the two hop-growing regions closest to the equator. Far and away the biggest hop crop comes from the northern strip of the world that lies between the 55th and 35th parallels, taking in southern Canada and the Pacific North-west of the United States, England, western, central and eastern Europe, and parts of the former Soviet Union and the Far East.

Germany is the world's biggest producer of hops (annual harvest 848,600 zentners), with the Hallertau region of Bavaria forming the largest single hop-growing region. Other large hop-growing areas include Spalt, Hersbruck and Tettnang, all in Bavaria, and the Elbe/Saale region from the former German Democratic Republic. There are tiny hop-growing areas further north in Baden near Heidelberg, the Eifel near Bitburg and in the Rhineland Palatinate near Bergzabern. The principal Bavarian varieties are Hallertauer Mittelfrüh, Hersbrucker, Perle, Tettnanger, Spalter, Brewers Gold and Northern Brewer, the last two bred from varieties developed in England. The Germans call their varieties 'noble hops', a term that has no scientific meaning but which stems from their superb aroma and low levels of alpha acid, ranging

As soon as the hops have been dried, they are pressed into large sacks known as 'pockets'. They will stay fresh and retain their bitterness and aroma for a couple of years. Hops are often compressed into pellets for ease of handling but many brewers prefer the whole hop flowers.

from 3.8 per cent in a Hersbrucker variety to 8 per cent in Northern Brewer, compared to 10 to 15 per cent in high alpha hops grown elsewhere.

Hop growers in the United States expect to overtake Germany and become the world's biggest producer by the second decade of the twenty-first century. The current annual harvest is 690,760 zentners. It will be a major achievement, for the hop plant has had a peripatetic existence in the US. English and Dutch settlers on the East Coast collected wild hops from the forests in the seventeenth century. They also imported hops from England and Holland but began to develop their own crops from cuttings. The first hop gardens owned by English settlers appeared in the Massachusetts region of New England in the late 1620s. New Hampshire became the major hop area but production throughout New England went into terminal decline at the time of the Civil War. Production switched to New York State, which supplied not only the burgeoning urban areas of New York City and Philadelphia but also the Midwest when the Erie Canal was built. But New York hops were prone to disease, and the entire crop was wiped out in 1927 by the fungus Peronospora. That, plus the dramatic decline in demand for hops as a result of Prohibition, put an end to hop growing on the East Coast. Hop cultivation had started in a small way in California and the Pacific North-west from the 1850s. Following the repeal of Prohibition and a return to pre-Prohibition levels of beer consumption, hop growing developed at a rapid pace in the Pacific North-west while California's acreage declined as a result of rising costs of land, increased urbanization and a shortage of labour to pick the crop.

Today hops are grown exclusively in Washington State, Oregon and Idaho. In Oregon's Willamette Valley, both the landscape, the climate and soil are similar to those in the German Hallertau, and as a result the region produces fine aroma hops, including the Willamette variety. Idaho was the last state to grow hops, with production centred in the area of Caldwell. Its climate and soil are similar to those of neighbouring Oregon. Washington State is now the biggest hop region of the United States, with production based in the Yakima Valley east of the Cascade Mountains. It has hot summers and there is often no rainfall in

Hop growers in Worcestershire, England, have developed dwarf hops half the height of conventional hops.

July and August. As a result, the hop fields have to be irrigated. Thanks to excellent climate, good soil and few problems of disease, hops from the Pacific North-west are of exceptional quality, have a healthy bright green colour and give pungent citric fruit bouquets and flavours to beer reminiscent of oranges and grapefruit. European hop growers, the Germans in particular, are critical of the aggressive character of American hops, which they say give a rough 'cat's pee' flavour to beer. Love them or hate them, American hop varieties are an important element of the beer renaissance in the United States and give craft brewers' ales and lagers stunning and distinctive aromas and flavours. The main American varieties are either developments of English and European hops or those specially bred in the US. Among the former are the Fuggle, introduced from England to Oregon as early as 1880, Perle, based on the German variety, Willamette, bred from the Fuggle, and Mount Hood, bred from the Hallertauer Mittelfrüh. Indigenous varieties are Cluster, the oldest American hop, Cascade, a medium-strength variety introduced in 1972, and Galena, Nugget and Chinook, high-alpha hops developed in the State Breeding Programme in Idaho and grown since 1978, 1983 and 1985 respectively. Chinook has a pronounced grapefruit aroma and flavour, and was bred from an English female Golding.

The Saaz or Zatec hop is the most prized in the world. Any brewer with pretensions to make a genuine Pilsner beer will import Saaz from the Czech Republic. With its delicate but firm bitterness and a superb 'noble hop' aroma, it is the perfect companion for the sweet, biscuity juices of a pale Pils malt. Bohemia was famous for its hops long before the rise of the Hallertau in neighbouring Bavaria. Hop cultivation began as early as the ninth century and was a sizeable industry by the fourteenth, encouraged by both the church and the German emperor. Alongside London and Nuremberg, the Bohemian town of Zatec (Saaz in German) became a major centre of the hop trade in the nineteenth century, described as the 'Golden Age' of the hop with the arrival of pale Pilsner beer. The annual harvest in the Czech Republic is 192,750 zentners, with the main bulk of the crop coming from the Zatec area and small amounts from Ustek and Trsice. They are all of the Zatec or Saaz variety: although the term Saaz is used worldwide, the Germans more accurately call the hop Saazer meaning 'of Saaz'. Saaz are also grown in the neighbouring Slovak Republic. The hop-growing areas are protected from extreme cold in winter by the Carpathian and Sudeten mountain chains. But the mountains make the area dry, and hops flourish only as a result of the red 'cinnamonic' soil, high in iron oxide, that retains unusually high levels of water. The Saaz hop is a low bittering variety, with less alpha acid than a Hersbrucker and considerably less than a Northern Brewer, both grown in Bavaria. In order to achieve the high level of bitterness in the classic Pilsner Urquell, large quantities of Saaz are needed.

Nobody knows for certain when hops were first grown commercially in England. They certainly grew wild during the time of the Roman occupation, for the Romans ate them as a delicacy like asparagus. But hops were not used in brewing until the sixteenth century. One theory says hops used in brewing arrived in south-east England in 1524 when King Henry VIII encouraged Flemish weavers to settle in the country and develop a cloth industry independent of continental Europe. J. Banlister, however, in his *Synopsis of Husbandry* written in 1799, put the date earlier at 1511 and used as proof a piece of contemporary doggerel: 'Turkey, carp, hops, pickerill and beer/Came into England all in a year'. It seems likely that small amounts of hops were either grown or imported into England earlier than the sixteenth century, but a flourishing industry did not start until a large body of Flemish

Short hops but long on flavour...Ruddles brewery in Rutland uses dwarf First Gold in its Bob's Gold ale, which has a fine citric aroma and flavour.

weavers, who spread from Kent across the River Dart into Essex and then into Norfolk and Suffolk, demanded bitter beer rather than heavy, sweet local ale. As commercial brewing grew, the businessmen who owned the breweries quickly grasped the fact that hopped beer stayed in good condition for longer and needed less malt than unhopped ale: hops made brewing more profitable. Hop growing spread rapidly as London and other industrial cities grew and large numbers of urban workers demanded copious amounts of beer. The plant was grown in Kent and the surrounding counties of Hampshire and Sussex while Herefordshire and Worcestershire supplied the thirsty needs of Birmingham, Wolverhampton and the Black Country.

Small amounts of hops were grown for a while in Scotland and Wales but harsh weather soon ended the experiment. Today, in spite of the spread of lager brewing and demands by the European Union to grow only unfertilized hops, English growers still concentrate on seeded varieties. It is not due to English cussedness or perversity but because the tougher nature of seeded hops means they are better equipped to withstand the difficult climate in England, with long, damp winters and often extremely wet summers, and the pests and diseases that attack the plant. It is undoubtedly true, however, that England's determination to stay with seeded hops has led to a massive decline in its once leading role as a hop exporter. The annual harvest today is 109,000 zentners compared to 300,000 in the 1930s.

The sturdiness of English hop varieties enables them to be grown in widely different types of soil. East Kent, where the much-prized East Kent Golding is grown, has deep chalky loam. Central Kent has deep and alluvial loams. The Weald of Kent has heavy soil and the more hilly terrain offers protection from wind and rain. The sandy, acidic areas of Kent that are not best suited to hop cultivation are designated as 'Bastard Kent'. The heavy soil of Herefordshire and Worcestershire is also good for growing hops. Until the eighteenth century, hop varieties were designated by their areas of cultivation, such as Canterbury and Farnham.

The two best-known English hops were named after the men who discovered and grew them. A Mr Golding found some Canterbury-type hops growing in his garden in Malling in Kent at the end of the eighteenth century. They were cultivated and found to have a high yield and a fine aroma. Within a century, Kent and Sussex had gone over almost entirely to Goldings. In 1875 Richard Fuggle introduced a new hop that was propagated when a hop picker on George Stace's farm in Horsmond, Kent, scattered some seeds on the ground. The Fuggle and the Golding survive today and are still the preferred varieties for scores of craft brewers in Britain, using the Fuggle for its bitterness and the Golding for its superb earthy, piny and peppery aroma.

Since the early part of the twentieth century, the South Eastern Agricultural College at Wye in Kent has been breeding new hop varieties that would be more resistant to pests and disease. Both Brewers Gold and Northern Brewer were created at Wye and eventually were grown in Belgium and the Bavarian Hallertau to meet the new demand for varieties with greater bitterness. In the mid-1970s Wye released new varieties that were even higher in alphas. Target and

Yeoman have bitter compounds of more than 10 per cent. Target now accounts for almost half the annual British hop crop but is in rapid decline as brewers and drinkers seek beers with more aromatic charm and less harsh 'hop bite'. The main English hops bred today are Target, Golding, Fuggle, Whitbread Golding Variety, Progress, Bramling Cross, Northdown, Challenger and Yeoman. The Whitbread Golding, despite its name, is a derivative of the Fuggle.

Wye College continues to work in the interests of hop growers, brewers and drinkers. In the 1990s, working with the ADAS Rosemaund research farm at Preston Wynne in Herefordshire, it cultivated new 'dwarf' hops that grow to just 2.4 metres (8 feet) compared to the conventional 4.8 metres (16 feet). Three varieties of dwarfs have been grown to date: First Gold, Herald and Pioneer. They are easier and cheaper to grow as they need a smaller support system of poles and wires. Dwarf hops are less likely to fall over in high winds and storms: while this is rarely a problem in England, whole crops have been destroyed in North America and central Europe by storms and typhoons. Picking dwarfs is also easier as a specially designed tractor can move down the path between two 'curtains' of hops and strip them both at the same time. Dwarf varieties are more resistant to disease and pests: ADAS is encouraging farmers in Herefordshire to grow Target on the boundaries of their fields to soak up pest attack and divert attention from the dwarf fields. Hop growers in the US and Japan are also experimenting with dwarf varieties.

Among other hop-growing countries, China is emerging as a major supplier as the country's brewing capacity expands. The annual harvest of 270,000 zentners puts China in third place behind Germany and the United States. The first hop gardens, in

the north east of the country, did not appear until the 1920s. Since the late 1950s, cultivation has expanded into the north west. Hop varieties have been cultivated principally from German and American varieties.

Slovenia, with an annual production of 70,000 zentners, is a small producer but its Styrian Golding is in great demand as an aroma hop. Several British brewers use Styrian Goldings to dry hop their ales. Slovenia was once part of the province of Styria during the Austro-Hungarian Empire. Following the break-up of the empire in the wake of World War I, Lower Styria joined the new Yugoslav republic and is now the independent country of Slovenia. (Upper Styria is part of Austria.) Hop farmers in Lower Styria tried without success to grow both Czech Saaz and German varieties but fared better when they received cuttings of the English Fuggle. Apparently the cuttings were mis-labelled 'Fuggles Goldings' and the name Golding was adopted. The modern Styrian Golding is a seedless hop and is much prized for its fine bouquet. The main hop-growing area is centred on the town of Zalec, a name remarkably similar to Zatec's in the Czech Republic.

Australia produces 58,820 zentners of hops a year and Tasmania accounts for more than 46,000 zentners of the total. Tasmania, almost identical in size to Bavaria, lies on the 42nd parallel and has a more moderate climate than the other hop-producing state of New South Wales. The father of Tasmanian hop growing is William Shoobridge, who brought hops from Kent in 1822 and planted them in Providence Valley near Hobart. After many years of growing American and English hop varieties, a hop research institute was set up in Ringwood near Melbourne in 1950. The aim was to develop new Australian hops for both domestic and overseas use. The main

Skimming the head of the yeast. Yeast recreates itself so there is never a risk of a brewer running short of supplies.

variety to come out of the institute is Pride of Ringwood. With an alpha content of 9–11 per cent, it is a high bittering variety but also has a fine aroma. In pelletized form, it has found success in other brewing countries. Tasmania is one of the few places to grow organic hops and they are in great demand from brewers. The Caledonian Brewery in Edinburgh imports organic Tasmanian Pride of Ringwood for its Golden Promise Ale.

HOP PROBLEMS

Growing hops is not a simple matter. The plant is especially prone to attack by disease and pests. In 1926 the fungal disease Peronospora destroyed almost the entire harvest in the Hallertau. The fungus makes the cones of the hop turn brown. Other diseases include powdery mildew that causes cone deformities; botrytis, which damages the tips of the cones; and Verticillium wilt that also turns the plant brown. The Hallertauer Mittelfrüh variety is so susceptible to wilt that it is now grown in only small amounts and is being replaced by new, hardier varieties. In England, the Fuggle is so open

to attack by pests and disease that it has virtually disappeared from its homeland of Kent and is now grown mainly in Worcestershire. Pests that attack and destroy hops include aphids and the red spider mite.

Research scientists attempt to tackle the problem of disease by breeding tougher new varieties. The stock response by farmers to pest attack is to reach for spray cans and pesticides. But research at the ADAS Rosemaund farm shows that the best way to prevent pests is to welcome predators such as ladybirds (ladybugs), lace wings, flies and parasitic wasps that kill aphids and spider mites. This is achieved by encouraging a natural environment of grass and plants to grow between the rows of hops in which predators can thrive, and to use organic mulches. It is remarkably short-sighted to drench hops and the soil in which they grow with pesticides and fertilisers that destroy the natural habitat of insects. The ladybird is the hop's best friend.

HOP BITTERNESS

The bitterness of hops is measured on a scale known as IBUs, standing for International Units of Bitterness, and is based on the level of alpha acid in a hop variety. The trend in the late twentieth century was towards hops high in alpha acid, a trend fuelled by both the growth of more bitter beers, both ales and lagers, and the fact that fewer hops need to be used if they are high in alphas. A century ago the alpha acid level in hops was around 5 per cent. Today some 'super' hops have levels as high as 17 or even 22 per cent. However, high alphas are in less demand as brewers concentrate on subtlety of bouquet and flavour. The hopping rate of a beer will depend on the type of hops used and varies between 85 grams (3 ounces) and over 198 grams (7 ounces) per 22 gallons (80 and 200 grams per hectolitre).

YEAST

Yeast converts malt sugars into alcohol but it is also a major contributor to the flavour of beer. A house yeast, cultured and stored in a brewery laboratory, will pick up and retain malt and hop characteristics and implant them in future brews.

Although beer has been brewed from the dawn of history, it was not until in the eighteenth century the Dutch scientist Anton von Leeuwenhoek and the Frenchman Louis Pasteur analysed yeast that its critical role in brewing was properly understood. Before then, fermentation was thought to be some kind of witchcraft. There was considerable scepticism at first when Pasteur, with the aid of a microscope, showed that the production of alcohol was the result of a natural chemical reaction in which yeast cells multiplied as they turned sugars into alcohol and carbon dioxide. He called the process 'la vie sans air' – life without air.

Yeast is a fungus, a single-cell plant that can convert a sugary liquid into equal proportions of alcohol and carbon dioxide. Some 3000 different brewers' yeast cultures are held in yeast banks throughout the world. With the exception of the family of Brettanomyces wild yeasts used to make Belgian lambic beers, brewers' yeasts are divided into two main categories: those used for warm-fermented ales and those used for cold-fermented lagers. Ale yeasts are known scientifically as *Saccharomyces cerevisiae*, which means 'sugar fungus ale', *cerevisiae* being the Latin word for ale. Lager yeasts were initially classified as *Saccharomyces carlsbergensis*, as the first pure culture was isolated in the Carlsberg brewery in Copenhagen, but as many types of lager yeast now exist, the family was reclassified in the 1970s as *Saccharomyces uvarum*.

The two types of yeast are often described as 'top fermenting' and 'bottom fermenting', as ale yeast rises to the surface of the wort during fermentation while lager yeast falls to the bottom. The terms are seriously misleading, for yeast of either type must work at all levels of the liquid in order to attack the maximum amount of sugar. During the first stages of fermentation, carbon dioxide takes yeast and protein to the top of the wort. Ale yeasts do not like being in a fatty liquid and so retain a thick head on top of the fermenting wort while lager yeasts thrive in such an environment and sink to the bottom of the vessel after initial head-forming activity. As brewers skim yeast head from the top of ale fermenters and from the bottom of lager vessels, natural selection chooses strains that work best for ale and lager production.

Lager yeasts tend to be powdery, stay in suspension in the fermenting beer and when they fall stick like glue to the bottom of the vessels. Ale yeasts on the other hand are

described as 'flocculant', which means the cells clump together and form a thick blanket on top of the wort. Ale fermentation is typically conducted at 12°C/54°F while lager yeast is tolerant of cold and will work at temperatures as low as 5°C/41°F. As a result, ale fermentation is faster and busier, the heat creating natural fruity compounds in the beer, while lager fermentation is slower; the long lagering process purges

As the yeast head is created, darker sections show the protein present in the sugar-rich wort. This yeast head is at the Hopf wheat beer brewery in Bavaria.

At the start of the fermentation process, hopped wort pours into the vessels where it is thoroughly mixed with the house yeast which begins to transform malt sugars into alcohol and carbon dioxide.

fruity 'esters' and produces a cleaner though less complex end product.

Yeast works with oxygen at the start of fermentation as there is plenty of dissolved oxygen in the wort. The brewer will aerate the wort before pitching the yeast to encourage yeast development. It works rapidly, with bubbles of gas rising to the surface and a brown slick quickly covering the surface. This stage is known as 'aerobic respiration', with the yeast developing with air. When all the oxygen is used up, the yeast reverts to 'anaerobic respiration', Pasteur's 'life without air'. Activity slows down but it is only during the anaeorbic stage that alcohol is produced. A dense and undulating head covers the wort while enzymes released by the yeast cells convert maltose and cane sugar into alcohol and carbon dioxide. Dextrins, also present in the wort from the mashing stage, cannot be fermented by brewers' yeast. The yeast enzymes are known as maltase (which attacks maltose to produce glucose), and invertase, which breaks down sucrose into glucose and fructose. The converted sugars are assimilated by the yeast, which is also busily reproducing itself as cells divide, fuse and create fresh spores. Yeast recreates itself so vigorously that there is never any danger of a brewery running out of supplies. The yeast head is skimmed off to encourage new yeast cells in suspension to continue to create alcohol. When there is virtually no yeast left in suspension (even an ale yeast will be overcome by alcohol and eventually sink to the bottom of the vessel) the brewer knows that primary fermentation is finished. Throughout the process he will have taken readings with a hydrometer to measure the sugar content of the wort.

When Pasteur first looked at yeast under a microscope he found that a typical culture would be made up of several strains, some of them competing with one another, while others were bacteria that impeded a good fermentation and gave a bad flavour to finished beer. When brewing was confined to the winter and early spring, bacteria would have been dormant and would not have affected the beer. But once brewers attempted to make beer all the year round, wild strains of yeast and bacteria were rampant in warm weather. As we have seen, it was the genius of Emil Christian Hansen in the Carlsberg Laboratory in Copenhagen that enabled the first pure yeast strain to be cultured and used world-wide.

It was the defining moment in the history of modern brewing. Between 1880 and 1890, brewing took the giant step from an abysmal ignorance of bacteria and microbiology to using pure yeast cultures. The impact of Hansen's work was not confined to lager brewing. Ale brewers, too, started to use pure cultures. The yeast in the Guinness brewery in Dublin, which had been multi-strain, with as many as five or six different cultures, was reduced to one. Some ale brewers prefer to use a two-strain yeast, with each strain working at different times and temperatures not only to convert effectively sugar to alcohol but also to ensure that the right fruity esters are created for flavour. The Bass ale yeast strain, perfected in Burton-on-Trent, is a two-strain culture while some Trappist brewers in Belgium, such as Orval, use a multi-strain one.

WATER

Brewers don't dismiss water lightly as an incidental liquid that is always on tap. Even the strongest beer is made up mainly of water – at least 90 per cent – and brewers treat it with reverence. For a start, they never call it water: that is the stuff they use for cleaning up after a brew. For brewing itself, they use 'liquor'. The type of water used is crucial if a brewer is producing a particular style of beer. You cannot make a genuine India Pale Ale with soft water, neither can you make a true Pilsner with a hard, flinty water like that of Burton-on-Trent. The total salts in Burton water amount to 1,226 parts per million. In Pilsen the figure is just 30.8. Before the Industrial Revolution and great advances in science, when it became possible to treat water with salts, brewers would set up their plants in areas where the water supply suited the style of beer they made. In Britain, London's soft waters, with a high chloride level, were ideal for brewing dark milds, porters and stouts, while the hard waters of Burton, Tadcaster in Yorkshire and Edinburgh, rich in gypsum and magnesium, were better suited to pale ale production. In the rainy climate of Ireland, Arthur Guinness had a plentiful supply of good brewing liquor on hand though, contrary to myth, it comes from the Wicklow Mountains, not the River Liffey that flows through Dublin. In Bavaria and Bohemia, the soft and almost salt-free waters allow great expression to the delicate aromas of 'noble' hops and the sweet juices of local barley malts, characteristics that are masked by flinty British brewing liquor.

As rain falls to earth it drains through the top soil, percolates through layers of minerals and porous rock, finds its way through cracks in non-porous rock until it settles on a table of impervious rock where it waits to be collected. It may force its way back to the surface in the form of a spring or overflow into a river. As it passes through the earth it absorbs mineral salts. The type and quantity of the salts depend on the rock formation in a given area. Soft water is the result of rain falling on to insoluble rock such as slate or granite. It cannot pick up mineral salts and is almost mineral free. Calcium bicarbonate, derived from chalk, is

Brewers want hard liquor (water) for ale brewing and soft liquor to make lager.

the most common cause of hardness in water. Brewers don't like it. Its ions (dissolved salts) impede fermentation, reduce the effect of more important sulphate ions and interfere with the clarity of the finished beer. Brewers make sure that only minimal amounts of calcium bicarbonate are present in their liquor.

Calcium sulphate (gypsum) on the other hand is a welcome guest in the brewery. It is highly beneficial to the brewing of pale ale. It helps create the right level of acidity in the mash, known as pH (power of hydrogen) and encourages enzymic activity as starches are turned to maltose in the mash tun. It ensures the best extraction of the aromas and flavours of hops, clarifies the

wort, encourages a powerful fermentation but discourages astringency in beer. Calcium sulphate also counters harshness in beer. Magnesium sulphate (Epsom salts) is also found in high levels in hard water. Yeast thrives on magnesium and helps account for the 'greedy' nature of traditional Burton yeast strains. The salts also help stabilize the wort during the copper boil with hops. London water contains high quantities of Sodium chloride – common salt; as a flavour enhancer, it improves the 'mouthfeel' of beer.

Today all brewers treat their brewing liquor to achieve absolute purity, passing it through filters several times to remove unwanted salts and impurities. In order to get the right flavour balance, good fermentation and use of raw materials, brewers in many countries will add small amounts of gypsum and Epsom salts.

TUCKERS MALTINGS

Tuckers Maltings
Teign Road, Osborne Park
Newton Abbot,
Devon TQ12 4AA
(phone 01626 334734)

Open between 10am and 3pm
(3.45pm public holidays in July, August and September), seven days a week between Easter and 31 October.

There are around eight tours a day, which include a visit to the Teignworthy Brewery on the site and a pint of ale.

The cost is around £3.95 per adult. Special rates for children, OAPs and goups. The maltings has a restaurant serving breakfast, lunch and cream tea.

Teignworthy Brewery
Teign Road, Osborne Park
Newton Abbot,
Devon TQ12 4AA
(phone 01626 332066)

3

BREWING STYLES

Brewing styles. . .or brewing families? Lager is far more than just a golden Pilsner. There are dark and red versions, too, found as far afield as Mexico and Japan. And both the Germans and the Dutch make powerful Bocks that recall the beers brewed by monks for the Lenten period. Ale has a vast range of sub styles, including pale ale and bitter, the hallmarks of English brewing, Scotch ales, golden, brown and 'sour red' beers from Belgium, old ales, barley wines, fashionable wheat beers from Bavaria and Belgium, plus porters and stouts that turned brewing into a commercial enterprise in the eighteenth century. There is a third family, one as old as time, using wild or spontaneous fermentation and found only in a tiny region around Brussels.

LAMBIC

The family of beer has its black sheep. Modern ales and lagers may differ in their methods of production but both are firmly rooted in the new technologies of the nineteenth and twentieth centuries. They are connected by the use of carefully cultivated, pure strains of yeast, whether warm or cold fermenting, designed to make beers that are consistent and free from the undesirable aromas and flavours imparted by wild yeasts and other untamed micro-organisms. But in a small area of Belgium, brewers set out to make beers that are deliberately infected with wild yeasts carried on the breeze, and by the bacteria encouraged to live in the fermentation cellars and even inside the oak tuns that hold the maturing beer.

This style of beer is known as lambic. It predates both the Industrial Revolution and the emergence of the modern state of Belgium. It is the last tenuous link with the earliest days of beer making when, once the cereal mash had been made, brewers stood back and watched in awe as wild yeast turned the sweet liquid into a life-enhancing alcoholic drink. No one knows for certain when lambic was first brewed. The roistering sixteenth-century peasants of Payottenland in the paintings of the Brueghels are drinking lambic or 'yellow beer' from their earthenware pots, not wine. But the beer style is far older than that. The Low Countries have for centuries been soft targets for invaders, offering easy access from the sea and a flat, traversible landscape. The Romans came in 57 BC and did battle with the Belgae, a branch of the Celtic people. After the Romans, the Normans invaded and they were followed by the Franks, the Germans, the Dutch, the Burgundians, the Austrians, the Spanish, the French and, once again, the Dutch. All of the invaders made alcohol, either wine,

The mash tun at the Cantillon Brewery where malted barley and wheat are blended.

cider or beer, and they would have been produced by some form of spontaneous fermentation. One of the fascinating aspects of lambic is that it is beery, vinous and cidery, a drink that crosses every bibulous boundary. Some historians argue that the Romans or earlier invaders may have brought a style of brewing that was ancient even then and not dissimilar to sikaru made by the Sumerians in Mesopotamia.

Over the ensuing centuries brewers, based on farms and in cottages, found that it was only in an area of some 500 square kilometres (193 square miles) in the valley of the River Senne, which includes Brussels and Payottenland, that the right blend of airborne spores existed to ensure good quality and consistent beers. It was from the woods, orchards and fields surrounding Brussels that nature provided the wherewithal to conjure up the most remarkable and idiosyncratic beer style known to man. Today a handful of surviving commercial brewers keep the guttering lambic torch alight. The style went into steep decline from the nineteenth century, with the

spread of Brussels into the surrounding countryside and the rise of breweries dedicated to ale and lager production for a large and more sophisticated urban population. But the development of beer connoisseurship in the 1980s and 1990s, with a profound interest in styles, created a new awareness of lambic. Protected by Belgian law since 1965, a European Union ordinance of 1992 and an *appellation contrôlée* from the influential European Beer Consumers' Union, lambic survives and even thrives. A bucolic beer confined for centuries to a tiny area of Belgium has now achieved recognition on a world scale.

If the origins of lambic are obscure, so is its name. One view is that the beer takes its name from four villages: Lembeek, Borcht-Lombeek, Onze-Lieve-Vrouw-Lombeek and Sint-Katelijne-Lombeek. One of the most respected blenders of lambic, Frank Boon, is based in Lembeek, which has had a guild of brewers since the fifteenth century and stages an annual pilgrimage to the shrine of the patron saint of lambic brewers, St Veronus, in Lembeek. Another suggestion is that lambic comes from the Spanish word *lambicado*, meaning 'carefully prepared'. The creation of the style as well as the name is also attributed to Duke Jean IV of Brabant who declared in 1428 that he was bored with the beer served at court and made a new type by macerating and boiling barley and hops in a pot still known as an alambic.

A straight, unblended lambic – flat, still, sour and sherry-like – is a rarity these days, though you will find it served on draught in cafés and bars attached to breweries. Much more common is gueuze, a blend of young and old lambics. The sugars in the young lambic start a secondary fermentation in bottle, creating a lively but short-lived head like champagne and a carbonated tingle in the mouth. There is yet more debate over the origins of the name. As a result of the foaming activity as the beer leaves the bottle, some argue that the word comes from geyser, which in turn derives from the Old Norse *geysa*, 'to gush'. But I was told by Marc van Campenhout of the Belle-Vue Brewery in Brussels that gueuze was a name given to poor people during the time of Spanish rule in the Low Countries. One thing that is beyond dispute is that gueuze was first produced commercially in the nineteenth century, probably to give lambic brewers a drink to challenge the new sparkling pale ales and lagers.

Other versions of lambic have equally intriguing names. Faro is a weak lambic, the result of washing the cereal mash a second time and then blending the finished beer with brown crystallized cane sugar. The name comes from the time of Charles V, the

sixteenth-century King of Spain, Burgundy and the Low Countries, and head of the Holy Roman Empire. His soldiers called the pale beer 'gold liquor' or 'barley liquor' – *farro* in Spanish. Fruit lambics are called kriek, from the Flemish for cherry (the French cerise is never used) or frambozen-framboise for raspberry.

Lambic is a type of wheat beer. Its protective laws and ordinances stipulate that at least 30 per cent of the mash must be unmalted wheat. Centuries ago, busy farmers who also brewed soon grasped the fact that barley malt offered sufficient starch and enzymes to produce a good sugary extract, while blending in some unmalted wheat would lower costs and also give an appealing tart and spicy flavour to the finished beer. Wheat adds great character to lambic. It is high in protein, which means that, as with conventional Belgian and German wheat beers, the end product is slightly hazy and has a rich, foaming head. Wheat starch produces a high level of dextrin, a type of sugar that cannot be fermented by conventional brewer's yeast

but which can be attacked by wild yeasts and bacteria, adding to the alcoholic strength and deepening aroma and flavour.

The brewing process begins with what is called 'turbid mashing'. The term 'turbid' stems from the fact that the wort produced by mashing is viscous and milky white, quite unlike the clear wort produced by ale and lager brewers. Pale malt, usually Pilsner malt, is blended with wheat and water with temperatures of 40°C–45°C (104°F–113°F). Boiling water is added, raising the temperature to 62°C (143°F). The liquid is then pumped to the brew kettle or copper. More boiling water is added to the mash tun and the temperature rises to 72°C (162°F), mashing the grist for a second time. The second batch of liquid also goes to the cooker where it is boiled for twenty minutes and is then pumped back to the mash tun for filtration. The wort returns to the brew kettle where it is boiled with hops for an exceptionally long four to five hours. The wort is heavily hopped but the hops have been aged for at least three years. The ageing of hops causes the alpha acids, the main bittering

Cantillon's brew kettle. Aged hops are boiled with the wort to act as a preservative.

agent, to oxidize and to lose much of their bitterness. The hop resins also oxidize and develop an unpleasant cheesy aroma but this is lost during long fermentation and storage. Brewers need the hops for the compounds in the resins that fight bacteria which could cause the beer to turn into malt vinegar. Belgian Brewers Gold hops are favoured by lambic producers, but as they are in short supply East Kent Goldings from England are also used.

The brewing of lambic follows certain time-honoured rituals. Production takes place only between October and April when outside temperatures remain at less than 15°C (59°F). If the temperature is too high, the wrong kind of spores can be carried on the breeze, affecting fermentation and the final flavour of the beer. When the hopped wort leaves the brew kettle, it is pumped to the attic of the brewery and run into a large, shallow tray known as a 'tun' or 'cool ship', made either from copper or stainless steel. Louvred windows are opened and fans are turned on to encourage yeasts in the air to enter and attack the sugars in the wort. Some tiles on the roof are even removed to help the spores come in. The wort is left in the cool ship overnight, when its temperature falls to less than 15°C (59°F) and it is inoculated by yeasts and other micro-flora. Jacques de Keersmaecker, managing director of Belle-Vue, who was born in a lambic brewery and has studied and produced the style all his life, describes the inoculation in the cool ship as 'the signature event in the creation of lambic, unique in beer making'.

The following day the wort is transferred to giant casks, made from oak or chestnut, which are stored in cool, dark cellars. The casks are open to the atmosphere. Cobwebs abound but the brewers are reluctant to disturb the environment and welcome the presence of spiders which kill fruit flies that would otherwise feed on the sugars in the fermenting beer and infect it. The casks are not new. They have previously held wine, usually port or sherry. Fresh wood would add unpleasant tannins to the beer. Each cask when it arrives in the brewery is meticulously cleaned and scraped inside and a sulphur wick is burnt to kill moulds that would give a putrid taste to the beer. But such cleaning and fumigating do not destroy the yeast cells and spores in the fibres of the wood that start fermentation. Belle-Vue has

Belle-Vue is the biggest of the lambic brewers and its many versions of gueuze and fruit lambics tend to be sweeter and more commercial than the classic interpretations.

The 'cool ship' in the roof at Belle-Vue. The wild yeasts enter through the louvred windows during the night and begin to attack the sugars in the wort.

15,000 casks, all bought from port makers. The casks are ranged on five floors and come in different sizes: 650-litre tuns, 250-litre pipes and 30-litre foudres (143, 55 and 6 gallons respectively). The oldest cask is 250 years, the average age is 50.

The fermentation that creates lambic is amazingly complex. It is often thought that it is the wild yeasts classified as Brettanomyces that create lambic but they are just part of an army of yeasts and bacteria that attack the sugars in the wort. Professor Hubert Verachtert and his colleagues at the University of Leuven have been studying the chemistry of lambic fermentation since the 1970s. To date, they have identified 100 different kinds of yeast colonies, 27 colonies of acetic bacteria and 38 colonies of lactic bacteria in a single batch of lambic. Fermentation involves four overlapping stages. In the first stage, the wild yeasts *Kloeckera apiculata* and enteric bacteria break down proteins by enzymic activity and produce a sweet, fruity aroma.

Secondly, Saccharomyces yeasts, untamed versions of brewer's yeast, produce alcohol and fruity esters similar to ale. During the third stage, lactic bacteria, mainly from the Pediococcus family, makes lactic acid which gives the beer its sour aroma and palate. It is only in the fourth stage of fermentation that Brettanomyces yeasts produce further chemical esters that add a fruity and vinous character to the beer. The second stage of fermentation starts after ten to fifteen days. It is violent and volcanic at first, with foam gushing out of the open bung hole on top of the cask. It continues for some seven months and overlaps with stage three. After eight months a sudden increase in yeast cells marks the start of the fourth and final stage of fermentation during which Brettanomyces yeasts make their vital contribution to the aroma and flavour of the beer. They also help to create a film on top of the beer similar to the 'flor' on sherry. This prevents the beer from oxidizing and turning into vinegar.

Tapping a cask in the cellars at Belle-Vue to check the development of a brew.

Lambic will stay in cask for as long as six years, though one-year-old versions are used for blending. As I toured the cellars at Belle-Vue I was given small glasses of lambic tapped from casks chalked to indicate the year and month they were filled. A month-old lambic had a yeasty aroma and bready taste: brewers call it 'green' or immature. A year-old version was sour on the nose, sweet and sour in the mouth and had a cheesy finish from the hops. At eighteen months the beer had taken on a delightful sherry colour, the musty 'horse blanket' aroma that is the typical contribution of Brettanomyces, a winey palate and a dry finish with still a hint of cheesy hops. At six and a half years the beer was much paler, had a sour, winey aroma, a sharp, tangy palate with a pronounced sherry character, and a sour and lactic finish.

When young and old lambic beers are

58

blended to make gueuze, unfermented sugars in the young beer start a fresh fermentation in the bottle. The result is a spritzy, foaming beer served from a bottle that has been corked with a wire cage in the manner of champagne. The blending requires enormous skill and careful tasting to get the balance right. The blenders must decide how much young lambic to marry with old: it is usually 60 per cent young, but the beer will have more character if as much old lambic is used as possible. Older lambic assimiliates sugars thoroughly, producing a well-attenuated and very dry beer with delightful winey and 'old sacks' aromas from the action of Brettanomyces. A beer using a higher proportion of young lambic will be softer and smoother; it is usually filtered and pasteurized for quick sale. Old blends are encouraged to go through a thorough bottle fermentation and are laid down for at least a year in cellars. Gueuze beers tend to have 5.5 per cent alcohol, a straight lambic about 4.5 per cent.

The most exotic versions of lambic are those in which a further fermentation is caused by the addition of fruit. The use of cherries and raspberries in brewing almost certainly predates the hop and recalls a time when farmer-brewers would use ingredients from surrounding fields and orchards to make beer. The fruit increases fermentability and adds a tartness to the finished beer that blends well with malt. Fruit fuses especially well with beers in which wheat, with its fruity, apple-like flavour, is featured. Small, hard cherries from the Schaarbeek suburb of Brussels are preferred, but they are now in short supply and have been replaced by a larger, fruitier, sweeter variety called Gorsem. The cherries are picked late in the season so that the fermentable sugars are well concentrated: it is a similar method to the 'noble rot' grapes used for some German wines. The cherries are added to the casks at the rate of one kilo to five litres (2.2 pounds to 1 gallon) of beer with some young lambic. The sugars in the fruit and the young beer create a new fermentation. The tannins on the skins add to the dryness of the finished beers while the pips impart further dryness and an almond-like character: the yeasts and bacteria eat right into the pips. Some producers of fruit lambics use syrups rather

Preparing the special type of Belgian cherries added to casks to make fruit lambic.

Belle-Vue's Séléction Lambic, a blended gueuze that dramatically improved the company's reputation.

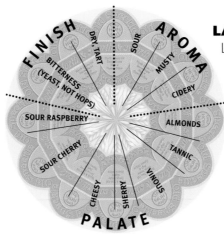

LAMBIC STYLE

Lambic and gueuze have pronounced sour and almost cidery aromas and flavours, while cherries and raspberries add spritzy sour fruit characteristics.

heady aromas of sour fruit, the quenching palates and shockingly dry finishes. At Belle-Vue I tasted a young kriek just a few months old with a cherry aroma, bitter fruit in the mouth and a pronounced cherry finish. A year-old kriek made with Schaarbeek fruit had a ruby-red colour, a sour palate and a finish packed with dry fruit. An eighteen-month-old kriek had a superb dry, earthy aroma, with bitter cherries in the mouth and a dry and winey finish.

than whole fruit. This is frowned on by purists. At Belle-Vue they use whole cherries in kriek but raspberry juice in framboise: whole raspberries disintegrate into a mush that blocks filters. Fruit lambics are usually left in cask for one to two years, and brewers blend and top up casks in order to marry young and old beers.

Drinkers who come fresh to fruit lambics have to overcome an inhibition that suggests they will taste something like alcoholic 'cherryade'. Once that belief is dispelled they can revel in the depth and complexity of the beers, and marvel at the tempting claret and pink colours in the glass, the

LAMBIC PRODUCERS AND GUEUZE BLENDERS

Belgor Brouwerij
Kerkstraat 17, 1881 Brussegem.
Brasserie Belle-Vue,
rue Delaunoy 58,
1080 Brussels

Frank Boon BV
Fonteinstraat 65,
1520 Lembeek

Cantillon Brouwerij
Gheudestraat 56, 1070 Brussels
(Phone 2 521 4928 for dates of opening days and brewery visits.)

De Keersmaeker Brouwerij
Brusselstraat 1, 1703 Kobbegem
(Beers labelled *Morte Subite* and *Eylenbosch. Morte Subite (Sudden Death)* beers are available in the À La Morte Subite café at 7 rue Montagnes aux Herbes Potagères in Brussels, near the Central Station.)

De Koninck Gueuzestekrij
Kerstaat 57, 1512 Dworp

De Troch Brouwerij
Langestraat 20, 1750, Schepdaal
(Owned by Interbrew, with similar beers to Belle-Vue.)

Drie Fonteinen
H. Teirlinckplein 3, 1650 Beersel

Girardin Brouwerij
Lindenberg 10, 1744 Sint-Ulriks-Kapelle

Hanssens Gueuzestekerij
Vroenenbosstraat 8, 152 Dworp

Lindemans Brouwerij
Lenniksebaan 257, 1712 Vlezenbeek

Moriau Geuezestekerij
Hoogstraat 1, 1600 Sint Pieters-Leeuw

Timmermans NV
Kerkstraat 11, 1711 Itterbeek

Vander Linden Brouwerij
Brouwerijstraat 2, 1500 Halle

Vandervelden Brouwerij
Laarheidestraat 230, 1650 Beersel

Van Honsebrouck Brouwerij
Oostrozebekestraat 43,
8770 Ingelmunster

Wets Gueuzestekerij
Steenweg op Halle 203,
1640 Sint Genesius

THE MIRACLE OF BRUSSELS

The classic lambic brewery is Cantillon in the backstreets of Anderlecht, known as the 'Liverpool of Brussels' as a result of the local passion for soccer. It is both a brewery and a museum, run with great passion by Jean-Pierre Van Roy, a descendant of the Cantillon family that blended gueuze in Lembeek in the eighteenth century and moved to Brussels in 1900. Robert and Marcel Van Roy started to brew lambic in 1937; they bought vessels from a brewery in Liège.

Van Roy is devoted to lambic and gueuze, and he is a stickler for tradition. He uses only whole fruit in his kriek and framboise and dismisses most of his competitors as makers of 'industrial gueuze'. He describes Cantillon as 'a living, working museum, the only artisanal brewery in Brussels'. He brews with a cast-iron mash tun, two copper brew kettles and a cool ship under the eaves of the roof.

He makes beer between November and April, producing around 60,000 bottles of beer a year. The temperature even in November can be too high or the wind too cold and strong, affecting the wild yeasts in the air and preventing fermentation. He says he has never made two identical brews.

Van Roy brews thirty times during the season. He mashes at six o'clock in the morning, blending malted barley and unmalted wheat in his mash tun in the ratio of 65 per cent malt to 35 per cent wheat. The water comes from the Brussels public supply. The mash lasts two and a half hours during which enzymes in the malt convert both the barley and wheat starches to sugar. Ten thousand litres (2200gallons) of sweet wort is pumped up a floor to the coppers and mixed with three-year-old cheesy and skunky Brewers Gold hops from Poperinge in the heart of the Belgian hop fields. The copper boil lasts for three hours, and during that time 10,000 litres of wort are reduced to 7500 (2200 to 1650

Serious work. . Jean-Pierre Van Roy is the classic lambic and gueuze brewer.

gallons) by evaporation. No brewing sugars are added. The hopped wort is cooled in holding tanks, then pumped to what Van Roy calls 'the tabernacle'. This is the tiny, cramped space under the eaves that houses the shallow, open copper vessel called the cool ship. The louvred windows are left open and a few tiles are removed from the roof to allow yeast spores easy circulation.

'We only use wild yeasts from heaven,' Van Roy says. 'Fermentation is the miracle of Brussels. We need dirty air to infect the beer,' he adds with disarming honesty. Fermentation begins during the night as the yeast spores are carried into the brewery loft on the warm wind. When the temperature of the inoculated wort reaches 18–20°C (64–68°F), it is racked into large oak casks called pipes bought from port makers in Portugal: the wine impregnated wood adds colour to the finished lambic, just as sherry casks add colour to Scotch whisky. Each cask has a letter and a number to mark the year and the 'gyle', the number of the brew.

The beer stays in cask for three years, during which time the yeasts and lacto-bacillii in the wood continue to turn sugars into alcohol. To make gueuze, Van Roy blends one- and three-year-old lambics. The corked bottles are stored horizontally, like champagne, and the sugars in the young lambic start a further fermentation. It takes two years to make gueuze.

Van Roy is unique among lambic and gueuze brewers by occasionally selling a straight, unblended bottled lambic; others sell only draught lambic. 'If I find one lambic is especially good, I don't blend it but bottle it and call it "Grand Cru",' he said. He occasionally adds sugar to an old lambic and markets it as faro, a style that was very popular before World War II but which has largely disappeared today. To make kriek or framboise, Van Roy adds 180 kilos (397

pounds) of either cherries or raspberries to young lambic in cask. The sugars in the fruit start a further fermentation and the beer is then bottled and laid down to mature.

I tasted a gueuze bottled in 1995. It had an aroma of almonds and sour, damson-like fruit, tart and dry in the mouth with a finish dominated by sour fruit. A lambic that had been in cask for three years and in bottle for a further year had a vinous, grapy aroma with some nuttiness. There was a dry fruit and a Fino sherry character on the palate and the finish was gentle, delicious and not over-sour. A framboise made in 1993 with the fruit added two years later was pink and gushed and foamed in the glass like pink champagne. It had sour raspberry fruit on the nose with more tart fruit in the mouth. The finish was wonderfully quenching and packed with fruit flavour. A 5 per cent Brabantiae is a blend of three different ages of lambic and is shockingly dry. Van Roy's classic, Rosé de Gambrinus, is a blend of cherries and raspberries and has a fruity, aromatic quality.

Cantillon specializes in saucy labels. Here the devil tempts Eve to try a fruit lambic blend.

ALE BREWING

I t may be a hangover from the days when brewing was the work of monks who fired their mash tuns at dawn before hurrying off to their devotions, but ale making is an occupation for early risers. Before its London plant became computerized, Guinness's brewing day would begin at 4.30 in the morning, when the head brewer would clamber into a raised wooden chair, in which only he was allowed to sit, and cry: 'Start the mash!' It is now more usual for brewing to start at 6.00 but it is still a daunting hour for many.

There are several vital checks to be made before barley malt meets its destiny. A member of the brewing staff tests the 'liquor', the water that comes either from wells on the site or from the public supply. The water will be filtered more than once to remove any impurities or unwanted chemicals, such as chlorine. Most ale brewers want a hard liquor and they will add gypsum (calcium sulphate) and Epsom salts (magnesium) to replicate the hard, flinty water of Burton-on-Trent and to get the correct level of acidity, the pH. The malt for brewing has to be crushed or 'cracked' in a mill. Various settings are used in the mill to produce different weights of cracked grain. Most of the malt is ground to flour but it is blended with coarser grits and the rough husks of the grain. The husks act as a natural filter in the mash tun. In the laboratory, a sample of the house yeast is studied to make sure it has no infections. Yeast cells must be white: blue cells are dead and indicate an insufficient number of healthy cells to start fermentation. Black rods among the cells means there is an infection and the yeast batch is scrapped.

The brewing process starts in a large round vessel called the mash tun, usually made of copper, cast iron or stainless steel and insulated with a slatted wooden jacket.

The mash tun, where malted barley and pure water are mixed, acts like a giant teapot.

It has a flat lid composed of two semicircles of wood raised by pulleys. In British breweries the tun is nicknamed 'the tea pot' as the infusion method of mashing is similar to making tea. Just as in good tea making, the mash tun is filled and drained with boiling water in preparation for a good infusion and to 'warm the pot'. Poised above the lid of the mash tun is a large tube called a Steel's Masher, linked to both a grist case holding the cracked grain and to the brewery's water supply. The masher is a Victorian device in which liquor and grist are mixed in the correct proportions and at the right temperature inside a cylinder with an Archimedean screw. Temperature is crucial during mashing: if it is too high, the enzymes in the malt will be killed; too low and they will work sluggishly and won't convert all the starch into sugar, while the malt will turn into paste. Liquor, heated to 75°C (167°F), floods into the tun and covers the base. The temperature is known as the 'strike heat'. The flow then thickens as the Steel's Masher releases malt, which lowers the temperature of the liquor to 65°C (149°F), the mash temperature. Malt and

liquor combined are called 'the goods', and if the temperature of the goods falls below 65° (149°F) more hot liquor is added. As well as pale malt, the grist may contain such darker malts as crystal, chocolate and black.

The thick, porridge-like mixture stands in the mash tun for around one and a quarter hours while saccharification, the conversion of starch into sugar, takes place. The conversion is the result of action by biological catalysts – enzymes – in the malt. The two most important enzymes are alpha-amylase, which convert starches into maltose and dextrins, and beta-amylase, which produces only maltose. Maltose is a highly fermentable malt sugar while dextrin cannot be fermented by brewer's yeast and gives 'body' to the finished beer, a pleasing roundness and richness of palate. The brewers check that saccharification is under way with the 'first runnings', similar to the tests made in both whisky and gin distilleries. Brass taps are fitted to the side of the mash tun. When they are opened, hot, cloudy, tawny liquid called the wort cascades into tall glasses. Experienced brewers can tell from the aroma and the taste of the liquid that sugar is being produced: it smells like malt loaf and is sweet and biscuity in the mouth. If there is any doubt about starch conversion, a few drops of iodine are added to the wort. If the iodine turns blue-black, then starch is still present. If it stays clear, then conversion has taken place.

When starch conversion is finished, the brewers must immediately end the mashing process to stop tannins extracted from the malt giving the wort a harsh flavour like stewed tea. More hot liquor is pumped into the tun to kill the enzymes. The slotted base of the vessel is opened and the wort (pronounced 'wurt', from the Old English *wyrt*, meaning root) drains through the thick cake of grain. To make sure no sugars are left behind, perforated tubes in the roof of the tun revolve and sprinkle or 'sparge' the grain with more hot liquor. The wort flows into a receiving 'back' below the mash tun and is then pumped to the coppers. Coppers work on a similar principle to a coffee percolator. The wort, heated to boiling temperature, gushes up a hollow column or callandria inside the copper and pours into the main body of the vessel. The constant flow from the callandria agitates all the liquid in the vessel. The boil last for around an hour and a half. Hops are added at the start of the boil, half way through and finally just a few minutes before the end of the process. As many of the aromatic and bittering qualities of the hops are distilled off during the boil, the final addition, known as 'late hopping', is vital to give a good hop character to the finished beer. The boiling wort extracts from the hops their acids, tannins and oils. At the same time, bacteria are killed along with any enzymes that have survived mashing and sparging, while some of the

malt sugars are caramelized to give colour and flavour to the beer. Depending on the recipe, brewing sugar may also be added during the copper boil to encourage a good fermentation and to produce the right balance of flavours demanded by the brewer. At the end of the boil, the hopped wort flows into a receiving vessel called the hop

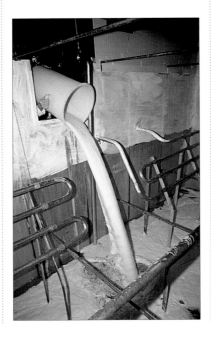

When the sugars have been extracted from the grain, the extract is boiled with hops in a copper or brew kettle.

back: *back* is an old Dutch word from which the term bucket is derived. Some brewers add additonal hops at this stage to give even greater aroma and bitterness to the beer. The spent hops from the copper cover the base of the vessel and filter out waste matter as the liquid flows to a cooler that brings the temperature of the wort down to 18°C (64°F) in preparation for fermentation.

The wort is now ready to meet its destiny. It is pumped to the fermenting rooms in the brewhouse. Fermenters may be round, square, open, enclosed or, occasionally, even tall conicals. But in Britain, the major ale-brewing country, traditional vessels are square in shape and open to the atmosphere: the great head of yeast developed during fermentation prevents any risk of infection from bacteria or wild strains. Many brewers still use wooden

Simple old technology in the form of a bucket is used to add yeast to a fermenter.

Taking a dip…a brewer measures the 'gravity' or sugar content of a brew at the start of the fermentation process.

fermenters but they are lined with polypropylene or copper to prevent bugs hiding in the wood and infecting the wort. The foaming wort, aerated to encourage yeast growth, runs into the vessels and yeast is then pitched and blended in the ratio of 0.45 kilos (1 pound) of yeast to every 4.5 litres (1 gallon) of beer. It takes two days for the yeast head to form. Gradually a dense white-brown rocky head builds that rises in great peaks: the dark streaks are proteins in the malt. Side boards sometimes have to be added to the vessels to stop the fermenting liquid over-running on to the floor.

Fermentation creates considerable heat. The temperature rises from 18°C to 22°C (64°F to 72°F). If it goes any higher, the yeast will get sleepy and refuse to convert all the sugars. To prevent this, cold water is pumped through coils in the fermenters. Fermentation lasts for about eight days: brewers like to give their worts 'two sabbaths' in contact with the yeast. From start to finish, the wort is constantly checked with hydrometers to check the specific gravity of the wort. The gravity falls as the sugars are consumed by the yeast and turned into alcohol and carbon

dioxide. The air above the fermenters is rich with the heady aromas of the natural chemical compounds or esters created by the yeast. Fermentation is complete when all or most of the fermentable sugars are converted. The 'green beer' is held in conditioning tanks for a few days to purge itself of rougher alcohols.

Several things can now happen. The beer may be filtered and pasteurized to kill

the yeast and run into either enclosed kegs or bottles, and filled with carefully measured doses of carbon dioxide. If it is to be the finest of warm-fermenting beer – real ale – none of these practices will be used. Instead the beer will be decanted or 'racked' into casks, often with the addition of priming sugar and further hops, and sent to pubs where it will enjoy a second fermentation that will develop more alcohol as well as ripe, mature flavours. A glutinous substance called finings made from isinglass is also added to the casks: it attracts yeast and proteins, and slowly drags them to the base of the cask to clarify the beer. The official name for real ale is 'cask-conditioned beer'. Beers that are bottled with living yeast, and which can be laid down for years to improve, are known as 'bottle conditioned'.

Off you go…a bung is knocked into a cask before it leaves for the pub where the beer undergoes a second fermentation.

PALE ALE

It is a common misconception that pale ale and bitter are one and the same beer styles. The misunderstanding is increased by the habit of British brewers of offering bottled versions of their premium or best draught bitters under the name of pale ale. The two styles overlap and inter-mingle but they are not the same. As we have seen in the first section, pale ale was developed out of India Pale Ale, a style created specifically for export. Once glass manufacture stopped being a craft and turned into a large-scale commercial operation, pale ale was bottled on a vast scale. Bass and its Burton neighbours Allsopp and Worthington led the way with bottled versions of their pale ales. In London Whitbread moved vigor-ously into bottled pale ale production. By 1912, the company bottled as much as 439,532 barrels or 45 per cent of its annual produc-tion and it was spending £12,000 a year, a vast sum for the day, on 'railway advertising' in the form of posters and cards aimed directly at middle-class commuters.

These bottled pale ales, often delivered direct to the doorstep alongside the milk, were sharply different in character from the new 'running beers' developed for the brewers' pub trade. Running beers were cask-conditioned and ran the gamut from pale to dark. But the pale versions, dubbed 'bitter' by drinkers, increasingly used the new type of stewed malt called crystal which, high in unfermentable dextrins, left sugar in the beer for body and roundness and gave bitter its now characteristic cop-per and amber tones.

It may, therefore, seem perverse to open the pale ale section with a beer found primarily on draught and which is called a bitter. But Marston's Pedigree Bitter is the

Most 'union set' fermentation systems have gone for a Burton, but Marstons in the home of pale ale remains true to the method. Liquor tanks on the top floor and malt mills below supply the mash tuns and coppers a floor down. Fermentation begins in open vessels but the liquid is then transferred to the union casks.

epitomy of pale ale brewing. It bridges the gap between India Pale Ales and the later pale ales. In eschewing the use of darker malts, it is the closest of any beer to the first pale ales of the nineteenth century. Above all, it is still lovingly craft-ed in a fermentation system known as the Burton unions which gives a unique complexity and subtlety of aroma and flavour to the finished product.

Marston, Thompson & Evershed started brewing in Burton in 1834 and moved to its present site, the Albion Brewery, in the town in 1898. Marstons, in common with all the

Burton brewers, adopted the union system of fermentation in order to cleanse its beers of yeast and offer a clear, bright and sparkling product to an increasingly sophis-ticated, educated and demanding public. Removing yeast was not an easy process. It could be skimmed from the top of ferment-ing vessels, but some remained in suspension with the result that some batches would be cloudy or hazy. The problem was solved by the union method. It was invented by the Liverpool brewer Peter Walker, another outsider who briefly

Brewing at Marstons' begins in a maltings where floor-malted barley unlocks its starches.

owned a plant in Burton. He placed trays or troughs above the oak casks in which the beer fermented. Fermenting beer rose from the casks through pipes into the troughs, which retained the yeast but, because they were slightly inclined, allowed the fermenting wort to run back into the casks. The method was called the 'union system' because all the separate parts – giant wooden casks, swan-necked pipes, troughs and cooling coils – were linked together or 'held in union'. The system had nothing to do with the influence of trade unions, though visitors to Marstons' brewery are amused to find that the local office of the Transport & General Workers' Union is situated next to the union fermentation rooms. The unions were effective but they were costly to run and capital-intensive, with constant repairs needed to the casks. In the twentieth century they were replaced by more cost-efficient systems, the most popular being a device called the parachute, a large metal funnel placed apex-down in the fermenter to collect the yeast. In Burton Ind Coope installed conventional fermenters, its unions reduced to a mural on the wall of the brewhouse. In the 1980s, Bass, the biggest brewer in the town, ripped out its union vessels and placed a few of them in their front car-park, an undignified end for such a fascinating brewing artefact.

Marstons remained faithful to the unions because it feels that only that system can produce the true flavour of a genuine pale ale. The company is so committed to the method that in the early 1990s it installed a third union room with thirty casks at a cost

Left: yeast and fermenting beer drip from a swan-necked pipe into the barm tray placed above the oak union casks.

Right: an aerial view of a barm tray showing the rich deposit of yeast left behind as the fermenting beer returns to the casks below.

of more than £1 million. This involved importing the highest quality memel oak from Germany. The wood was fashioned into giant casks by a specialist firm of coopers near Manchester. Marstons still employs its own coopers at Burton to repair the casks: this occasionally involves closing down one whole union 'set' in order to take out a cask and replace damaged or leaking staves.

Fermentation at Marstons begins in open square vessels sited in rooms above the union sets. The open vessels are unusually shallow. Head brewer Paul Bayley says that one of the many curious characteristics of yeast developed in the union system is that it will refuse to work in a conventional deep vessel. His yeast is multi-strain (at least two and possibly four strains) and he describes it as 'greedy', voraciously turning malt sugars into alcohol. Thirty-six hours after primary fermentation has started, the wort is 'dropped' or pumped to the union casks below, action that aerates the wort and encourages it to continue its hungry work. Each oak cask holds 144 gallons (6.546 hectolitres). A union set is made up of two rows of casks, eight casks to a row, with a trough set above them. The trough is called the 'barm tray', *barm* being an old dialect word from the High German for yeast. Each cask is cooled by water pumped through internal pipes or attemperators. As fermentation continues, carbon dioxide drives wort and yeast up swan-neck pipes inserted into the bung of each cask: the curved necks of the pipes overhang the barm tray. The wort runs down the slight incline of the tray and back into the cask through union pipes, while some of the yeast sediments into the tray. By the time fermentation has finished, nearly all the yeast has been collected in the troughs, leaving clear beer in the casks. Taps at the base of each cask are then opened, the green or rough beer runs into further

troughs below and from there into a collecting back or tank. It stands in the tank for a day to purge itself of rough alcohols, then is decanted into casks and delivered to pubs where it enjoys a second fermentation.

The end result, Marstons' Pedigree Bitter (4.5 per cent alcohol by volume with 26 units of bitterness) is a beer of marvellous

A cathedral dedicated to beer...the union rooms at Marstons are silent save for the drip-drip of beer and yeast as they flow into the barm trays and the hiss of gas created by fermentation.

Held in union...the oak casks are linked together by an intricate framework of pipes, tubes and troughs.

68

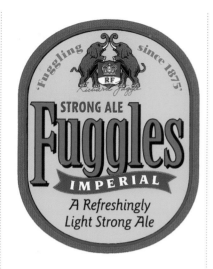

Hop and glory. . .a faithful re-creation of an India Pale Ale brewed by Whitbread using only the traditional English hop variety, the Fuggle.

delicacy and complexity. The aroma, known locally as the 'Burton snatch', has a powerful 'burning match' sulphuriness from the gypsum in the brewing liquor. This slowly thins to reveal biscuity malt, resiny hops and delicate fruit. The fruit is a clearly definable hint of apple, which also used to be evident on the aroma and palate of Draught Bass when it was brewed in unions. The fruitiness lingers in the mouth and on the finish, balanced by a robust hop bitterness from Fuggles, Goldings and Whitbread Goldings Variety. The beer also has an intriguing hint of sourness, which adds to its quenching nature: I suspect this is derived from the brewing liquor and is retained by the house yeast. Finally, the beer is dry, the result of yeast activity which turns most of the sugars to alcohol. The malt comes from England's finest barley, Maris Otter. Paul Bayley adds 17 per cent glucose sugar during the copper boil. Bayley

defends this use of a high level of brewing sugar on the grounds that it is traditional to the recipe. An all-malt brew, he says, would be too rich and would unbalance the beer, the hops in particular.

The small Yorkshire town of Tadcaster is known as the 'Burton of the North'. It has a plentiful supply of hard brewing water from an underground lake of limestone water. It also has three breweries, two of which are named Smith. It was a schism in the Smith family at the turn of the century that resulted in John Smith walking up the hill to open his Magnet Brewery, which is now part of the Scottish Courage group. The Samuel Smith branch of the family has stayed determinedly independent and claims, with justifiable pride, that its Old Brewery, built in 1758, is the oldest in Yorkshire. Sam Smiths uses wooden casks for its cask-conditioned ales, employs its own coopers and delivers to local pubs with horse-drawn

Jim Kerr, manager of the Castle Eden Brewery near Durham in north-east England where Fuggles Imperial was first brewed. Castle Eden was once a family-owned company called Nimmos, famous throughout the north east for its ales, but became part of Whitbread, which announced it would close the plant in the autumn of 1998.

drays. Smiths has remained loyal to the 'Yorkshire square' method of fermentation. The squares not only cleanse fermenting beer of yeast but also help to produce high levels of carbonation that in turn lead to the thick collar of foam on a pint that is demanded by any self-respecting Yorkshire drinker.

The first brewery in Yorkshire to build stone squares was opened by Bentley & Shaw of Huddersfield. It is thought the inspiration came from the radical scientist Dr Joseph Priestley who had unravelled the mysteries of 'fixed air' (carbon dioxide) and created carbonated water as a result of living next door to a brewery in Leeds. While most modern squares are made of stainless steel, Samuel Smiths uses Welsh slate. The vessels are designed to tackle the

Cool beer, hot air. . .London Olympia, scene of the annual Great British Beer Festival run by the Campaign for Real Ale, a showcase for cask-conditioned ale.

problem of the particular yeast strains used in Yorkshire. Unlike the Burton yeasts, which greedily attack malt sugars, Yorkshire strains are 'flocculant': the cells clump together and separate from the fermenting beer. Unless the yeast is roused on a regular basis, it will not attenuate far, leaving a high level of unfermented sugar in the finished

Hop Back Summer Lightning, a superb pale ale brewed by one of the new small craft breweries that have expanded choice for British beer drinkers.

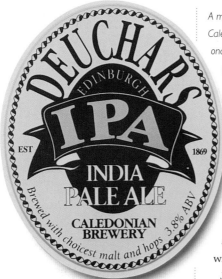

A multi-award winning IPA brewed by the Caledonian Brewery in Edinburgh, a city that once rivalled Burton as a major exporter of pale ale.

beer. The Yorkshire square is a two-storey vessel, with the chambers connected by a manhole with a raised rim. The bottom deck is filled with wort and yeast. As fermentation progresses, yeast and wort rise through the manhole into the open top storey, known as the barm deck. The yeast is trapped by the rim while the wort runs back to the bottom chamber through pipes. Every couple of hours, yeast and wort are pumped back into the top deck to aerate liquid and yeast. When fermentation is complete, the manhole is closed while the green beer is left in the bottom chamber to condition for two days. Yeast is recovered from the top deck. Beers brewed by the method are noticeably full bodied as a result of the presence of unfermented sugars.

Samuel Smith's Old Brewery Pale Ale is 5.2 per cent alcohol by volume and is brewed from pale malt with a high level of crystal (10 per cent), giving the beer both an amber colour (35 units) and a nutty and fruity/winy character. The hops are Fuggles for bitterness and Goldings for aroma and create 26 bitterness units. The company has

phased out the use of brewing sugars and other adjuncts. In spite of the relatively low bitterness units, the beer has a pronounced hoppy appeal. There are rich malt, dark fruit and spicy hops on the aroma, a big malt and fruit palate and a long, complex finish dominated by ripe fruit and hops, and ending dry and bitter with hints of oak and vanilla.

John Gilbert was an active member of the Campaign for Real Ale in London and a dedicated home brewer. He turned his skills to commercial use by setting up the Hop Back five-barrel micro-brewery in 1987 attached to the Wyndham Arms pub in the cathedral city of Salisbury. The success of his beers led Gilbert to build a new 50-barrel plant in 1992 on an industrial estate outside Salisbury. He now owns half-a-dozen pubs and he has installed a bottling line to widen distribution of his beers. His flagbearer is Hop Back Summer Lightning, which has won more than fifty awards at beer festivals, including winner of the Strong Bitter class in the 1992 Champion Beer of Britain competition organized by CAMRA. In one fell swoop or swallow, Summer Lightning destroys the rather snobby attitude of bigger brewers towards the new breed of micros, which suggests that craft beers lack polish and are poorly balanced. Summer Lightning is a beer of great finesse and complexity, interweaving malt, hops and fruit into a remarkable melange of aromas and flavours. It is 5 per cent alcohol by volume and, with just a pinch of crystal malt blended with Pipkin, it is a truly straw-coloured ale of the palest

variety. Hops are Challenger and East Kent Goldings used in pellet form. It has a massive aroma of peppery, resiny hops and citric fruit (Challenger have a pronounced lemon quality which they imprint on the yeast), the palate is intensely hoppy with more tart, citric fruit, and the finish begins bitter-sweet and becomes dry and dominated by more hop and fruit flavours. Bitterness rating is 28. As the name implies, it is a wonderful summer refresher but it is brewed all the year round and is available in both cask-conditioned and bottle-conditioned versions.

If Salisbury is grand then Edinburgh, the Scottish capital, is snooty, as any Glaswegian would agree. Yet behind the austere façade of stately houses, monuments and broad avenues lies a brewing tradition that gave the city the nickname of 'Auld Reekie' (Old Smelly). When one of the last

Thomas Cooper, Yorkshire-born brewer who took pale ale to Australia.

remaining independent breweries in the city was due to close in 1987, Russell Sharp gave up an executive post with the Chevas Regal whisky distillery to return to Edinburgh to launch a buy-out to save Caledonian. He succeeded brilliantly, overcame a major fire in 1995 and made the brewery the revered standard bearer of the Scottish brewing renaissance. As well as a large portfolio of traditional Scottish ales (see Scotch Ale section), Sharp has recreated a brilliant inter-pretation of India Pale Ale.

Edinburgh had deep, hard-water wells stretching from Holyrood in the east of the city through the Canongate, the Cowgate and Grassmarket to Fountainbridge in the west. With a plentiful supply of liquor similar to Burton's, the city's brewers hurried to make their own versions of pale

ale in the nineteenth century in order to cash in on the lucrative export trade. Robert Deuchar was one of the best-known of the pale ale brewers and his beer has been lovingly recreated by Russell Sharp and his colleagues. R&D Deuchar's IPA is 3.8 per cent alcohol by volume and is brewed from Pipkin pale malt with small additions of crystal and wheat malt for body and clarity. It has 15–17 units of colour. Fuggles and Goldings whole flower hops produce 34 to 36 units of bitterness, high for a Scottish ale. The quenching and clean palate of the beer is the result of Caledonian's deep-bed mashing system that extracts the maximum malt sugars. The wort is boiled in coppers that are fired by direct flames. The burnished coppers with detached hoods are a prized possession and are thought to be the only

Before Coopers' Sparkling Ale became a cult beer in Australia, local deliveries were made by horse-drawn drays. In a land famous for its ice-cold lagers, Coopers' was dismissed as an out-dated joke, but it now enjoys an international following.

ones in Britain still fired by direct heat. Russell Sharp says that his wort and hops are 'properly boiled, not stewed, as you get with stainless steel and steam heat'. Deuchar's IPA blossoms with Goldings hops and citric fruit, with tart fruit, biscuity malt and peppery hops in the mouth, and a long yet delicate bitter-sweet and brilliantly refreshing and satisfying finish.

Australia has a split beer personality. The early settlers took an ale culture with them but it was supplanted by lager in the

72

Thomas Cooper and his wife Ann, the daughter of an innkeeper, emigrated from Yorkshire to Australia in 1852. Thomas worked as a shoemaker and later a dairyman while his wife brewed at home, using the skills her father had taught her. Once, when she was taken ill, Thomas brewed some ale as a tonic. His friends were impressed with his efforts and he decided to brew commercially. When Ann died, he remarried and produced the prodigious number of sixteen children, sufficient to found a brewing dynasty.

Sparkling Ale, 5.8 per cent alcohol by volume, reminds me in its complexity, colour and fruity-hoppiness of the Orval Trappist ale from Belgium. It is brewed from local pale and crystal malts and hopped with Pride of Ringwood pellets from Victoria and Tasmania. Liquid cane sugar comprises

around 18 per cent of the grist. Units of bitterness are 25, colour 10–11. Sparkling Ale used to be fermented in wood and cleansed of yeast by dropping the beer into oak hogsheads known as puncheons, where a secondary fermentation took place. But 'progress' in the form of conical stainless-steel fermenting vessels arrived. Long-standing lovers of the beer say it has lost a little of its complexity as a result. Today, when primary fermentation is over, the beer is centrifuged and blended with fermenting beer and sugar to encourage a second fermentation in keg or bottle. The beer is matured at a warm temperature for six weeks before it leaves the brewery. It has a big peppery hop character and bursts with tart fruit, with a pronounced hint of apple. The finish is dry and hoppy with a good balance of fruit.

The real ale message spreads...Coopers' picked up the revivalist term from the Old Country and used it to promote its sedimented bottled ale.

twentieth century. Even so, such international brands as Castlemaine XXXX are still called 'bitter' in their homeland even though they are brewed with lager yeast. There are brew-pubs in Fremantle, Melbourne, Perth and Sydney producing ale, but the one commercial company that has kept the flickering ale flame alive in Australia is Coopers of Adelaide. Coopers' Sparkling Ale is now a national cult drink, but for years it was drunk only by a handful of aficionados and was considered a joke by most beer drinkers, especially as its heavy yeast sediment meant that it was cloudy rather than sparkling in the glass unless poured with enormous care.

David Geary was one of the earliest of the new wave craft brewers in the United States. His Pale Ale, launched in 1986, was based on his experience as a brewer in Britain.

David Geary in Portland, Maine, produces one of the finest interpretations of pale ale thanks to a close relationship with British brewers. Geary sold medical equipment until he met Peter Maxwell Stuart, the laird and brewer at Traquair House in the Scottish Borders. Maxwell Stuart, who had restored a brewhouse of great antiquity on his estate, visited the United States in 1982 to promote his Traquair House Ale. When David Geary met him, he found the noble Scot to be 'an inspiration: I thought the whole idea of brewing was amazing'. Micro-brewing was in its infancy in the US and Geary accepted an offer from Maxwell Stuart to learn his brewing skills at Traquair House. As well as his apprenticeship in Scotland, he worked at a dozen or so other British breweries and studied at the world-famous Heriot Watt school of brewing and distilling in Edinburgh.

Back in the US, Geary had further British help in building his brewery. Peter Austin, known as the 'father of the micro-brewing revolution' in England, has installed breweries throughout the world, including China and France. He also launched one of the first and most successful small breweries, Ringwood in Hampshire. With another English micro-brewer, Alan Pugsley, Austin helped Geary to build a plant with equipment imported from Britain, including classic open fermenters. Geary's Pale Ale was launched in 1986, and a decade later he doubled his capacity with two new 100-barrel fermenters. The beer is made from pale, crystal and chocolate malts imported from Britain, with American hop varieties. It is 4.5 per cent volume/3.6 per cent weight and has a pronounced citric fruit aroma, a mellow and well-balanced malt-and-hops palate, and a finish that begins fruity and becomes dry and hop-accented. Geary also brews a

Come fill the flowing bowl...Taylor's Landlord has a fiercely traditional air.

Hampshire Special Ale (5.6–7 per cent) for the winter months with a label showing boats frozen in the River Maine. This warming, spicy, fruity-hoppy ale is available in cask-conditioned form in one bar, the Great Lost Bear, in Portland. Hampshire Special is racked into casks, tapped and vented and allowed to mature, another result of Geary's hands-across-the-sea relationship with British practitioners.

In San Francisco, the Anchor Brewery is best known for its Steam Beer, an American classic. But owner Fritz Maytag has a small and beautifully crafted portfolio of beer, of which Liberty Ale is a brilliant reworking of the English pale ale style. As well as saving and building Anchor's business, Maytag immersed himself in the craft of brewing and the world's great styles. Among his many overseas trips was a protracted journey round the great pale ale brewers of England in the 1970s, including Marstons of Burton, Timothy Taylor in Keighley, Yorkshire and Youngs of London. Inspired by their products, he returned to the US to create a pale ale.

Maytag is a fierce American patriot and he produced Liberty Ale in 1975 to commemorate the ride on horseback two hundred years earlier by Paul Revere from Boston to Lexington to warn leaders of the American Revolution that the British army was on the march. Not surprisingly, Liberty Ale is a very American interpretation of the pale ale style. No sugars are used. It is an all-malt beer and a pale American malt produces a flaxen colour. It is 6 per cent alcohol by volume, 4.8 by weight. American

Fritz Maytag, founder of the Anchor Brewery in San Francisco, visited several British pale ale breweries to help fashion his distinctive beers. Liberty Ale bursts with fruity and spicy American hop aromas and flavours.

hops add a distinctive tasteprint to the beer. Maytag uses Cascade from the Pacific North-west, a variety positively booming with a pronounced citric lemon fruitiness. The beer is not dry hopped in the English manner but there is an addition of Cascades to the maturation tank. The finished ale is spicy and lemony on the aroma and palate with a long, dry and hoppy finish. It is a big, bold and assertive beer.

Charles Finkel runs the Pike Brewery in the modish harbour area of Seattle, backed by a well-thumbed library and small brewery museum. He brews both a Pale Ale and an East India Pale Ale, rightly differen-tiating between the styles. Finkel uses a generous level of crystal malt in his Pale Ale, accounting for 20 per cent of the grist. Pale malt is imported floor-malted Maris Otter. East Kent Goldings hops also make the long journey from England to the Emerald City, close to the Canadian border. At 5.5 per cent alcohol by volume, 4.5 by weight, the beer has a rich amber colour, a peppery hop aroma, a biscuity and nutty palate, with spicy hops and dark fruit on the finish. At first sight, Pike East India Pale Ale (7 per cent by volume, 6 by weight) has an odd composition of pale, carapils and Munich malts, the last two being a European version of English crystal and a Munich malt that gives the city's lagers their burnished gold colour. But Finkel has done his homework. In the nineteenth century, British ships often brought supplies of barley and malt from other countries: the 'white malt' sometimes referred to was an imported Pilsner variety. Finkel uses Chinook hops from the Pacific North-west, British Columbian from Canada and East Kent Goldings. This superb ale is tawny gold in colour, has an immense aroma of grapefruit from the Chinook, with more tart fruit in the mouth, and a long hoppy-fruity finish.

PALE ALE STYLE
Profound hop attack and a deep bitterness balanced by biscuity malt are the hallmarks of the style that has had a lasting impact on British and North American brewing practice.

A beer from Seattle that uses English malt and Goldings hops to create the right balance of flavours.

PALE ALE PRODUCERS

Anchor Brewing Co.
1705 Mariposa Street,
San Francisco CA 94107

Bass Brewers
137 High Street,
Burton-on-Trent DE14 1JZ

Caledonian Brewing Company Ltd
42 Slateford Road, Edinburgh EH11 1PH

Castle Eden Brewery
PO Box 13, Castle Eden,
Co. Durham TS27 4SX

Cooper's Brewery Ltd
9 Statenborough Street, Leabrook, Adelaide SA 5068

D.L. Geary Brewing Company

38 Evergreen Drive, Portland ME 04103

Marston, Thompson & Evershed Plc
Shobnall Road,
Burton-on-Trent DE14 2BW

Pike Brewery
1432 Western Avenue,
Seattle WA 622-1880.

Samuel Smith Old Brewery
High Street, Tadcaster,
North Yorkshire LS24 9SB

Timothy Taylor & Co. Knowle Spring Brewery
Keighley, Yorkshire BD21 1AN

BITTER

Bitter is a British phenomenon. W.L. Tizard, the author of the influential *Theory and Practice of Brewing*, noted in an edition dated 1857 that brewers were replacing porter with 'bitter ale'. He was referring to the pale ales brewed for export in Burton-on-Trent. But the term 'bitter' was used adjectivally: it was not until the following century that it came into use as a noun to describe a particular style of beer. Frustratingly, there is little evidence to pinpoint the precise time of its arrival. After that passing reference in the mid-nineteenth century, the term seems to have gone out of use until the brewers built their substantial tied estates of directly owned

Above: A few of the hundreds of coopers employed by Bass in the nineteenth century to fashion wooden containers for draught ale.

Below: Young's of Wandsworth, brewers of hoppy, tangy beers, still deliver casks of ale to some south London pubs by horse-drawn drays.

public houses and fashioned 'running beers' to sell in them. From the early years of the twentieth century, pale ale came to mean a bottled beer while bitter was a draught ale. 'Running beer' was a term that covered all the casked beers in a pub and 'bitter' was coined to differentiate it from less heavily hopped mild brown ales.

Pale ale and bitter went their separate ways. While some brewers, notably Bass, Guinness and Worthington, continued to make bottled beers that matured in glass and threw a sediment, most adopted filtration and pasteurization to produce star-bright beers with a long shelf life. Bitter remained a naturally conditioned ale that enjoyed a second fermentation in cask in the pub cellar and had low levels of CO_2. Today such beers would be called 'real ales'. While the rest of the world hurried to serve brewery-conditioned ales and lagers – chilled, filtered, pasteurized and pumped to the bar by carbon dioxide pressure – the British doggedly stayed loyal to a method that decreed that brewing wasn't completed in the brewery but continued in the pub. Pub and brewery were locked in a close

Adnams' Bitter from Southwold in Suffolk doesn't guarantee to improve a golfer's handicap but it does deliver a rich, fruity-hoppy aroma and flavour and a hint of salt and seaweed.

relationship. It enabled the brewer to monitor the progress of his beer in the pub. He could train cellar staff in the arcane rituals of knocking venting pegs into bung holes, measuring the rate of escape of natural CO_2, taking samples to watch the slow clearing of the still-working beer, and then, as soon as perfect clarity and palate were achieved, emptying the cask within three to four days before oxidation set in.

Bitter is usually darker (ranging from straw-coloured through copper, amber and tawny) than pale ales as a result of the crystal malts used to give the beer 'body' and to hasten maturation.

Bitter overtook mild ale in popularity in the 1950s and then came under sustained attack from a new type of ale called 'keg'. A rash of mergers created for the first time in Britain a handful of giant brewers anxious to flood the market with heavily advertised national brands. Hype and long shelf life, the latter the result of filtration and pasteurization, replaced maturity and flavour. Keg beer sparked one of the world's best-known consumer revolts. The Campaign for Real Ale (Camra for short) spoke for millions of pubgoers when it rubbished keg beers and urged brewers to return to the tried and trusted ways of cask conditioning. The campaign, which reached 52,000 members in 1998, is still a potent force in Britain. It organizes hundreds of beer festivals each year, showpieces for cask ale, and vigorously lobbies brewers and British and European parliaments. It is true to say that the beers in this section have survived and thrived only as a result of Camra's activity.

'BITTER' STYLE

Bitter developed as a draught version of pale ale but has become a style in its own right. Many brewers add crystal malt for roundness and body: it gives a nutty and biscuity note to bitter. Yeast and hops combine to add rich fruit aromas and flavours.

Thoroughbred beer. . . Ken Don, head brewer at Young's of Wandsworth, offers a glass of bitter to one of the brewery's dray horses. But Dobbin, unlike London pubgoers, seems to prefer the feed offered by the brewery horseman.

Adnams, in common with other East Anglian brewers, enjoys easy access to the finest malting barley in a region known as the grain basket of England. The brewery has one of the finest locations in the country in the coastal town of Southwold, dominated by an inshore, whitewashed lighthouse. Adnams once drew brewing liquor from a well beneath the North Sea. Although the water became contaminated and the public supply is now used, Adnams' beers have a salty, seaweedy character that bonds the brewery to the sea. Brewhouse and fermenting room are fiercely traditional, with burnished mash tuns and coppers, and high-sided wooden fermenting vessels. Adnams Bitter (3.8 per cent alcohol) is brewed from Maris Otter pale malt,

brewing sugar and a dash of caramel for colour. It has 26 units of colour. Challenger, Fuggles and Goldings whole hops create 33 units of bitterness. The beer is dry hopped in the cask with Goldings. The brewery's house yeast gives the beer a pronounced aroma of citric fruit balanced by spicy and peppery hops. The palate is a superb balance of rich, juicy malt, tart hops and citric fruit, with a long, rounded finish dominated by bitter hops but underpinned by sweet, biscuity malt and citric fruit.

London, once one of the great brewing cities, has declined as a result of mergers and closures as well as the problems of moving beer around the traffic-congested streets. Quality beer survives thanks to the efforts of two family-owned companies, Fullers of

Chiswick and Youngs of Wandsworth. The two breweries produce beers of great distinction and dissimilarity: Fullers' have a pronounced malty-fruity character balanced by complex hops flavours while Youngs' are no-nonsense ales, tangy and bitter, reflecting the proximity of south London to the hop fields of neighbouring Kent.

Fuller, Smith & Turner is on a site where brewing has taken place for some three hundred years. The present company, with Fullers and Turners still in control, dates from the 1820s. Behind the wisteria-girt offices there is a modern, functional brewhouse. Fullers produces three bitters, all based on similar recipes employing Alexis pale malt, crystal malt, flaked maize and caramel with Challenger, Goldings,

Northdown and Target hops. Chiswick Bitter's humble alcohol rating of 3.5 per cent allows the hops full expression, with 28 units of bitterness. The beer has a pronounced aroma of piny, resiny hops with light citric fruit. The palate has a clean, quenching balance of malt and hops, and there are more light fruit notes in the delicate finish. London Pride started life as Chiswick Pride but now enjoys greater recognition as the brewery's flagship product. Unlike Chiswick Bitter and the premium ESB, London Pride is not dry hopped in cask and therefore has greater malt character. It is a fascinatingly complex beer with a firm malty and fruity aroma underpinned by hops. It is bitter-sweet in the mouth and has a long finish that inter-

weaves between firm maltiness, spicy hops and a dash of bitter orange fruit. ESB – Extra Special Bitter – has won an array of awards from Camra beer festivals. Dry hopped with Goldings, the 5.8 per cent beer bursts on the nose with an explosion of malt, hops and marmalade fruit. There is an enormous attack of rich malt, hop resins and ripe

Shepherd Neame is Britain's oldest brewery and celebrated its 300th birthday in 1998. Based in Faversham, it has first call on the fine, bitter hops grown in the surrounding Kent countryside.

80

fruit in the mouth, and a deep finish dominated by peppery Goldings and great wafts of orange, lemon and gooseberry fruit. This is not a beer for the faint-hearted.

Young & Co. of Wandsworth is a robustly independent family brewery where a belief in traditional values is handed down from one generation to the next. A brewery on the banks of the River Wandle was founded in 1675 and came into Youngs' sole ownership in 1884. Beer lovers have great affection for the company because in the 1970s it set its face firmly against keg beer and determinedly concentrated on cask-conditioned ales. Other brewers derided Youngs but its directors and staff had the last laugh, becoming a highly successful company that rode the crest of the real ale revival. It is a remarkable brewery. Surrounded by traffic-snarled roads, it manages to be a haven of almost sylvan tranquillity. Large and amiable dray horses are stabled there, for Young's still delivers by horse-drawn vehicles to some local pubs. Ducks and geese greet visitors and a young ram, the brewery mascot, is paraded round the yard. Ale is brewed in traditional mash tuns, coppers and open fermenters while such Victorian artefacts as beam engines are proudly displayed to the endless throngs of tourists. Above all, it is a working brewery producing sublime beer.

Londoners are not renowned for understatement yet Youngs' best-selling bitter is universally ordered as 'a pint of Ordinary'. The curious soubriquet is used to distinguish the beer from its stronger stablemate, Special Bitter, but in every other respect it is a far from ordinary beer. At 3.7 per cent alcohol, it is extremely pale, with just 14 colour units. The belt-and-braces of Youngs' bitters is Maris Otter malting barley: the company has to pay a premium for the malt but says the extra pennies on production

costs are worth it to enable the yeast to work in harmony with the malt and to ensure the right balance of flavours. Small amounts of torrefied barley and brewing sugar are added. Fuggles and Goldings, used as whole blossoms, create 33 units of bitterness. The beer has a no-holds-barred peppery and resiny Goldings aroma with orange fruit from the house yeast. Hops and citric fruit dominate the mouth while the finish is bitter, quenching and dry with more orange fruit. Special Bitter, 4.6 per cent, clearly comes from the same stable yet is a radically different beer. It has been transformed in recent years from a rich but overly malty ale into one beautifully balanced by the simple expedient of dry hopping it in cask with Target. Special has 20 units of colour, 32 of bitterness. A

Brakspears brewery beside the River Thames uses a rare 'dropping system' of fermentation to cleanse its beers of yeast.

peppery hop aroma balanced by ripe citric fruit is followed by a mellow maltiness in the mouth and a big finish packed with hops and citric fruit.

Shepherd Neame is a company of impressive antiquity. It is England's oldest brewery, dating from 1698, though records suggest brewing has gone on there since the twelfth century. It is based in the Kentish market town of Faversham, in the heart of hop-growing country. The importance of hops to both brewery and region can be measured by the moulded hop design that surrounds the entrance to the main offices. There is no stinting on locally grown

Going dotty for a pint. . .the classic image of the English pub, with pints of bitter refreshing drinkers as they play a game of dominoes.

Goldings and Target varieties. Master Brew Bitter (3.7 per cent) and Best Bitter (4.1 per cent) both make generous use of Halcyon pale malt and crystal malt. Both are dry hopped and have bitterness units of 37 and 41 respectively. The Bitter is a hymn of praise to the hop, from its piny, resiny aroma, through a biscuity malt palate, to the bitter, tangy, fruity finish. Best Bitter has greater malt character and more pungent fruit but still has that all-pervading spicy, peppery hop note. A premium bitter, Spitfire Ale (4.7 per cent), commemorates the Battle of Britain fighter pilots who fought with German Messerschmitts in the skies over Kent during World War II. It is a big, bold beer packed with ripe malt, citric fruit and resiny hops.

W.H. Brakspear is a picturesque waterside brewery in Henley, owned by an old Thames Valley family since 1799 that is distantly related to Nicholas Breakspear, the only English Pope. It uses a fermentation method known as the 'dropping system', an effective way to cleanse beer of yeast. Primary fermentation starts in the conventional open squares on the first floor of the brewhouse. When the conversion of sugar to alcohol is under way, with a good rocky head on top of the wort, it is dropped by gravity into a second bank of fermenters. It is a brilliantly simple yet effective method that leaves behind all the 'trub' or spent matter such as used hops and dead yeast cells. The wort is thoroughly aerated and roused, and a new and cleaner yeast head soon forms as fermentation continues. Brakspear Bitter and Special are beers with complex malt and hop grists, made up of Maris Otter pale malt, Pipkin crystal and

black malts and invert sugar, with Challenger, Fuggles, Goldings and Styrian Goldings hops. Both beers are dry hopped in cask and have, respectively, 38 and 46 units of bitterness. The amber Bitter has a wholemeal biscuit and orange peel aroma, full-flavoured malt and floral hops in the mouth, and a long, lingering bitter-sweet finish. Special is a full-bodied, copper-coloured ale with malt and fruit aromas and flavours, with banana and orange in the finish and a good balance of hops.

The Yorkshire, family-owned brewery of Timothy Taylor in Keighley has the rugged independence and belief in traditional values that is typical of this bluff

Landlord the hopped wort circulates over a
deep bed of Styrians after the copper boil.
As a result the beer has a profound citric
note from nose to finish. It blends with
Worcestershire Fuggles and East Kent
Goldings to give a deep bitter character to
the beer which balances the full Golden
Promise malt, the only cereal used, a Scottish
malting barley with a juicy quality.

Across the Pennines, Joseph Holt in
Manchester is one of the most idiosyncratic breweries in Britain. Founded in 1849,
it remains family-owned and is a highly
profitable company, with a tied estate of
around 120 pubs. But as far as the outside
world is concerned, it could be run by
Trappist monks, so reluctant is the company to make any public pronouncements.
It still delivers beer to its pubs in fifty-four
gallon hogsheads and refuses to metricate.
The 4 per cent Bitter is made from a blend
of Halcyon, Pipkin and Triumph pale malts,
a touch of black malt, flaked maize and light
invert sugar. The hops are Goldings and
Northdown in blossom form and they
create 40 units of bitterness. The beer has
a superb bouquet of peppery hops and
citric fruit, there is a brilliant balance of malt
and hops in the mouth, and a long, bitter,
hoppy finish with a lingering tart fruitiness.

Cask-conditioned bitter is available in
Canada thanks to a connection with an old
brewing family in south-west England. The
Arkells of Swindon founded their brewery
in 1843, and a member of the family left
England to found a community in Guelph,
64 kilometres (40 miles) from Toronto.
Guelph, with a good supply of hard spring
water, was once a major brewing town.
When the Wellington County brewery

region. Based in mellow stone buildings, the
evocatively named Knowle Spring Brewery
(the spring supplies brewing liquor and also
waters the chairman's whisky) has won
many prizes for its ales. Its Landlord Best
Bitter (4.3 per cent) has been named
Champion Beer of Britain three times by the

Campaign for Real Ale, a richly deserved
prize for such an outstanding and complex
ale. The beer's unique signature comes from
the use of Styrian Goldings. The Slovenian
hop, a Fuggle derivative despite the name,
is now widely used in Britain as an
aromatic late addition, but in the case of

opened there, it named one of its beers Arkell Best Bitter in honour of both the local hero and the brewery in England that bears his name. The bitter, in bottle and on draught, is brewed with imported English malts, East Kent Goldings and Styrian Goldings. The hops impart a big peppery, , citric character to the beer, which balances full, sweet malt in the mouth. The finish is long, bitter-sweet, hoppy and fruity. As a result of another connection through the name of the brewery, Wellington also brews an Iron Duke Pale and Iron Duke Porter.

British Columbia is home to many British ex-patriates. Many of them enjoy the beautifully crafted ales in Spinnakers, a

Swan's Hotel brewery in Victoria, BC is called Buckerfield's and produces pale, brown and

Scotch ales plus an oatmeal stout for Canadians and many British ex-patriates..

spacious tavern-cum-brewery on the edge of Victoria. Paul Hadfield brews a clutch of draught ales of which his biggest seller is Spinnaker Ale (4.2 per cent). It is made from pale and crystal malts and hopped with Cascades from Washington State and Centennials from Oregon. The beer has an apple fruit aroma, more tangy fruit in the mouth and has a light dry finish. Mount Tolmie (4.2 per cent) has caramalt, chocolate and crystal blended with pale malt. Mount Hood hops are added in the copper and the beer is dry hopped with Cascades. It has a citric fruit aroma, sharp dark fruit in the mouth and a very dry and bitter finish. Doc Hadfield's Pale Ale, also 4.2 per cent, uses Mount Hood for aroma and bitterness. It has a resiny, piny aroma, with citric fruit in the mouth and a light, dry finish.

BITTER BREWERS

Adnams & Co.
Sole Bay Brewery, East Green,
Southwold, Suffolk IP18 6JW

W.H. Brakspear & Sons Plc
The Brewery, New Street,
Henley-on-Thames, Oxon RG9 2BU

Fuller, Smith & Turner
Griffin Brewery, Chiswick Lane South,
Chiswick, London W4 2QB

Joseph Holt Plc
Derby Brewery, Empire Street,
Cheetham, Manchester M3 1JD

Shepherd Neame Ltd
17 Court Street, Faversham,
Kent ME13 7AX

Timothy Taylor & Co.
Knowle Spring Brewery, Keighley,
West Yorkshire BD21 1AW

Young & Co.
The Ram Brewery, High Street,
Wandsworth, London SW18 4JD

Wellington County Brewery
950 Woodlawn Road West, Guelph,
Ontario N1K 1B8

MILD AND BROWN ALE

As Britain's industrial base has narrowed and declined, mild ale, the beer style that refreshed and replenished generations of blue-collar workers, has retreated to a few areas where work is still synonymous with foundries, car making and, very occasionally, digging coal. Until the 1950s, mild outsold bitter. In 1959 it accounted for a formidable 42 per cent of beer consumption. Now it makes up just a tiny fraction of total beer sales.

Mild today is considered to be a synonym for weak, which is one reason for its decline. Originally, mildness was a reference to the fact that the style was less heavily hopped than a pale ale. Unfermented brewing sugars were left in the beer to give sweetness to the flavour and to restore lost energies to drinkers who had spent eight hours or more engaged in hard manual labour. In Herbert's *Art of Brewing* published in 1871, the typical gravity of a mild ale was given as 1070°, close to 7 per cent alcohol in modern terms. At the turn of the century, the average strength of mild was 1055°. It suffered from a drastic lowering of strength in World War I and later from the international trend towards paler alcoholic drinks. In Britain, as brewers attempted to attract younger people of both sexes into pubs, mild was seen as having an outdated 'cloth-cap' image.

The last major area for mild drinking is the region known as the Black Country, based around Wolverhampton in the West Midlands. The name Black Country is a half-affectionate, half-ironic one that stems from the countless factory chimneys that belched black smoke when the region was the powerhouse of English industry based on foundries and coal mines. It is in the Black Country that the taste of a true Victorian mild can still be tasted. The Beacon Hotel in Sedgley was built in 1850, complete with a

THE ROYAL NAVY AMENITY SHIP
"MENESTHEUS"

~ BEER ~

ENGLISH MILD ALE

Brewed in

Davy Jones Brewery

"THE WORLD'S ONLY
FLOATING BREWERY"

On Sale at all BARS of the AMENITY SHIP
9d per Pint   SUPPLIES UNLIMITED

Operated By
NAVY, ARMY & AIR FORCE INSTITUTES
SPONSORED BY BOARD OF ADMIRALTY

Lilliputian brewery in the yard at the back. Sarah Hughes bought the hotel in 1921 and ran it for thirty years, handing it on to her son and daughters when she died in 1951. The brewery had produced a strong dark mild, based on Victorian recipes. The Hughes family closed the brewing operation in 1958 but Sarah Hughes's grandson, John, decided to begin brewing again in 1987 when he discovered her recipe in a cigar box locked in a bank security vault. All the old wooden vessels had rotted away

Fighting spirit. . .in World War II, on the instructions of Prime Minister Winston Churchill, troops were supplied with Mild Ale from a brewery based in a Royal Navy ship.

and had to be replaced by stainless-steel ones, faced with wood.

To watch the brewing process, you have to clamber up narrow wooden stairs to the cramped area at the top dominated by a mash tun. Maris Otter pale malt is blended with 10 per cent crystal. After mashing and sparging, the wort is dropped a few feet into a tiny underback or receiving vessel and from there into the original, open-topped copper where it is boiled with Fuggles and Goldings hops. After the boil, the hopped wort runs into the hopback (receiving vessel) where it clarifies and is then pumped to five fermenters converted from cellar tanks bought from the now-closed Ansells Brewery in Birmingham.

John Hughes has restored the hotel and turned it into a Victorian shrine, complete with taproom, smoke-room and snug, all with gas lamps, open fires and tiled floors. Each room is supplied with beer from a central servery, with glasses pushed through hatches. In the glasses there is Sarah Hughes's Dark Ruby Mild, 6 per cent alcohol. It has a rich and fruity nose, with blackcurrant dominating, laced with an earthy Fuggles aroma: it is the Bordeaux of the beer world. The palate is complex, summoning up every dark fruit imaginable. The finish becomes dry with a lot of Fuggles hop character.

The Victorian Highgate Brewery in Walsall stands incongruously among streets of staid suburban houses. But when the brewery was built in 1895 Walsall was the centre of the local leather-making industry and the brewery's mild ale refreshed generations of workers in hot and steamy factories. It became part of the large Mitchells & Butlers group based in nearby Birmingham, which later merged with Bass. In the mid-1990s Bass sold the plant for a notional sum to one of its employees, Steve Nuttall. He has busily expanded sales, bought some pubs of his own and added several other beers to the Highgate portfolio. But Highgate Mild remains his bread-and-butter brand, produced in an antique 'tower' brewery, where production flows from floor to floor, with mashing at the top,

Mild doesn't mean weak. . .the Dark Ruby Mild brewed in Sedgley in the West Midlands is based on a Victorian recipe and is 6 per cent alcohol.

coppers below and fermenters a further floor down. Mashing is in two ancient tuns, originally made from wood and relined with stainless steel but retaining hand-raised wooden lids. The malt grist is ground in a wooden mill and then sieved to remove stones and other detritus in a wooden shuttle known as 'the coffin' that runs on leather pulleys. The boil and hop addition take place in two gleaming coppers with internal heating callandrias topped by

The Beacon Hotel, home to Sarah Hughes's mild, is a shrine to Victorian pub architecture and has a fine kitchen range in the Tap Room.

It may be Mild but it does have hops...the Highgate Brewery in Walsall has two fine copper kettles.

company, founded in 1881 by Daniel Batham when he lost his job as a coal-miner. The Bathams had been in business for seventy years before they first brewed a pale beer. Today Best Bitter is the main product but Mild Ale has revived a little. Mild and bitter are 'parti-gyle' beers: Tim Batham brews his 4.3 per cent bitter from Maris Otter malt, with Fuggles and Northdown hops in the copper. A portion of the beer is watered down to 3.6 per cent to make the mild. Caramel is added in the fermenter and Batham puts in twice as much yeast for mild as for bitter: the acidity of the wort is lower in the mild as a result of the added liquor and it is important to get a vigorous

Highgate for many years was a mild-only brewery. The horse on the label recalls the time when Walsall was famous for its leather factories.

funnels called 'Chinese hats'. The fine fermenting room is packed with a variety of round and square vessels, once made from wood but now lined to keep bugs from the brew. The recipe for Highgate Mild calls for 2 tonnes of Halcyon pale malt, 65 kilos (143 pounds) of black and 15-20 kilos (33-4 pounds) of crystal for every one hundred barrels brewed. Maltose sugar and caramel are also used for fermentability and colour. Brewing liquor, rich in iron, comes from a bore hole on the site. Hops are Fuggles and Goldings. The colour rating is 75, the bitterness units 22. The head brewer describes the yeast strain, handed down from one generation to the next since the brewery opened, as 'a beast'. It is a four-strain yeast, each strain attacking elements of the sugars at different times during fermentation. The beer has a modest alcohol rating of 3.2 per cent but it nevertheless has a rich and deep aroma and flavour, with a tangy hint of iron from the

liquor, dark fruit, chocolate and licorice in the mouth, and a dry, nutty finish with a delicate balance of hops.

The Vine pub in Brierley Hill near Dudley has a striking barley-white exterior with the legend 'Batham's Genuine Home Brewed Mild & Bitter Beers' above the bar windows and a quotation from Shakespeare's *Two Gentlemen of Verona* on a fascia board above the top storey: 'Blessing of your heart: you brew good ale'. The pub is the brewery tap for Batham's Delph Brewery, a small company that owns just nine pubs in the area. Don't ask for the Vine if you go there: it is known to all and sundry as the 'Bull and Bladder', for a butcher's shop and slaughterhouse were on the site for years. The brothers Tim and Matthew Batham are the fifth generation of the family to run the

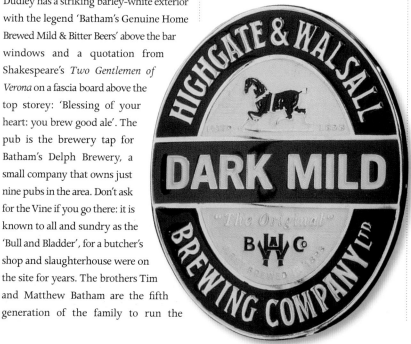

fermentation under way. Finally, the mild is racked into casks and heavily primed with brewing sugar to ensure a powerful second fermentation. The beer is dry hopped in the cask with Goldings and has an unusually big hop character for the style. There is a dark winy fruitiness on the palate with blackcurrant dominating. The finish is bitter-sweet, becoming dry and quenching.

The biggest producer of mild by far in the Midlands is the large Wolverhampton & Dudley group, Britain's biggest regional brewer, owning 850 pubs and producing Banks's beer. Mild outsells bitter, an astonishing achievement in this day and age, and the beer is even advertised on television. The attention to detail at Banks's is awe-inspiring. Its copper mash tuns and kettles gleam from regular buffing, floor-malted Maris Otter barley comes from the brewery's own maltings, and hops are the finest English Fuggles and Goldings with Bramling Cross from British Columbia: hops are added late in the boil but not in the cask. The 3.5 per cent tawny mild, with 40 units of colour and 25 of bitterness, uses caramel for colour rather than dark malt. Head brewer Richard Westwood claims caramel is tasteless, but I find it gives a distinctive vinous, port-wine character to the beer, which has a delicate hop aroma with light fruit notes. The fruit begins to blossom in the mouth, vying for attention with the rich malt. The finish has a pronounced vanilla character ending with a pleasing wineyness.

A rare pale 'light mild', with the mysterious name of AK, is brewed by McMullen in Hertford, run by a family with some Irish ancestry who began brewing in 1827. Four years later McMullen launched AK, which remains their biggest-selling ale today. In the nineteenth century many brewers offered both light and dark milds, but the advent of pale ale reduced demand

for the lighter versions. McMullen has stood firm against every modern trend since the 1960s and then, just as there was renewed interest in mild, it dropped the name and repositioned the brand as 'Original AK Bitter'. To its legion of aficionados it remains AK Mild. Once there were many breweries with milds called AK. No one is certain what the letters stand for. I believe the name derives from the practice of branding casks to indicate the type of beer and its strength. From medieval times, the letter 'X' was used on casks to signify strength. If you cut an X vertically, you get a K. I suspect that AK meant the first (A) brew in a series of mild ales (K). But no doubt, like the origins of the name porter, the debate will rumble on.

McMullen has one of the finest traditional brewhouses in the country and a cool, dimly lit fermenting room packed with high-sided wooden vessels. AK is brewed from Halcyon pale malt, flaked maize, maltose syrup and a touch (1 per cent) of chocolate malt. The beer has a floral hop aroma from Goldings and Whitbread Goldings Variety balanced by rich fruit and vanilla. There are sweet malt, fruit and hops in the mouth followed by a dry finish with orange peel and chocolate notes.

In Liverpool, the Robert Cain Brewery, based in a vast, red-brick Victorian plant, brews a complex, aromatic and creamy Dark

Beer fit for a Bard. . .Batham's brew-pub has a quotation from the Two Gentlemen of Verona *across the lintel.*

Mild that drinks stronger than its modest 3.2 per cent alcohol. Head brewer Paul Jefferies believes that the character of the beer was determined at the turn of the century by the enormous popularity of Dublin-brewed Guinness among the large Irish population. In an area infamous for poverty and sweatshops, not everyone could afford Guinness, and dark mild would have been an acceptable alternative. The use of roasted barley with pale and chocolate malts supports his theory. The finished beer is heavily primed with dark liquid sugar, made by Tate & Lyle from molasses, which gives a pronounced licorice flavour. The hops are Goldings and Target. As a result of the priming sugar, added at the rate of four pints per barrel, casks have to be stored in cool

areas of pub cellars. 'Otherwise', says Paul Jefferies, 'the casks will blow their taps!'

In the Welsh capital, Cardiff, another dockside city with a past rooted in iron, steel and coal-mining, the Red Dragon Dark brewed by the family-owned Brains company is the most famous ale of the Principality and has slaked the thirsts of miners and Rugby fans for decades. It is 3.5 per cent alcohol, brewed from pale and chocolate malts, and invert and glucose sugars, with Fuggles and Goldings whole flower hops. It is a fine 'quaffing' beer, with chocolate and delicate hops on the aroma, dark malt in the mouth and a smooth, creamy, lightly hoppy finish.

One of England's oddest beer styles is a brown ale that isn't. It is confined to the

What's in a name? No one knows for sure why McMullen's light mild is called AK, but Fergus McMullen (right) and two happy drinkers help celebrate the ale's growing success.

north east, where the most famous version is Newcastle Brown Ale, brewed in a city with more shipping and coal-mining connections. It is the biggest-selling bottled ale in Britain and is exported widely to the US (where it is sold on draught) and to Russia. Unlike brown and mild ales brewed elsewhere in England, Newcastle Brown Ale was formulated to counter the popularity of pale ale. The russet-coloured beer was developed for Newcastle Breweries in the 1920s by the suitably named Dr Porter, as the beer is a blend of two brews: a strong dark ale is not sold commercially but is used solely for blending with a paler beer. The malts are pale and crystal. A blend of English hops create just 24 units of bitterness. With an alcohol rating of 4.7 per cent, this is a malt-accented beer with a chewy, nutty flavour and a hint of vanilla.

Another characterful north-east brown ale, Double Maxim, is brewed by Vaux of Sunderland, the Wearside town once famous for its shipbuilding. Vaux is a Norman French name but the pronuncia-tion is rendered 'Vorx' on Wearside. A member of the ruling family, Captain Ernest Vaux, led a daring raid during the Boer War using a Maxim machine-gun. On his return to Sunderland he was honoured with a beer called Maxim. A stronger version, called Double Maxim, was introduced in 1938. It is brewed from pale and crystal malts with a touch of caramel and is primed with sugar. Fuggles is the sole hop variety used. It is 4.2 per cent alcohol and has an earthy Fuggles aroma, is rich and nutty in the mouth and becomes dry in the finish with some light, tart fruit. It has 22 units of bitterness. After years of lobbying by the local branch of Camra, Vaux produces a cask-conditioned and a bottled version of the beer.

Mild may be virtually dead in London but a famous Cockney brown ale has survived, albeit produced today in the West Country town of Trowbridge in Wiltshire. Manns Brown Ale was once brewed by the large Mann, Crossman & Paulin company in Whitechapel, East London and was one of

Robert Cain's Brewery in Liverpool is a magnificent Victorian red brick complex that produces a Dark Mild that once rivalled Dublin-brewed Guinness in popularity.

Brains Dark, a revered mild ale brewed in Cardiff and popular throughout the South Wales valleys.

its major brands. When Manns became part of the Grand Metropolitan/Watney brewing giant in the 1960s, the Whitechapel plant was closed. Manns Brown Ale led a peripatetic life for several years until GrandMet sold all its breweries and the beer ended up with the newly independent Ushers Brewery in Trowbridge. Brown Ale still accounts for more than 100,000 barrels of beer a year, a 'nice little earner' as they say in London. The beer has an extremely modest 2.8 per cent alcohol but has a good rounded flavour due to the use of roasted barley along with pale malt and wheat malt. It is lightly hopped with Targets, which balance the sweetness and creaminess of the malts. The brand is likely to decline slowly as its loyal market of older working-class Londoners dies off. Ushers has acutely tagged that market by using the archetypal

Above: Newcastle Brown Ale is actually russet-coloured and was brewed to counter the popularity of pale ale in the 1920s. The malty, nutty beer is Britain's biggest-selling bottled ale.

Below: Same beer, different bottles. . .a collection of bottles for Vaux Double Maxim brown ale in the Sunderland brewery's museum. Double Maxim was introduced in 1938.

blue-collar cartoon character, Andy Capp, in its promotions.

In the US, the ground-breaking Brooklyn Brewery in New York City produces a big, bold interpretation of brown ale. Brooklyn Brown (4.8 per cent weight/6 volume) is made from pale, crystal, chocolate and black malts and is generously hopped with Cascades and Northern Brewer as well as being dry hopped in the keg. Rich chocolate and espresso coffee dominate the aroma and palate, balanced by great hop character. The beer was contract brewed for several years but in 1996 the company opened up its own plant and restored a brewing tradition to Brooklyn that had been destroyed first by Prohibition and then by waves of closures in the 1950s and 1960s.

Nothing's too good for the working class...the archetypal cloth cap and muffler drinker, Andy Capp, is used to promote a now rare example of a London Cockney brown ale. It's all a bit confusing, for the beer is now brewed in rural Wiltshire and Andy Capp is a cartoon Geordie from the far north east.

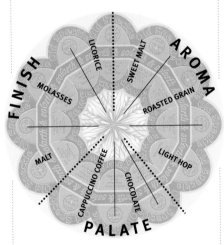

MILD AND BROWN ALE STYLE

Gentle hops, rich biscuity malt and light fruit are the hallmarks of a style that dominated English brewing until the 1950s. The original aim of Mild Ale was to refresh industrial and agricultural workers and replenish lost body sugars.

MILD AND BROWN ALE PRODUCERS

Daniel Batham & Son Ltd
Brewery, Delph Road, Brierley Hill,
West Midlands DY5 2TN

S.A. Brain & Co. Ltd
The Old Brewery, 49 St Mary Street,
Cardiff CF1 1SP

Brooklyn Brewery
118 N 11th Street, Brooklyn,
New York 11211

Robert Cain & Co. Ltd
Stanhope Street,
Liverpool L8 5XJ

Highgate & Walsall Brewing Company Ltd
Sandymount Road, Walsall,
West Midlands WS1 3AP

Sarah Hughes Brewery
Beacon Hotel, 129 Bilston Street,
Sedgley, Dudley,
West Midlands DY3 1JE

McMullen & Sons Ltd
Hertford Brewery,
26 Old Cross,
Hertford SG14 1RD

Scottish & Newcastle Plc
Tyne Brewery, Gallowgate,
Newcastle upon Tyne NE99 1RA

Ushers of Trowbridge Plc
Directors House,
68 Fore Street,
Trowbridge, Wilts BA14 8JF

Vaux Breweries Ltd
Sunderland,
Tyne & Wear SR1 3AN

Wolverhampton & Dudley Breweries Plc
PO Box 26,
Park Brewery,
Bath Road,
Wolverhampton,
West Midlands WV1 4NY

OLD ALE

Old ale suffers from two confusions. Many writers lump it together with barley wine, while others assume it must be a beer of fearsome strength. While the term 'barley wine' smacks of sheer vinous power, an old ale need not necessarily overburden the hydrometer. It is a beer that acquires its maturity, flavour, ripe condition and smooth flavour by ageing. Centuries ago, such ageing took place in great oak tuns. Today it is more likely to be in a bottle or a brewery conditioning tank. Historically, it was beer brewed for blending, usually with a younger and more spritzy pale or brown ale. Old or 'stale' ale was one of the key constituents of the early porter beers, a blend of pale, young brown and old ale.

The vatting of beer has long since disappeared and the finest versions of old ale are now those which mature and improve on their yeasty lees in a bottle. Others are produced for the winter and Christmas period, cask-conditioned ales that gain in palate and flavour as the weeks pass by. McMullen of Hertford produces a winter beer called Stronghart, a 7 per cent alcohol old ale brewed from Halcyon pale malt, crystal malt, flaked maize and maltose syrup. A single hop is used, Whitbread Goldings Variety, which creates 33 units of bitterness. One Christmas I had a small glass of the beer on a regular basis until the one cask in the pub ran dry. Over a period of a month, it was fascinating to trace the changes in the beer as it developed ever more pronounced flavours of raisins and sultanas. Towards the end of its life there was an aroma and palate best summed up as port wine with hops.

As a result of the seasonal nature of the style, some breweries use the base old ale as the source for other beers. At the classic Highgate Tower brewery in Walsall, already noted for its dark mild, Highgate Old Ale is

brewed at 5.1 per cent alcohol and is then watered down to make the 3.2 per cent mild. The old ale is brewed from pale, crystal and black malts with caramel for colour and some brewing syrup. Whole flower Challenger and Progress hops create 30 units of bitterness. The beer has tempting aromas of dark malt, chocolate and coffee, with chewy malt and chocolate in the mouth and a bitter-sweet finish dominated by sultana fruit and hops.

The connection between old ales and mild ale is stressed by Mike Powell-Evans, head brewer at Adnams in Southwold, Suffolk. He says his Old (4.1 per cent) is no

Highgate's Old Ale is a stronger version of its famous Dark Mild.

more than a strong mild, a claim he also makes for his redoubtable Tally-Ho 7 per cent barley wine. Adnams Old (pale and crystal malts, brewing syrup and caramel, with Fuggles and Goldings whole hops) has a rich malt aroma with light hop notes, juicy malt in the mouth and a chewy malt and hops finish with the unmistakable orange fruit from the house yeast.

A long way removed from an old ale with such a modest strength is Vintage Harvest Ale from the John Willy Lees

Brewery in Manchester. This remarkable ale registers 11.5 per cent and I sometimes wonder whether the measurement is made by the Richter Scale rather than a brewer's gauge. Conventional brewer's yeast will give up at around 12 per cent, overcome by the alcohol. Head brewer Giles Dennis takes the first barley and hops of the harvest to fashion a new vintage every autumn. He uses Maris Otter barley and East Kent Goldings and ferments the ale in open copper vessels. The beer is stored in the brewery until it is released in bottled and cask-conditioned versions on 1 December. Although he uses only Maris Otter pale malt, the finished beer has a burnished copper colour as a result of the caramelization of the brewing sugars during the long copper boil. Harvest Ale has 30 units of colour and 34 units of bitterness. Giles Dennis recommends that the bottled version should be laid down for several years to improve. The beer in bottle is pasteurized but this does not prevent a melding of aromas and flavours.

It is a brave brewer who alludes to a tom cat in the name of his beer, for beers with off flavours or those which have been badly pasteurized have an aroma all too reminiscent of a tom's 'spray'. But Lees's near neighbour, Frederic Robinson of Stockport, boldly places a winking feline at the centre of its beer mats and labels for Old Tom, an 8.5 per cent old ale. The beer has been brewed since 1838 and is almost as old as the brewery. Details of the ale have been found in the brewer's handwritten notes dating from 1899. It was only available on draught then, but is now sold in bottle as well. Robinson's is a fiercely traditional brewery with copper brewing vessels, tiled walls and a firm belief in the virtue of whole hops rather than compressed pellets. Old Tom is the result of a mash of Halcyon and

Pipkin pale malts, crystal malt, flaked maize, torrefied wheat and caramel for colour, boiled with Goldings and Northdown hops and dry hopped in the cask with a further addition of Goldings. It has a heady aroma of ripe dark fruit, fat malt and peppery hops in the mouth, and a long finish reminiscent of port wine with a balance of spicy hops.

Another old ale that comes in both cask and bottled versions has won many prizes at Camra-run beer festivals. Theakston's Old Peculier is a beer with both an odd name and an even odder spelling. The brewery is in the ancient town of Masham in the Yorkshire Dales, an accessible part of the

rugged Pennine mountains that form the backbone of northern England. Masham, surrounded by hills dotted with grazing sheep, became a leading centre of the medieval wool trade. Its commercial importance gave it a degree of independence, and the citizens were permitted by the bishops of York during the Norman period to establish their own ecclesiastical court to administer law and order. The Masham court was known as a 'peculier' as it was outside the

So old it's got whiskers…Robinson's Old Tom dates from 1838 and dates back almost to the beginnings of the Stockport brewery.

jurisdiction of the bishops. The court, made up of 24 local men, still sits to choose churchwardens and make small local grants. When the Theakston family bought the Black Bull pub with its own brewery in 1827, it was inevitable that they should make a beer using such a memorable name. Fifty years later Theakstons built a new brewery and maltings, and then in the 1920s merged with another local brewer called Lightfoot. Today Theakstons is part of the giant Scottish Courage group and the Masham site is as much a visitors' centre as a brewery.

The Masham brewery has a cast-iron mash tun with an oak jacket, a second-hand copper with a triangular flue, an open coolship for cooling the wort, and rooms packed with high-sided fermenters, some of them made of slate. Old Peculier, 5.6 per cent, is made from pale and crystal malts and some torrefied wheat, brewing sugar and caramel. A blend of hops is used but Fuggles is the main variety: head brewer Hugh Curley is a devotee of the Fuggle, with its earthy, uncompromising bitterness. The beer is dry hopped with Fuggles, has 29 units of bitterness and 95 of colour. The mixed strain house yeast gives a pronounced softness of palate and intense fruit character to all the brewery's ales. Old Peculier has a winey aroma of blackcurrant fruit balanced by peppery hops. Toffee and roast malt dominate the mouth while the finish is roasty, fruity and hoppy.

The two great classics of the old ale style both come from south-west England. George Gale & Company is a family-owned business in Horndean in Hampshire, once an important stop on the coach route from London to Portsmouth. The brewery started life in the Ship and Bell public house that now stands alongside the present site. Its Prize Old Ale was developed by a brewer from Yorkshire in the 1920s; he may have been

Gale's bottle-conditioned Old Ale is brewed in Hampshire but may have been modelled on a Yorkshire style called Stingo.

prompted by the Yorkshire style of strong ale called 'Stingo'. POA, as it is known for short, is the only regular British beer produced in hand-corked bottles. Unlike some brewers, Gale's head brewer Derek Lowe recommends that the beer should be laid down for five years but will not commit himself beyond that length of time. One of his predecessors, however, thought the beer would be at its best after twenty years.

POA is brewed with the other ales in a delightful and slightly higgledy-piggledy brewhouse with a cast-iron mash tun, a 1920s copper and a fermenting room with both square and round wooden vessels dating from the 1920s. The Old Ale is 9 per cent alcohol. It is brewed with Maris Otter pale malt, which makes up 98 per cent of the

grist, and a touch of black malt and wheat. Fuggles and Goldings create a massive 47.5 units of bitterness. The beer is dry hopped with Styrian Goldings. The wort is boiled for two hours, which caramelizes some of the brewing sugar, resulting in a tawny colour in the glass. The beer used to be conditioned in wooden hogsheads but Derek Lowe has switched to modern conditioning tanks. He says it gives the beer a cleaner palate and avoids the need to blend different batches. Conditioning lasts for at least six months and may take a year. More house yeast (a multi-strain) is added just before bottling. All aspects of bottling – washing, rinsing, filling, corking and sticking on the labels – are done by hand. While the bottles are declared at 9 per cent alcohol, the beer may reach 10 or 11 per cent as a result of a second fermentation. It has a stunning aroma of spicy hops and ripe fruit, including a hint of apple from the yeast strain. A well-matured POA will develop a pronounced Calvados character. There is a faint hint of sourness in the finish, perhaps from the brewery's own well water, a touch of chocolate from the dark malt and a pungent fruity, hoppy finish.

The Thomas Hardy red-brick Victorian brewery in Dorchester produces the most celebrated of all old ales. Thomas Hardy's Ale was first brewed in 1968 for a literary festival to commemorate the work of Hardy, author of such famous Wessex novels as *Far from the Madding Crowd* and *Tess of the D'Urbervilles*. In *The Mayor of Casterbridge*, Hardy had waxed lyrial about the ales of the town, his nom de plume for Dorchester: 'luminous as an autumn sunset, full in body yet brisk as a volcano'. Head brewer Roger Wharton does not think Thomas Hardy's Ale is based on a nineteenth-century recipe but it is unchanged since it was first brewed in 1968. The ale has a starting gravity of 1125° and reaches 12 per cent alcohol, possibly slightly more after bottle conditioning. Old bottle labels used to recommend laying the beer down for twenty years but Roger Wharton is cautious about supporting such claims. He says the beer is in good drinking form after one year and will improve year by year. When I took part in a vertical tasting of vintage Thomas Hardy's Ale with former brewery chairman Christopher Pope, I found the changes year by year were quite fascinating, with vinous and sherry notes dominating the older vintages. In Mr Pope's memorable description, one vintage had the character of 'a library of old leather-bound books'. Another reminded me powerfully of the aroma of fresh tobacco. Some of the older vintages had drawn corks rather than crown caps, which may have led to some slight oxidation of the beer.

Thomas Hardy's Ale is brewed from 100 per cent Pipkin pale malt. The russet colour of the beer is the result of a long copper boil which darkens the wort and caramelizes

The Thomas Hardy Brewery in Dorchester is home to a world-famous old ale.

some of the sugars. Brewing liquor comes from the Blackdown Hills and is hard and chalky: the chalk is removed and the water slightly softened. Hops are a complex grist of Challenger, Goldings and Northdown whole flowers with dry hopping in cask with Styrian Goldings. The beer has a mighty 75 units of bitterness. It is fermented in a 75-barrel vessel that allows room for a large head of yeast to build up. The wort is repitched with yeast several times in order to keep fermentation going: the high level of alcohol encourages the yeast to go to sleep on the job. The mixed yeast strain gives all the Thomas Hardy beers a rich, soft fruitiness reminiscent of pear drop and banana. In a beer of 12 per cent this develops into a sherry or Madeira wineyness.

After fermentation the beer is matured at room temperature for three months in glass-lined tanks. It is bottled without the addition of sugars or fresh yeast. Just fifty barrels of the ale are made at a time. It is impossible to give a definitive description of an ale that develops such stunning aromas and flavours over the years and which varies widely from vintage to vintage. The best advice is to buy several vintages (they are available from the brewery) and organize your own tasting.

Greene King's Strong Suffolk Ale is a palpable link with the 'staled' and aged old ales of the eighteenth century. The brewery is in the ancient town of Bury St Edmunds, a place of great antiquity and charm, Georgian buildings blending with the ancient gate-house and the remains of its walls. The last brewery in the town was founded in the early eighteenth century but may be even older. It was bought at the turn of the following century by Benjamin Greene, who had trained with Sam

First brewed in 1968, each vintage of Thomas Hardy's Ale varies from the previous one.

Whitbread and had learned the skills of making porter and stout, and blending them from young and aged ales. Greene later merged his brewery with rival Kings that stood on the same street. The brewhouse has fine traditional copper vessels, is supplied with liquor from its own wells and malts its own pale malt to exacting standards.

To find the most fascinating vessels in the brewery, you have to scramble up perilous ladders and walkways until you reach the tops of two large oak vats. Made of untreated wood, each one holds sixty barrels of beer. A powerful 12 per cent ale called Old 5X is stored in the vats for two to five years. It is not sold commercially but used for blending with the brewery's barley wine known as St Edmund, its Winter Ale and

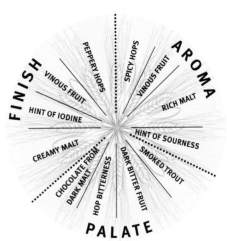

OLD ALE STYLE

Ripe malt aromas, big hop bitterness and a rich fruitiness are typical characteristics of a style that dates from a time when ales were aged in wooden vats for a year or more.

Oak vats in Greene King's brewery store a beer that is blended to become Strong Suffolk Ale.

most notably, the Strong Suffolk. The lids of the vats that hold Old 5X are covered with 'marl', the Suffolk dialect word for the local chalky soil. The marl protects the ale and stops wild yeasts infecting it, but drunk straight (as I did in the brewers' sample room) it has slight lactic sourness and oakiness from the wood. To make Strong Suffolk, it is blended with a 5 per cent beer called BPA, Best Pale Ale. The beers are brewed from Pipkin and Halcyon pale malts with some crystal, and hopped with Challenger, Northdown and Target. The blend is bottled at 6 per cent and has a rich apple oaky aroma and palate balanced by spicy and peppery hops and a tart, iodine note in the finish. The beer is filtered and pasteurized but improves slightly in bottle.

OLD ALE BREWERS

Adnams & Co.
Sole Bay Brewery, East Green,
Southwold,
Suffolk IP18 6JW

Boston Beer Company
The Brewery,
30 Germania Street,
Boston, Massachusetts 02130

George Gale & Co.
The Hampshire Brewery,
London Road,
Horndean,
Hants PO8 0DA

Greene King Plc
Westgate Brewery, Westgate Street,
Bury Str Edmunds,
Suffolk IP33 1QT

Thomas Hardy Brewing Ltd
Weymouth Avenue,
Dorchester DT1 1QT

Highgate & Walsall Brewing Company
Sandymount Road, Walsall,
West Midlands WS1 3A.

J W Lees & Co.
Greengate Brewery,
Middleton Junction,
Manchester M24 2AX

McMullen & Sons Ltd
The Hertford Brewery,
26 Old Cross,
Hertford SG14 1RD

Frederic Robinson Ltd
Unicorn Brewery,
Lower Hillgate,
Stockport,
Cheshire SK1 1JJ

T & R Theakston Ltd
Wellgarth, Masham, Ripon,
North Yorkshire HG4 4YD

BARLEY WINE

Brewers have always made strong ales but the term 'barley wine' came into use only in the eighteenth century in order to counter the impact of imported wines, mainly from France. English brewers found themselves under attack from Bordeaux and Burgundy and fought back with strong ales they hoped would please the insularity and jingoism of the island race. The new technologies of the Industrial Revolution made it possible to make strong but pale beers, distinct from the dark milds and porters drunk by the working class. The increasing use of lightly cured pale malt and the scientific culturing of pure strains of yeast gave brewers far greater control over the production of strong beers of reliable and consistent quality. These beers were described as October beers (brewed in the spring and stored until the autumn), malt liquors and malt wines. Eventually they were brought together under the generic title of barley wine.

Thomas Astley, author of *The London and Country Brewer* published in 1742, recommended that malt liquors should be vatted for at least nine months before tapping. A century later, William Tizard, in his *Theory and Practice of Brewing*, said strong ales should be brewed from the best and palest malts to a gravity of between 1085° and 1112°, and then aged for at least a year and preferably two. But once the vatting of strong ales went out of fashion as a result of commercial pressure and high rates of excise duty, barley wines retained their strength but in all but a handful of cases lost the ageing process.

The leading British barley wine for many years was Bass No.1, available only in small nip bottles with labels bearing the famous Bass red diamond trade mark and point-of-sale posters that declared the ale 'warms and

nourishes, has no reaction, is famous for its flavour, has the character of a rare wine'. The title 'No.1' signified that this was the strongest of all Bass's many brands at 10.5 per cent alcohol. Enormous pride and care went into the brewing of the beer. The head brewer and maltster would 'walk the piece' in the maltings, meaning they picked their way through the germinating barley in order to choose the ripest and finest malt. Only pale malt was used: the russet colour of the finished beer was the result of an astonishing twelve-hour copper boil during which the sugars darkened and caramelized; 2.7 kilos (6 pounds) of Fuggles and Goldings hops were used for each barrel of beer in order to balance the rich sweetness of the malt sugars. The fermenting beer had to be constantly roused and repitched with yeast

Steve Wellington tests the strength of a new batch of Bass No. 1 barley wine.

in order to achieve the required strength. After fermentation, the beer was matured in hogsheads for an entire winter in the brewery yard at Burton. If the winter was hard, the beer would sometimes freeze and then burst its casks when it melted. Bass clerical workers would rush to scoop up the alcoholic slush and then warm it over their office fires.

There was great anguish when Bass stopped production of No.1 on the grounds of 'lack of demand'. Anguish turned to joy when the beer made a comeback in 1996, though it now requires a trip to the Bass Museum in Burton-on-Trent to sample it. The museum includes a tiny 1920s pilot brewing plant formerly used by Bass's subsidiary Mitchells & Butlers in Birmingham to try out new recipes. The brewery was installed in the museum in the 1970s purely as an exhibit, but in 1994 a former Bass brewer, Steve Wellington, was invited to brew small amounts in order to show visitors the brewing process and to provide beer for the museum bar. Two years later Bass No.1 appeared from the tiny plant that can make just sixty barrels of beer a week. The equipment includes two teak-clad fermenters dating from 1853 and a superb copper that empties the hopped wort into a collecting vessel below. The tiny amounts of Bass No.1 produced by Mr Wellington are far removed from the beer's hey-day when 1000 barrels a year were bottled. But at least this flag-bearer of a noble style has returned and is made available in draught form for the Bass Musuem bar. When a panel of Camra tasters sampled seven barley wines for the campaign's newspaper *What's Brewing* in December 1996, Bass No.1 came top, scoring 216 points out of a maximum 250. The tasters admired its 'molasses and peppery hop aroma, glacé fruit palate and rich warming finish'. They found a distinct hint of caramelized oranges in the finish.

Barley wine's profile was given a boost in August 1995 when a beer called Norman's Conquest won the coveted title of Camra's Champion Beer of Britain. It had to beat such mainstream styles as mild, bitter and stout to achieve its victory. Norman's Conquest is a serious beer with a punny name. It is brewed by Chris Norman with a starting gravity of 1066°: the year 1066 marked the Norman invasion of England. Mr Norman is a former airline pilot who brewed at home in his spare time and took early retirement to turn his hobby into a full-time job. With his wife Helen, he lives in a remote Somerset village, West Lydford. The Normans' company is called Cottage Brewing because, Chris points out, it is a true cottage industry. Brewing takes place in his garage, converted to accommodate a five-barrel plant, though the clamour for his beers following the award to Norman's Conquest led to the brew-length being doubled to ten barrels. The beers are conditioned in a converted, temperature-controlled garden shed. Norman's Conquest is 7 per cent, on the low side for a barley wine, but the rich and warming alcohol belies the modest strength.

Tiny brewing vessels in the Burton Museum used to recreate old beers including barley wine.

It is brewed from pale malt with crystal and pale chocolate malts for colour and body, and is hopped with Challenger (34 units of bitterness). The hops balance the sweet and juicy malt with a tart citric fruitiness reminiscent of grapefruit. The palate is spicy while both the aroma and finish have a plum jam fruitiness. Norman's Conquest was available first in cask-conditioned form but its success encouraged the Normans to produce it in a bottle-conditioned version as well.

Fuller's Golden Pride is 9.2 per cent alcohol and has a delectably smooth and honeyish quality from Alexis pale and crystal malts. The house yeast gives a pronounced fruitiness, with Seville oranges leading the pack. A complex hop grist of Challenger, Goldings, Northdown and Target balances the richness of the malt.

The devil has the best beers... Youngs' Old Nick is a cult beer in Scandinavia but is not popular in America's 'Bible Belt'.

Finally, the big, long finish is packed with peppery hops, ripe grain and vinous fruit. Fuller's keeps alive the old tradition of rolling casks of barley wine round the brewery yard in order to encourage the yeast to keep on working. Every autumn a portion of a batch of Golden Pride is racked into a 54-gallon hogshead, which is rolled once a week for three months. Finally the beer is decanted from the hogshead into small 20.4-litre (4.5-gallon)

casks known as pins, which get a further addition of hops.

Fullers' near neighbour, Youngs of Wandsworth, suggests that the devil has the best beer as well as the best tunes. Old Nick barley wine (7.25 per cent) is not only popular in the company's own trading area but has become a cult beer in Scandinavia, where drinkers for decades have been deprived of the ability to enjoy strong beers as a result of government clampdowns. It is also a big seller in the United States, though the depiction of a lascivious devil on the label has not helped sales in the 'Bible Belt' areas. Old Nick is an appealing russet colour (75–80 colour units) due to the generous use of crystal malt with Maris Otter pale. The hops are Fuggles and Goldings, which create 50–55 bitterness units. It has a biscuity aroma balanced by tart hops, with vinous fruit and hops in the mouth and a long bitter-sweet finish with the malt and fruit held in check by Fuggles bitterness.

The most memorable barley wine I have tasted in the United States is Sierra Nevada's Big Foot. The Sierra Nevada Brewing Company, based in the university town of Chico, northern California, was one of the

Giles Dennis, head brewer at J.W. Lees Brewery near Manchester, brews an annual vintage Harvest Ale of 11.5 per cent alcohol that has a massive attack of fruit and hops.

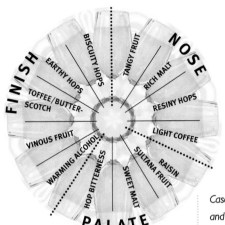

BARLEY WINE STYLE
Rich vinous fruit, sometimes reminiscent of pear drops, balanced by a huge perfumy hop bitterness and sweet, juicy malt are the benchmarks of a style created to offer a home-grown alternative to French wine.

Cascade, Centennial and Nugget hops from the Pacific North-west are carefully weighed and balanced to achieve the right levels of aroma and flavour in Big Foot Barley wine.

earliest new-wave micros. It was founded in 1981 by Ken Grossman and Paul Camusi, with Grossman making the leap from home-brewing to full-blown commercial production. Big Foot, brewed in the winter and early spring, is bottle conditioned and, at 8.48 per cent weight/12 per cent volume, is one of the strongest beers brewed in the US. It has a deep aroma of hops and dark malt, massive alcohol and hops in the mouth and a long, fruity and hoppy finish. The hops are Nugget for bitterness, with a late addition of Cascades for aroma. Further Cascades and Centennials are added during a month-long conditioning in the brewery. The beer stays in good condition for up to two years.

In Seattle, Charles Finkel's Pike Brewery produces a big, assertive, warming, roasty and toasty barley wine called Old Bawdy, so called because the brewery is on the site of a former brothel or bawdy house.

Making tracks...Sierra Nevada's barley wine is bottle conditioned and is one of the strongest beers made in the United States. It is packed with malt, hops and fruit flavours.

BARLEY WINE BREWERS

Bass No. 1 Barley Wine
contact Bass Museum, Horninglow Street, Burton-on-Trent, Staffs DE14 1YQ, tel: 01283 511000.
Museum opens every day except Xmas Day, 26 December and 1 January

Cottage Brewing Company
The Old Cheese Dairy, Lovington, Castle Cary, Somerset BA7 7PS

Fuller, Smith & Turner PLC
Griffin Brewery, Chiswick Lane South, Chiswick, London W4 2QB

Pike Brewing
140 Lakeside Avenue, Suite 300, Seattle, Washington 98122

Sierra Nevada Brewing Co.
1075 E 20th Street, Chico, California 95928

Young & Co.
Ram Brewery, High Street, Wandsworth, London SW18 4JD

J.W. Lees & Co.
Greengate Brewery, Middleton Junction, Manchester M24 2AX

STOUT AND PORTER

Stout and porter are the vogue beers of the moment. This is true of Britain in particular, the country that gave birth to the style. The British are the biggest consumers of stout. In 1995 Guinness brewed more stout at its Park Royal brewery in London than at any time since the plant opened in the 1930s. Beamish and Murphy, the other Irish stout brewers, are enjoying steady growth in Britain, while an increasing number of British brewers have dusted off old recipe books to recreate some fascinating versions of porter and stout, often in cask-conditioned or bottle-conditioned form. The enthusiasm for the style has also enveloped the craft brewers of the United States, who are keen to brew again many of the beers that were lost during Prohibition. Porter and stout also pop up in the most unlikely places: in the torrid heat of the Caribbean islands, the icy cold of Scandinavia and the Baltic States, in Anglophone Africa, in Japan and high in the mountains of Sri Lanka, all testimony to the world-wide influence of the style when it was at the peak of popularity in the nineteenth century and was driven by the steam engine of British imperialism.

The interest in porter and stout in Britain and the United States has been aided by the work of the family-owned Samuel Smith Brewery in Tadcaster, Yorkshire. Sam Smith is best known in England for its Old Brewery Pale Ale, but in the 1980s it introduced a porter and two stouts, available only in bottle on both sides of the Atlantic. The range comprises Taddy Porter ('Taddy' being the nickname for Tadcaster), Celebrated Oatmeal Stout and Imperial Stout. The porter (5 per cent alcohol) has a coffee and tart fruit aroma, more fruit and bitter hops in the mouth, and a long, dry finish packed with dark fruit, hops and roasted malt. Oatmeal Stout (5 per cent) has a smooth and silky palate with hints of chocolate and espresso coffee on the nose, and nuts and roasted grain in the finish.

Sam Smith describes its Imperial Stout (7 per cent) as an ideal digestif, the perfect replacement for Cognac. It even recommends serving it in a brandy balloon and suggests it should accompany Stilton and walnuts, baked sultana and lemon cheesecake, caviar, apricot-glazed bread-and-butter pudding, chocolate-baked Alaska, and chocolate trifle with roasted almonds. It will not be overpowered by any dish, with its highly complex roast barley aroma, a flavour of burnt dark raisin and sultana fruit, a deceptively smooth cappuccino finish with a hint of lactic sourness, creamy malt, sour fruit and spicy hops from traditional Fuggles and Goldings.

By a quirk of history, the John Smith's Brewery adjacent to Sam Smith's also brews an imperial stout, the most fascinating example of the breed. John Smith's is now part of the Scottish Courage group but at the turn of the century the Smiths were related. A row in the family forced John Smith to leave the Old Brewery and walk up the hill to launch his Magnet Brewery. Imperial Russian Stout reached the Magnet Brewery by a circuitous route. When porter and stout dominated London brewing, some ten breweries in the capital made stout for

A poster for Guinness during World War II… despite shortages of raw materials, the quality of the stout was unchanged. The expression 'Guinness is good for you' was withdrawn by government pressure after the war in both the United States and Britain but remains in the memories of generations of stout drinkers.

A bottle of Guinness with the Irish harp on the label became recognized world-wide as symbols of both quality and Ireland's struggle for nationhood.

used in a conventional beer. It has an aroma of fresh leather and licorice, with bitter black chocolate in the mouth, and an intense finish packed with bitter dark fruit and hops. There is an oily, tarry note that is the hallmark of the style.

Craft brewers producing porters and stouts of note include Titanic of Stoke-on-

Deep Shaft Stout, bottle conditioned, is one of the new breed of dark beers from British craft breweries.

export to the Baltic States and Russia. The most prominent of the breweries was owned by the Thrale family and was subsequently bought by a Scottish-American Quaker called Barclay, a member of the family that achieved great success as Barclays the bankers. The international connections were maintained when the brewery was taken over by John Courage, a Scot of French Huguenot descent. Barclay's Imperial Russian Stout had a long journey from London to Danzig and then into the Baltic en route to Imperial Russia. The voyage was especially hazardous during the Napoleonic wars when French forces blockaded the Baltic ports. In spite of these difficulties, supplies did get through and the beer became a cult drink at the court of the Tsars, and cases were sent to Russian troops fighting in the Crimea. In order to cope with demand, Barclay's agent in the region, a Belgian called Le Coq, built a brewery in Tartu, Estonia, to make Russian stout. In 1917 the Bolsheviks

nationalized the brewery. It survived the years of Soviet rule and has now been privatized. It plans to brew dark beer again now it is free from a command economy structure that forced the brewery to concentrate on thin lagers.

Even when the trade with Russia ended, Barclay and later Courage continued to brew small batches of Imperial Russian Stout. When it was brewed in London, it was matured in oak casks for a year before being bottled. Production was moved to John Smith's in Tadcaster when the Courage brewery closed. It is now sold after only a brief conditioning period and it is advisable to lay the beer down for at least a few months before drinking it as it is not filtered and will improve on its sediment of yeast. The 10 per cent alcohol beer is brewed from pale, amber and black malts with a touch of Pilsner malt. An enormous amount of Target hops – 11 kilos (24 pounds) per barrel – are used; that is four times the quantity of hops

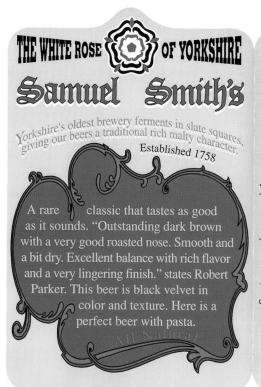

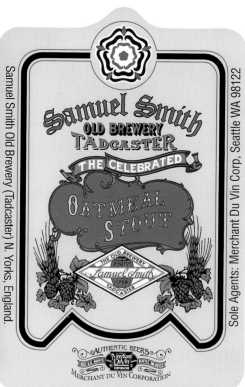

Samuel Smith ferments in traditional Yorkshire 'squares' and has used them to fashion a range of porters and stouts that have been acclaimed in both Britain and the United States. Oatmeal gives a delicious creamy note to stout.

Trent, RCH in Weston-super-Mare in Somerset, and Freeminer in Gloucestershire. All have won prizes at Camra beer festivals. Titanic is in the Stoke suburb of Burslem, home of John Smith, the hapless captain of the ill-fated *Titanic*: beers in the range include Lifeboat Ale, Wreckage and Captain Smith's Strong Ale. The 4.5 per cent Stout is brewed from Maris Otter pale malt, flaked wheat and a generous dose of roasted barley which gives the beer a dry Irish character. Hops are Goldings and two American varieties, Willamette and Yakima. The aroma has roasted grain, dark fruit and peppery hops, there is a fine balance of creamy malt and hops in the mouth, followed by a dry finish with chocolate and coffee notes. The beer has an intriguing bitter-sweet appeal due to the careful balance of grains and hops, with a delicious creaminess from the flaked wheat.

RCH, which has expanded from a brew-pub in a hotel in Burnham-on-Sea, gives its porter the most unappealing name: Old Slug

(4.5 per cent). Black malt blended with pale and crystal develop a sour, lactic note. Hops are Fuggles and Goldings. The beer has a woody, grainy and dark fruit aroma, with coffee and bitter fruit in the mouth. The finish is tart and bitter with more sour fruit. It is dark brown in colour which, allied to the lactic note, makes it one of the most fascinating interpretations of the early versions of the style. It is available in cask and bottle, as is the beer from Freeminer. The brewery is in the Forest of Dean where open-cast mines are still worked. Deep Shaft Stout is a powerful 6.2 per cent alcohol brewed from Maris Otter pale malt, malted oats and roast barley. Hops are Fuggles and Goldings and the beer is dry hopped in cask. Bitterness units are 45 to 50. It is an uncompromising beer with a black coffee and hops aroma, biscuits and charcoal in the mouth, and a big bitter, hoppy finish with dark malt and fruit.

Nutritional stouts were once vogue beers throughout the British Isles. Not only oats

but also oysters and milk sugar were added to stout to offer alternatives to the bitter, dry and roasty style from Ireland. The most famous survivor of the milk stout style is Mackeson. It is made with the addition of lactose, a by-product of cheese making, and is made up of 95 per cent milk sugars. It cannot be fermented by conventional brewer's yeast and leaves carbohydrates and calories in the beer.

Mackeson was founded in 1669 during the reign of Charles II. In the nineteenth century it brewed an India Pale Ale and several other beers but it made its fortune with its milk stout. It was bought by Whitbread which turned it into a national brand. By the 1960s sales were so enormous that they accounted for more than half of Whitbread's total output. By this time 'milk' had been withdrawn from the label as a result of a post-war government ruling that claims that beer contained milk were misleading. The stout is brewed from pale and chocolate malts, caramel and around 9 per cent lactose. The lactose is added in the form of powder to the copper during the boil with hops. The lack of fermentability of the milk sugar is stressed by the fact that while the stout has a starting gravity of 1042°, the finished alcohol rating is just 3 per cent. The starting gravity measures the sugars present in the wort prior to fermentation and 1042° would normally ferment out to around 4 per cent alcohol. Target hops produce 26 units of bitterness. The dark, almost jet-black beer has a coffeeish aroma and palate reminiscent of post-war coffee essence. There is a light fruitiness on the palate and a distinct hint of that old children's confectionery known as milk drops.

Oats have long been used in stout in Scotland, dating from the time when beer, bread and porridge were made in the home. The Broughton Brewery in the Borders makes Scottish Oatmeal Stout (3.8 per cent), brewed with pale malt, oatmeal and roasted barley with Fuggles and Goldings hops. It has 130 units of colour and 28 of bitterness. There is creamy sweetness from the oatmeal in the mouth with roasted coffee beans, followed by a dry, creamy and lightly fruity finish. In the once great brewing town of Alloa, Maclays produces a 4.5 per cent Oat Malt Stout. The stout is arguably the classic version of the Scottish style, based on an 1895 recipe. The oats are malted, not used as raw grain, and account for 22 per cent of the grist, which also includes Maris Otter pale malt, roast barley and chocolate malt. The only hop used is the Fuggle. The colour rating is 50 units, bitterness 35. The stout has an enticing aroma of rich hops and roast grain, and there is a subtle malty sweetness in the mouth and a bitter-sweet finish with a hint of dark chocolate.

Even chocoholics would be hard pressed to claim that chocolate is nutritious but it makes an intriguing addition to stout. When the South London brewers Youngs launched a Double Chocolate Stout in March 1997 it found it had a runaway success on its hands. It is 5 per cent alcohol and is a typical Young's beer, made from Maris Otter malt, Fuggles and Goldings hops and the tart fruit character of the house yeast. The additions are chocolate malt, roasted until it resembles coffee beans and liquid chocolate, which is added during the copper boil. The beer has a pronounced aroma of dark chocolate and is rich, smooth and slightly creamy in the mouth. There is a good underpinning of bitter Fuggles and peppery Goldings on the finish.

Oyster Stout is yet another nutritious version of the style. In Victorian times stout and oysters were part of the staple diet of Londoners. Oysters grew in abundance in the estuary of the River Thames and were cheap to buy until over-dredging and pollution killed them off. Stout has always been a robust companion for fish: the acidity of the beer points up the delicate flavours of fish and blends well with the saltiness and fleshiness of oysters and other shell fish. In Ireland fish restaurants still serve stout and oysters, and both Guinness and Murphy stage annual oyster festivals. Many British brewers produced oyster stouts as the perfect accompaniment for shell fish. Some went a step further and added oysters to the beer. The style lingered on into the 1960s and then disappeared. It was revived in 1995 by Marstons' of Burton-on-Trent

Mackeson was once the biggest brand brewed by Whitbread. 'Milk stout', made with the addition of lactose, is a term that can no longer be used in case drinkers think it contains real milk.

with a 4.5 per cent Oyster Stout, now available regularly in bottle, a beer with a sulphury, hoppy and bitter chocolate aroma, a complex palate of dark fruit, roasted grain and hops, and a big hoppy-fruity finish. All it lacks are oysters.

For a taste of the real thing you will have to go to Dublin and drink the 4.8 per cent Oyster Stout brewed in the Porter House Brewing Company in Parliament Street. It is a brew-pub with a ten-barrel plant. The three-storey building has bars and a restaurant. It is elegantly decked out with marble floors, a mass of stripped pine and a vast collection of beer bottles in cabinets on each floor. The brewing equipment can be viewed through windows, with malt mill, liquor tank and mash tun at the top, copper in the middle and fermenters on the ground floor. The Porter House was opened in 1996 by two cousins, Liam LaHart and Oliver Hughes. Porter House Oyster Stout is brewed from pale malt, roast barley, black malt and flaked barley. Hops are Galena, Nugget and East Kent Goldings. The flesh from Dublin Bay oysters are added during the copper boil. The stout has a powerful fishy aroma, a bitter quinine and iodine flavour and a dark malt, hops and fishy finish. It is the perfect companion for the fish and sea food dishes in the restaurant, which include generous helpings of mussels.

The pub's porter (4.3 per cent) is called Plain, the old Dublin name for the style, immortalized in the poem 'A Pint of Plain is Your Only Man' by Flann O'Brien in 1939. It is brewed from pale malt, flaked barley, roast barley, and black and crystal malts. The hops are the same as for Oyster Stout. There is a late addition of hops at the end of the copper boil for extra aroma. There are bitter hops and roasted grain on the aroma and palate, with a long espresso coffee finish and tart fruit and hops. The most

First brewed in 1997, Young's stout with real chocolate became an instant success.

impressive beer is Wrasslers 4X Stout (5 per cent) with a grist made up of pale, crystal and roast malts, wheat malt, flaked barley and roast barley. Hops are again Galena, Nugget and Goldings. It is based on an early 1900s recipe from the defunct Deasy's of West Cork, which was the favourite beer of Michael Collins, founder of the Irish Free State. Wrasslers 4X has a big coffee and chocolate aroma and palate, and a hoppy-fruity finish with a powerful hint of burnt currants.

A short walk from the Porter House Brewing Company brings you to the gates and the vast bulk of Guinness, one of the world's greatest and certainly best-known breweries, whose name is synonymous with the very word stout. More than nineteen versions of Guinness are brewed throughout the world and ten million pints are drunk every day. Among the brands, the most fascinating one and a peerless example of the style is Guinness Foreign Extra Stout. Not only is it sold in 55 countries and brewed under licence in 44 but it is also a palpable link with the earliest days of entire butt, porter and stout. In the traditions of the early brewers of porter, it is a blend of young and aged beers. The aged stout is truly 'stale'. It is stored for two to three months in the cellars of the Dublin brewery during which time it picks up lactic flavours from the action of wild Brettanomyces yeasts. It is blended with young stout and the bottles are then stored for a further month before going on sale.

FES, as the beer is known for short, is made from pale malt, 25 per cent flaked barley and 10 per cent roasted barley. Flaked barley aids head-retention on the finished beer and adds a pleasing grainy flavour. Roasted barley is cured in a kiln to a high temperature and looks and tastes like coffee beans. It is used for colour and for a bitter fruit and coffee aroma and flavour. The hops are a blend of varieties, including Galena, Nugget and Target. The finished beer is 7.5 per cent alcohol with bitterness units in the 60s. The complex stout has a toasty, roasty, winey and woody aroma, a full bitter-sweet palate with great hop character, and a finish that becomes dry and hoppy with hints of bitter chocolate, coffee, licorice and sour fruit, including unripened bananas. And on the nose there is a musty aroma that brewers call 'horse blanket', the result of the action of wild yeasts.

Variations on the theme of FES originate in Dublin. It is a massive brand in Africa,

where Guinness owns several breweries (three in Nigeria alone) and also licenses other companies to make the beer for them. It is also made under licence in the Caribbean. The strength of the beer is a uniform 8 per cent. The African breweries make a standard beer from pale malt and then blend it with an unfermented hopped wort that has been boiled and evaporated. An even stronger version is made for the Belgian market. It has a dark fruit aroma with great hop attack, burnt raisins in the mouth and a long bitter-sweet finish packed with dark fruit and hops.

Scandinavia has a rich heritage of porters and stouts, unsurprising given the popularity of the style in the last century in the neighbouring Baltic States and Russia. One of the world's classic dark beers is brewed by Pripps, the major brewing group in Sweden. Carnegie Porter takes its name from a young Scottish brewer named David Carnegie who emigrated to Sweden in 1836 and opened a brewery in Gothenburg. Pripps, now based on the outskirts of Stockholm, also originated in Gothenburg and eventually bought Carnegie's company. When the brewery closed in the early 1990s,

production was moved to Stockholm and a beer that had been so invisible for years that it was available for a time only on doctor's prescription began to get some welcome promotion. At first it was sold only in a 3.5 per cent version, a strength that does not begin to do it justice (this strength is still used when it is sold on draught in pubs). Then in 1985 Pripps brought back the original 5.6 per cent version. This is a superb beer with a dark malt aroma reminiscent of rich cake, a cappuccino coffee palate and a finish that becomes dry with more dark malt, hops and a hint of port wine or Madeira. Pripps has added a vintage version of the porter. It is matured for six months in the brewery and is then bottle-matured for a further six months. Although it is filtered and pasteurized before release, the brewers believe it will improve in bottle, developing a port wine note.

Another porter also now available in an annual vintage version comes from the Sinebrychoff Brewery in Helsinki, Finland. Koff Porter, at 7.2 per cent, belongs in the

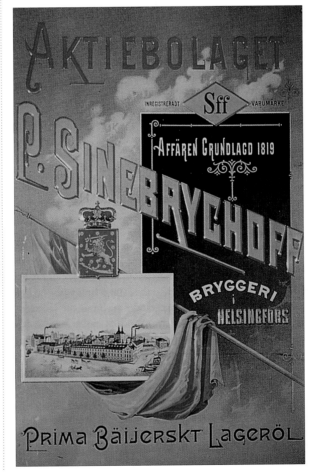

Above left: A Scot named David Carnegie took the art of porter brewing to Sweden in the mid-nineteenth century. It is still brewed and appears as an annual vintage.

Left: Sinebrychoff of Helsinki added a porter to its range in 1952, using the yeast saved and cultured from a bottle of Guinness. It is the strongest beer brewed in Finland and belongs to the imperial stout class.

Left: *Carlsberg of Copenhagen is best known for its pale lager but it brews an 'imperial stout porter', albeit by cold fermentation.*
Right: *High in the mountains of Sri Lanka, bottle-conditioned Lion Stout comes from a brewery founded by a British tea planter.*

strongest beer made in Finland. It is brewed from four malts and German Northern Brewer and Hersbrucker hops. The colour rating is 250–300, bitterness units 50. It is conditioned at warm temperature for six weeks, bottled without filtration but then pasteurized. It has a big, slightly oily body, a deep roasty, vinous and bitter aroma, and a long finish packed with dark fruit, roasted grain and bitter hops. The annual vintage brew comes in an attractive club-shaped bottle.

In Denmark, Carlsberg brews another member of the imperial stout family. If this is surprising, given the company's pre-eminence in the world of lager brewing, the founder, J.C. Jacobsen, started as an ale brewer; moreover, he would have seen the popularity of imported British porters and stouts, and was also a great admirer of British brewing skills. The label of the beer calls it both an Imperial Stout and a Porter for good measure. It also includes the enigmatic letters 'Gl', short for Gammel or 'old', a reference to the original Old Brewery. The Imperial Stout Porter is a hefty 7.8 per cent and is made from pale and roasted malts with German Hallertauer hops. It has rich dark fruit, bitter coffee and scorched vanilla notes. It is fermented with the house lager yeast and purists could argue that is not a true stout. It is nevertheless a wonderfully full-bodied, robust and complex beer.

Beer has such a short history in Japan (the first breweries were set up with American help in the 1860s) that it is surprising to find samples of stout in the

imperial stout class and owes its curious name to the Finns well-nurtured dislike of the 'Big Bear' next door. The brewery was founded in 1819 by a Russian called Nikolai Sinebrychoff but the locals call it 'Koff' to disguise the Russian name. The brewery started with warm fermented ales but as early as 1853 had switched to brown Munich-style lagers. A century later, when the Olympics were staged in Helsinki in 1952, the brewery decided to bring back one of its earliest brews, Koff Porter. It had no ale yeast available and the brewers claim they solved the problem by saving the yeasty deposit from a bottle of Guinness export stout and making a culture that is still going strong today. Koff Porter is the

country. But the new Japanese brewers brewed it with enthusiasm as they flexed their muscles and attempted to make all known varieties of beer. The most remarkable example of Japanese stout comes from Asahi. The 8 per cent beer is not only a true warm fermented stout but uses a wild Brettanomyces yeast culture during fermentation to give it a sour and lactic note. It has a big, powerful palate laced with dark fruit and hops, a dry and pungent aroma, and a long, soft, vinous finish with hints of rich, dark cake. Kirin Stout, also 8 per cent, is cold fermented, bitter-sweet and with dark toffee notes. Sapporo's Yebisu Stout is named after a Shinto god and is soft, mellow and easy-drinking.

The island of Sri Lanka, the former British colony of Ceylon, produces some characterful stouts. McCallum's Three Coins Brewery in the suburbs of Colombo makes a 6 per cent Sando Stout named after the famous Hungarian circus strongman Eugene Sando, whose image was also used on the labels of Murphy's Stout in Ireland. The Colombo beer is now cold fermented and is made from pale, crystal and chocolate malts from England and Germany, with Czech hops. It is rich, fruity and hoppy. A more characterful interpretation of the style comes from the Ceylon Brewery high in the mountains at Nuwara Eliya in the tea-planting region, close to the holy city of Kandy. Lion Stout (6.2 per cent) is a true warm-fermented beer from a brewery founded by tea planters to refresh themselves during their labours. Brewing liquor comes from the nearby Lovers Leap waterfall while Czech, Danish and English malts, Styrian hops and an English ale yeast are transported up precarious roads 3,500 feet above sea level. Lion Stout is served in cask-conditioned form, drawn by handpump, the Beer Shop in Nuwara Eliya and in UKD Silva's pub in Kandy. A bottle-conditioned version (7.5 per cent) is exported and has rich chocolate, bitter coffee and hops on the aroma and palate.

In Australia a stout tradition is not altogether lost under the ice floes of sweet, ice-cold lager. Cooper & Sons of Adelaide produces a bottle-conditioned Stout (6.8 per cent) with a pronounced chocolate and coffee character. It is slightly oily on the tongue from the use of roasted malt that is blended with pale and crystal. Cooper's dedication to tradition is well known but it comes as a shock to find Australia's Big Two brewers also producing stout. Both Foster's and Castlemaine honour the tradition. Foster's of New South Wales makes a true, warm-fermented Sheaf Stout brewed from pale and crystal malts and roasted barley. It is 5.7 per cent alcohol with 200 colour units and 35 bitterness units. It is almost jet black in colour, has an aroma of roasted malt and hops, an oily, perfumy palate, and a long, bitter and slightly winey finish.

Foster's great rival, Castlemaine Perkins of Brisbane, Queensland, famous for XXXX lager, produces Carbine Stout. The brand was registered in 1925 by the then independent Perkins Brewery. It is named after a famous racehorse from the late nineteenth century whose blood line can be traced to 70 per cent of Australian thoroughbreds racing today. Carbine won the Melbourne Cup in 1890 and went on to win a further 32 other races. Carbine Stout (5.1 per cent) was

first brewed from pale, amber, crystal and black malts with cane sugar and was fermented with an ale yeast. In the 1950s it was reformulated with a simplified grist and a lager yeast. More recently Castlemaine Perkins has revitalized the brand with more traditional ingredients such as roast barley and malted wheat. It has a big roasted grain aroma and palate and a dry finish.

The craft brewing frenzy in the United States has seen dozens of porters and stouts appear and flourish. Two of the pivotal figures in the American brewing revolution, Fritz Maytag at Anchor Brewing in San Francisco, and Bert Grant at Yakima Brewing, have both fashioned fine interpretations of the style. Anchor Porter (5.7 per cent volume/4.6 per cent weight) is brewed from pale, dark and roasted malts. It has a cappuccino coffee aroma and palate and a big hop character from the use of American Cascades. In Washington State, Grant's Perfect Porter (4.8 per cent volume/3.4 per cent weight) is brewed from five different malts, including Scottish peated malt, which gives it an appealing smoky flavour. It is dry hopped in cask, has 30 bitterness units and is aged in oak casks in the proper porter fashion. The result is a beer with an intense bitter chocolate aroma and palate, and a dry, tart and fruity finish with a good underpinning of hops. Grant's Imperial Stout belongs to the Victorian London tradition. It is 7 per cent volume/ 5.4 per weight and reaches a mouth-puckering 100 units of bitterness. As well as dark and roasted malts, the brewery uses a touch of honey, an old American traditions to encourage a good fermentation. This big-bodied beer has aromas and flavours redolent of licorice, fresh leather and coffee,

Cooper's of Adelaide makes a bottle-conditioned stout packed with coffee and chocolate flavour.

Named after a legendary racehorse, Carbine Stout was first brewed in the 1920s and has recently been restored to something of its original glory with the use of roast barley.

200,000 barrels-a-year operation with a restaurant, bar and beer garden on site. A seasonal Yuletide Porter (5.6 per cent volume/4.5 per cent weight) uses pale, caramel (crystal) and black malts with flaked barley and is hopped with Cascade and Cluster varieties. It has a roasty, creamy aroma and palate with a dry, malty, fruity and spicy finish. Black Hawk Stout is a regular brew made from the same grist as the porter but one degree stronger.

In neighbouring Fort Bragg, North Coast Brewing makes an Old No. 38 Stout (5.5 per cent volume/4.4 per cent weight), named after a retired steam locomotive on the local railroad and advertised as 'water, malt, hops, yeast and that's all'. Roasted barley is blended with pale and crystal malts to produce a 'Dublin Dry Stout' packed with roasted grain and bitter chocolate character. It has won silver and bronze medals in both the World Beer Championships and at the Great American Beer Festival. Old Rasputin Russian Stout (9.6 per cent volume/7.7 per cent weight) is a fully paid-up member of the imperial family, bursting with intense aromas and flavours of dark grain, bitter

with hints of apple fruit. Rogue Ales of Newport, Oregon, won gold medals for its Shakespeare Stout and Mocha Porter in the World Beer Championships staged in Chicago in 1996. The Porter (5.3 per cent volume/4.25 per cent weight) has 54 units

Pete Slosberg's porter recalls the earliest days of American brewing when maple syrup encouraged a good fermentation.

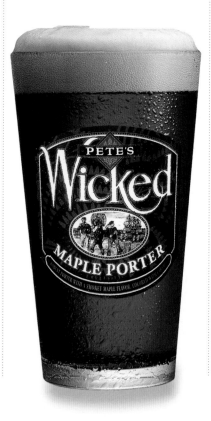

of bitterness, is unfiltered and brewed from pale, English chocolate malt from Beeston in Nottingham, black, Munich, carastan and crystal malts, Centennial and Perle hop varieties and an ale yeast. It is dark ruddy brown in colour and has a powerful sour fruit and bitter hops aroma. There is tart fruit in the mouth and hops, followed by a long and quenching finish packed with dark winey fruit and a late burst of hops. If a beer called stout existed in William Shakespeare's time, it would have meant a strong beer not a black one. The beer named in honour of the Bard is brewed with pale, crystal and chocolate malts with rolled oats and roasted barley. It is 6.1 per cent volume/4.9 per cent weight and throws a dense orange-brown foam, has a smooth chocolate aroma with a creamy note from the oats, burnt currants and bitter hops in the mouth and a long finish dominated by hops, dark fruit, roasted grain and silky oats.

The Mendocino Brewing Company in Hopland, California, is 90 miles north of San Francisco in vine- rather than hop-growing country: hops were grown there until they were forced out by vine growers. Mendocino is a sizeable

Anchor Porter from San Francisco has an appealing Cascade hop aroma and a cappuccino coffee palate.

fruit, coffee and chocolate. Pete's Brewing of Palo Alto, California, has a contract-brewed Maple Porter from Stroh of St Paul, Minnesota. The 5.4 per cent volume/4.3 per cent weight beer uses maple syrup along with dark roasted malts. It has a dark toffee aroma, a rich bitter-sweet palate balanced by piny hops, and creamy, fruity finish.

On the East Coast, brewmaster Garrett Oliver at the Brooklyn Brewery in New York City makes a top-fermenting Black Chocolate Stout for the Christmas and New Year period. The first batch was such a sensation when it crossed the Brooklyn Bridge to Manhattan that each vintage is now eagerly awaited every festive season. It is 8 per cent volume/6.8 per cent weight and has a smooth, creamy, mouth-filling chocolate character from dark malt and a big hoppy finish.

The Midwest was once a major force in American brewing. At the turn of the century, Cleveland, Ohio, had close to thirty breweries. The number had declined to just one by 1984, and even that company closed. In 1988 two brothers, Patrick and Daniel Conway, launched the Great Lakes Brewing Co. in a three-storey building dating from 1860. The company has expanded, adding a restaurant and beer garden. Edmund Fitzgerald Porter (5.4 per cent volume/4.7 per cent weight) is not pasteurized, to give maximum freshness of taste. It is brewed from two-row pale, crystal and chocolate malts and roasted barley, and is hopped with Cascade, Northern Brewer and Willamette (60 bitterness units). It is smooth drinking, with good floral hops on the nose, dark grain and chocolate in the mouth and a quenching,

It's a long way from London but Alaskan Smoked Porter may be the closest to the original style.

gently fruity finish. The name comes from a freighter that sank with all hands in the Great Lakes in 1975. The brewery also makes occasional Oatmeal and Imperial Stouts.

The Alaskan Brewing Co. of Juneau has won many awards for its Smoked Porter (5.5 per cent volume/4.4 per cent weight). It is made from two-row Klages pale malt, black,

Great Lakes porter has three hop varieties and chocolate malt and roast barley in its makeup. It is named after a freighter that sank with all hands in 1975.

chocolate and two varieties of crystal, with Chinook and Willamette hops. A smoke-house is just across the road from the brewery and the dark malts are taken there,

spread on racks and smoked over alder wood for three days. The finished beer, brewed once a year in winter and then vintage dated, has an intense smoky aroma and palate overlain by spicy hops and dark malt and chocolate. The smoked rich darks malts, allied to an intense bitterness, mean that a beer brewed close to the Arctic Circle is the closest we may yet come to the original porters of eighteenth-century London.

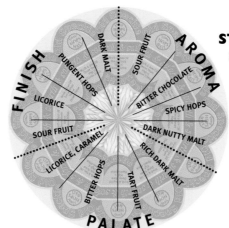

STOUT AND PORTER STYLE

Roasty, tart, tangy, hoppy and bitterly fruity, with chocolate and coffee notes, porters and stouts are complex but also wonderfully refreshing.

PORTER AND STOUT BREWERS

Alaskan Brewing Co.
5429 Shaune Drive, Juneau, Alaska 99801

Anchor Brewing Co.
1705 Mariposa Street, San Francisco, California 94107

Asahi Breweries
23-1 Azumabashi 1-chome, Sumida-ku, Tokyo 130

Brooklyn Brewery
118 N 11th Street, Brooklyn, New York 11211

Broughton Ales Ltd
The Brewery, Broughton, Biggar, Borders ML12 6HQ

Carlsberg Brewery
100 Vesterfaelldvej DK 1799, Copenhagen, Denmark

Castlemaine Perkins
11 Finchley Street, Milton QLD 4064

Ceylon Brewery
Nuwara Eliya, Kandy, Sri Lanka

Cooper's Brewery Ltd
9 Statenborough Street, Leabrook, Adelaide SA 5068

Foster's/Carlton & United Breweries Ltd
1 Bouverie Street, Carlton VIC 3053

Freeminer Brewery Ltd
The Laurels, Sling, Coleford, Forest of Dean, Glos GL16 7LZ

Grant's Yakima Brewing Co.
1803 Presson Place, Yakima, Washington 98903

Great Lakes Brewing Co.
2516 Market Street, Cleveland, Ohio 44113

Arthur Guinness & Son
St James's Gate, Dublin 8

Kirin Brewery Co.
26-1, Jingumae 6-chome, Shibuya-ku, Tokyo 150

Mackeson, Whitbread Beer Company
Porter Tun House,
Capability Green, Luton, Beds LU1 3LS

McCallum's Brewery
299 Union Place, Colombo, Sri Lanka

Maclay & Co. Ltd
Thistle Brewery, Alloa,
Clackmannanshire FK10 1ED

Marston, Thompson & Evershed Plc
Shobnall Road, Burton-on-Trent,
Staffs DE14 2BW

Mendocino Brewing Co.
13351 Highway 101 S. Hopland,
California 95449

North Coast Brewing Co.
455 N Main Street, Fort Bragg,
California 95437

Pete's Brewing
514 High Street, Palo Alto,
California 94301

Porter House Brewing Co.
6-18 Parliament Street, Dublin 7

A. B. Pripps
Bryggerier, Bryggerivagen 10, 16186,
Stockholm, Bromma, Sweden

RCH Brewery
West Hewish, Weston-super-Mare,
Somerset BS24 6RR

Rogue Ales
2320 OSU Drive, Newport,
Oregon 97365

Sapporo Breweries
7-10-1 Ginza, Chuo-ku,
Tokyo 104

John Smith's Magnet Brewery
High Street, Tadcaster,
North Yorkshire LS24 9SA

Samuel Smith Old Brewery
High Street, Tadcaster,
North Yorkshire LS24 9SB

Oy Sinebrychoff AB
Alikergvantie 40, 04250, Kerava, Finland

Titanic Brewery
Unit G, Harvey Works,
Lingard Street, Burslem,
Stoke-on-Trent,
Staffordshire ST6 1ED

Young & Co. Plc
Ram Brewery, High Street,
Wandsworth,
London SW18 4JD

SCOTCH ALE

Scotland has a cold climate but the hardy barley plant grows in some abundance, providing the raw material for both beer and the 'water of life', whisky. Brewing was for centuries a domestic affair in town and country, and barley was augmented with other produce from the fields, such as oats (also used to make the hearty dish of porridge), wheat and heather. Hops did not flourish in such a sun-starved country. They were expensive to import from England and were not taken taken up by brewers until much later than those south of the border.

It was the absence of hops that led to a breakthrough in Scottish brewing and the appearance of a powerful commercial industry. When French aristocrats settled in Edinburgh during the early nineteenth century to escape the revolution, they took to drinking the strongest and well-matured version of local ale, which they called 'Scottish Burgundy'. When supplies of real Burgundy and claret were cut off during the Napoleonic Wars, a commercial brewing industry developed, first to supply the local market with palatable, well-brewed beers and then later to provide the large number of Scots who had emigrated to North America, the Caribbean and Australasia with beer from home.

Scottish ale is rich, warming and heavy, a kind of liquid version of porridge. Black and chocolate malts as well as roasted barley are blended with pale malt. Ales are brewed in a different manner from their English counterparts. The copper boil is brief: when few hops are used it is important not to distil off the plant's delicate aromas and flavours. Fermentation is at a much lower temperature of 10°C/50°F, compared with 20°C/68°F in

Edinburgh's Caledonian Brewery is a pace-setter in the revival of brewing traditional styles.

Caledonian makes a rare example of organic beer called Golden Promise.

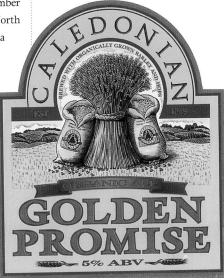

England. As a result, the yeast works slowly; it does not create a vast head nor does it need to be skimmed and eventually settles at the bottom of the vessel. This method of brewing is empirical and predates refrigeration: in earlier times, brewing took place only in the winter months when the biting cold would have forced yeast to work slowly and sluggishly. The similarities to early lager brewing are obvious, but nevertheless Scottish beers are members of the ale family. Unlike lager beers, they are not fully attenuated or brewed out, leaving malt sugars for body, roundness and depth. In the nineteenth and early twentieth centuries, so much Scottish beer was exported that the term 'Export' became a style in its own right, a strong, amber-red, malty and lightly hopped beer: McEwan's Export is still a major brand for the Scottish & Newcastle group. The Scottish brewing industry was confined to the Lowlands where the finest malting barley grew; barley further north tends to be of poorer quality but is suitable for whisky distilling. Mergers, takeovers and closures threatened to snuff out the tradition of Scottish ale until the new generation of small craft brewers sparked a revival in the 1980s and 1990s.

The Caledonian Brewery in Edinburgh has already been mentioned for its Deuchar's IPA. It also brews a full range of Scottish ales ranging from a dark, malty 60 Shilling (3.2 per cent), brewed from Pipkin pale, crystal, amber, black and wheat malts, and Fuggles and Goldings whole hops (45 units of colour, 31 units of bitterness), a biscuity and hoppy 70 Shilling (3.5 per cent; 41 colour units, 29 bitterness) and a fruity, malty 80 Shilling with a hint of chocolate from chocolate malt (4.1 per cent; 26 colour units, 35 bitterness).

Many people consider that the 80 Shilling ale brewed by the Belhaven Brewery in the picturesque seaside town of

Full steam ahead. . .Caledonian recalls the great days of steam with a beer dedicated to Britain's most famous train.

Dunbar near the English border to be the classic of the style. Brewing in Dunbar can be traced back to the fourteenth century, when monks made ale there. It is a handsome site, based around old maltings buildings mellowed by smoke, with some fascinating brewing artefacts in a small museum. Belhaven 80 Shilling is 4.1 per cent

alcohol, with 33 units of colour and 29 bitterness units. It is brewed from Pipkin pale, black and crystal malts with some brewing sugar. The hops are Whitbread Goldings Variety for bitterness and Fuggles and Goldings for aroma in pellet form. It is a complex beer with aromas of rich malt, hops, toasted grain and gooseberry fruit, juicy malt and tart hops in the mouth, and a long, dry malty finish with more hints of gooseberry. Among the Belhaven portfolio is a 90 Shilling winter ale (7.2 per cent), which in bottled form is known as Fowler's Wee Heavy. A wee (small) heavy indicates a strong ale sold in a nip bottle containing a third of a pint. Belhaven's St Andrew's Ale (4.5 per cent) has a lot of peppery hop character for a Scottish ale and is dry hopped in cask (36 units of bitterness).

Broughton is another Borders brewery based in a small town of the same name that was the birthplace of John Buchan, author of such gung-ho novels as *The Thirty-Nine Steps* and *Greenmantle*, the latter giving its name to the brewery's flagship beer, Greenmantle Ale (3.9 per cent). A touch of roasted barley is blended with pale malt, and the hops are Fuggles and Goldings (34 colour units, 24 bitterness). It is a remarkably fruity beer with a pronounced orange and lemon aroma, fruit and malt in the mouth, and a long, lingering, bitter-sweet finish with more tart fruit. Broughton also brews a traditional 80 Shilling (4.2 per cent) and a powerful Old Jock (6.7 per cent) with spicy and vinous aromas, malt, fruit and butterscotch in the mouth and a big bitter-sweet finish.

The most fascinating brewery in Scotland is Traquair House near Peebles. It is the oldest inhabited stately home in the country, the 'quair' in the name being an ancient Scots word for a burn or stream that runs into the River Tweed, the border

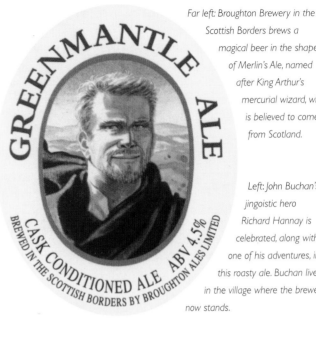

Far left: Broughton Brewery in the Scottish Borders brews a magical beer in the shape of Merlin's Ale, named after King Arthur's mercurial wizard, who is believed to come from Scotland.

Left: John Buchan's jingoistic hero Richard Hannay is celebrated, along with one of his adventures, in this roasty ale. Buchan lived in the village where the brewery now stands.

between Scotland and England. Mary Queen of Scots stayed at Traquair and Prince Charles Edward Stuart (Bonnie Prince Charlie) visited the house to raise support for his Jacobite rebellion. Traquair House is owned by the Maxwell Stuarts, members of the Catholic Stuart clan. They keep the main Bear Gates to the house locked until a Stuart regains the throne of the United Kingdom. Parts of the imposing, white-faced and turreted house date from the twelfth century. It was rebuilt in the seventeenth century, and a brewing copper was added to the brewhouse in 1738. At some time the brewery went into disuse and its outbuildings were cluttered with jumble. When the twentieth laird (lord) of Traquair, Peter Maxwell Stuart, acquired the title in 1965, he discovered the brewery and was fired with determination to make beer there again. The house is open to visitors and he felt a working medieval brewery would be an added attraction.

With the help of Sandy Hunter, a renowned brewer at Belhaven in Dunbar, he restored the vessels and started to produce small batches of Traquair House Ale. At 7.2 per cent, it is typical of the strong ales once

At 6.7 per cent alcohol, Old Jock packs a punch. It is a fine interpretation of the style known as 80 shilling.

THE SHILLING

The term shilling in Scottish beer names comes from the old, pre-decimalization unit of currency used in Britain. In the nineteenth century, Scottish brewers invoiced their beer in shillings, the stronger the beer, the higher the rate of shillings. A 60 Shilling is the lowest strength beer available, roughly equivalent to an English mild. A 70 Shilling is similar to a pale ale or bitter, 80 Shilling approximates to a best or premium bitter while 90 Shilling is a strong ale or a 'wee heavy' in bottle. To add to the confusion, the Scots also call 60 Shilling 'light' (even though it may be dark in colour), the 70 Shilling 'heavy' and the 80 Shilling 'Export'.

Above: Traquair House is the oldest inhabited stately home in Scotland. Its main gates stay locked until a member of the Stuart clan returns to the British throne.

Left: The restored brewhouse at Traquair House. The original house brewery was built in 1738 and lay disused for many years until the Laird reopened it and brewed the powerful Traquair House Ale.

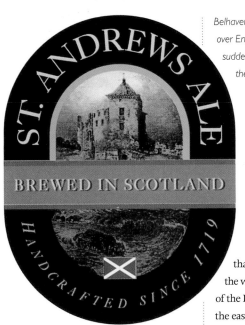

Belhaven's St Andrews' Ale recalls a victory over English forces when the flag of St Andrew suddenly appeared in the sky above the battlefield.

to mark the marriage of Lady Catherine, and a spiced Jacobite Ale in 1995 to commemorate Bonnie Prince Charlie's ill-fated march on London.

In the United States, Bert Grant at the Yakima Brewing Company says without a shred of self-doubt that his Scottish Ale is 'the best beer in the world'. Grant's brewery is in the heart of the Pacific North-west's hop country, on the eastern side of the Cascade Mountains. Grant has three passports: he was born in Scotland, grew up in Canada, where he worked as a chemist for Canadian Breweries, and migrated across the border to work for Stroh in Detroit before moving to Yakima to build a hop-processing plant. His home-

brewing efforts met with such enthusiasm that he decided to brew full time. He started in the old Yakima Opera House and eventually moved to a greenfield site on the edge of town. His Scottish Ale is 4.5 per cent weight/5.6 volume. He uses a generous amount of crystal malt alongside the pale, giving the beer a burnished amber colour and a nutty roastiness in the mouth. The hoppiness (45 units of bitterness) comes from Cascades in the brew kettle and Willamettes for dry hopping. The beer has a rich sultana fruitiness balanced by pungent hops on the aroma, and a dry and fruity finish. It has 45 units of bitterness. Grant sold his company in 1996 but remains a consultant, and the new owners are giving all his beers greater promotion throughout the US.

It's a long way from Caledonia but Scottish-born Bert Grant brews a fine interpretation of the style in his brewery in Yakima in the heart of the Washington hop fields.

brewed throughout Scotland and much admired by French emigrés. It is brewed from pale malt with just a touch of black malt. Its russet colour is the result of some caramelization of sugars during the boil in an open copper. The only hop used is East Kent Goldings. Fermentation used to be exclusively in oak vessels, but Lady Catherine Maxwell Stuart, who took over the house and brewery when her father died in 1990, has added some more modern vessels to cope with demand. As well as being on sale in the tea-room in the grounds and throughout Britain, the beer is also exported to Japan and the United States. It has a vast aroma of malt, hops, dark chocolate and spices, there are ripe fruit and bitter hops in the mouth, while the long finish is packed with pineapple fruit, chocolate, malt and peppery Goldings. Traquair House also brews a draught Bear Ale at 5 per cent, a fruity and hoppy Scots 'heavy' available in the Traquair Arms Hotel in the neighbouring village of Innerleithen, and occasional ales, such as a Wedding Ale

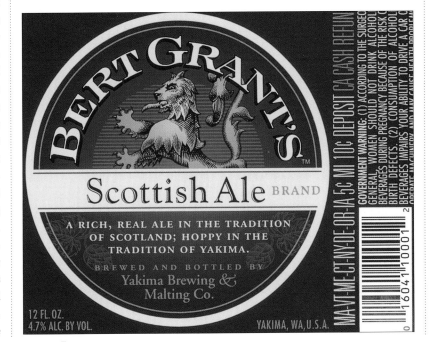

Born in Scotland, raised in Canada, now brewing in the US, Bert Grant has not forgotten his brewing and sartorial roots.

Nat Collins at the Woodstock Brewery in Kingston, New York State, brews one of the strongest Scottish-style ales in the world. His Braveheart Scotch Ale, inspired by the Mel Gibson movie, is 8.8 per cent weight/11 per cent volume. Collins says he is brewing a Scotch Ale in the nineteenth-century tradition. He uses two-row pale malt and carapils with some roasted barley. The hops are Cascade, Northern Brewer and Tettnanger. It has a deep brown colour, a big collar of foam, a massive assault of ripe fruit and malt on the nose, smooth malt in the mouth, and a big bitter-sweet, malty-fruity finish. Collins brews just one batch of the beer a year and would like to add some smoked malt if he can find a supplier.

SCOTCH ALE BREWERS

Belhaven Brewery Co. Ltd
Spott Road, Dunbar, Lothian EH42 1RS

Broughton Ales Ltd
The Brewery, Broughton, Biggar,
Borders ML12 6HQ

Caledonian Brewing Company Ltd
42 Slateford Road,
Edinburgh EH11 1PH

Grant's Yakima Brewing Co.
1803 Presson Place, Yakima,
Washington 98903

McEwan, Scottish & Newcastle Plc
11 Holyrood, Edinburgh,
Lothian EH8 8YS

Traquair House Brewery
Traquair Estate, Innerleithen,
Peeblesshire EH44 6PW

Woodstock Brewing Co.
20 St James Street, PO Box 5021,
Kingston, NY 12402

SCOTCH ALE STYLE

A roasted grain character with chocolate notes from dark malt and a gentle hop bitterness mark out the style of a beer brewed for a cold climate and likened to liquid alcoholic porridge.

WHEAT BEERS

Bavaria was the country to develop the lagering of beer on a commercial scale, using cold-fermenting yeast cultures. Yet the beer style that predates lager refused to go away. The use of wheat in brewing is an ancient custom. Lambic, the world's oldest surviving method of brewing, is a type of wheat beer. The roots of the style lie in rural communities where farmer-brewers used the cereals in the fields for food and drink. They knew that barley made the best beer while wheat made better bread. Wheat is a difficult grain to brew with. It lacks a husk and can gelatinize and clog up the brewing vessels. But wheat also gives deliciously spicy and fruity flavours to beer. As barley malt contains a husk, it acts as a natural filter in the mashing vessel and and so when used together, barley can counter the stickiness of wheat grains. The high level of natural enzymes in barley malt meant that unmalted wheat could be used, and its starches converted to sugar by the barley enzymes.

The arrival of lager brewing and the commercialization of all types of beer

A beer fit for a king…a statue of Ludwig of Bavaria welcomes visitors to the Schneider wheat beer brewery.

effectively sidelined wheat as a brewing grain. If barley was the best grain for brewing, why bother with a cereal that was a nuisance? Today, despite the resurgence of wheat beer in Belgium and Germany, the cereal accounts for only one per cent of the total grain used in brewing world-wide. In Belgium the style disappeared from view until one enterprising brewer revived it. Only in Bavaria did wheat beer hang on, even though it was dismissed as 'an old ladies' drink' until the 1980s.

Bavaria is famous not only for the first lager beers but also for the sixteenth-century 'pure beer law', the Reinheitsgebot, that now covers the whole of reunited Germany. The law was the work of the Bavarian royal family, the House of Wittelsbach. In 1516 the dukes Wilhelm IV and Ludwig X introduced the pure beer law or Reinheitsgebot at the assembly of the

The original Schneider brewery in Munich was granted a licence by the royal family to make commercial wheat beer.

The cool and elegant brewhouse at Schneider where half a million tonnes of barley and wheat are used annually.

Estates of the Realm in Ingolstadt. It laid down that only barley malt, yeast and water could be used to make beer. The decision was not entirely altruistic. The Bavarian royal family, in the best feudal traditions, held a monopoly over the growing of barley and did not want the monopoly undermined by the use of other cereals and sugars.

Hops were added to the law when they began to be widely used in brewing, but wheat was excluded for several centuries. The Wittelsbachs and their court drank wheat beer and they were determined that no one else should sample it. The hoi-polloi could put up with brown beers made from wood-cured malts but the king, queen, dukes and princes would enjoy the paler pleasures of wheat beer, just as they ate refined white bread while the masses made do with brown.

The aristocratic mystique surrounding

wheat beer was broken only in 1850 when the royal family licensed a Munich brewer named Georg Schneider to brew the style. He brewed first in the world-famous Hofbräuhaus (Royal Court Brewhouse) and later moved to the Tal, the Dale, just off the city's main square. In spite of the growth of lager brewing, Schneider was sufficiently successful to need a second brewery, which he bought in Kelheim in the heart of the Hallertau hop-growing region. The brewery in the Tal was destroyed by Allied bombs during World War II, though a large tavern stands there today selling Schneider's specialities.

The Kelheim brewery is a blend of Spanish and Gothic architecture. Built in 1607, it is the oldest continuously operating wheat beer plant in the world. It is run today by Georg Schneider V, his wife Margaret and their son, another Georg, who is being groomed for the succession. The

Schneider's main brand, Weisse, has a bronze colour from the use of Vienna and dark malts.

Dr Andreas Wideneder, brewmaster at the Hopf brewery in Upper Bavaria. Hopf is a specialist wheat beer company owned by Hans Hopf whose name is close to the German for hops – Hopfen.

company produces 300,000 hectolitres (6.6 million gallons) a year and ninety per cent of that is a 5.4 per cent Weisse. It also produces Aventinus, an 8 per cent doppel-bock, or double strong wheat beer. There is also a recent addition to the portfolio, a lighter Weizen Hell. 'Hell' in Bavaria means a light beer, while *Weisse* (white) and *Weizen* (wheat) are interchangeable terms in wheat beer labelling. Schneider uses half a million tonnes of local barley and wheat a year. Both grains are malted as raw grain and therefore cannot be used under the strictures of the Reinheitsgebot. They are blended in the proportion of 60 per cent wheat malt to 40 per cent barley. Some Vienna and dark malts are added to give the Weisse its attractive

Stubby closed fermenters at Hopf. The warm fermenting yeast culture creates a vast head that can be glimpsed through the visors at the top of the fermenters.

bronze-copper colour. Hersbrucker hops from the Hallertau are in pellet form with a little hop extract. Weisse has just 14 units of bitterness: hops are used primarily for their

preservative quality and too much bitter-ness would overpower the classic spicy, fruity character of a wheat beer. Hard water comes from a local well and is softened by removing some of the salts.

The modern brewhouse was installed in the late 1980s. It has stainless-steel mashing vessels standing on marble floors. A double decoction method is used, which means that portions of the mash are pumped from one vessel to another, heated to a higher temperature and then returned to the first vessel. Hops are added in two stages during the copper boil, and the hopped wort is then pumped to the fermentation hall with sixteen stainless-steel vats. The atmosphere is ripe with heady fruit aromas as the yeast goes to work on the malt sugars, with banana and apple dominating. The single-strain yeast culture has been used for as long as anyone in the brewery can remember and it is treated like holy water. Twice a day, the yeast is skimmed from the top of the fermenters, cleaned and pitched back into the fermenting wort. Fermentation lasts between three to five days at 20°C/68°F. The beer is not filtered and is bottled at a warm temperature. Yeast and some unfermented wort to give the right balance of yeast to sugar are added. The beer is matured for a

Spaten's Franziskaner wheat beers threaten to overtake its lagers in popularity. The wheat beers were originally brewed on a site next to a Franciscan monastery.

week at 20°C/68°F. This produces a lively carbonation as a secondary fermentation begins. The beer then has fourteen days of cold conditioning at 8°C/46°F to stabilize it.

Georg Schneider VI was at pains to stress that bottle conditioning uses the house

warm-fermenting yeast. He is critical of other Bavarian wheat beer brewers who have responded to the surge in demand by cutting corners. They use a lager yeast in the bottle which adds to stability and shelf life but flattens some of the rich fruity and spicy flavours. Some even filter and pasteurize the beer after primary fermentation before reseeding with lager yeast and adding some sediment to give an impression of natural cloudiness.

The unfiltered Schneider Weisse ('*mit Hefe*' on the label means 'with yeast'; '*kristall*' is filtered beer) has a pronounced banana, cloves and nutmeg aroma with a tart and slightly acidic flavour in the mouth and a creamy, fruity finish. The bubblegum characteristic that many drinkers find in wheat beer is due to the phenols and guaicols produced by a true wheat beer

An old storage cask with a halo of hops greet visitors to Prince Luitpold's Martha brewery in Fürstenfeldbruck.

yeast. These compounds are similar to those found in tropical tree sap used to make chewing gum, including Juicy Fruit. The magnificent Aventinus is bronze-red in colour thanks to the generous use of well-cured caramalt. It has a rich spices and chocolate aroma and palate, with more spices, fruit and cloves in the finish. It is the perfect nightcap. The brewery prefers its beers to be drunk within eight months, but says they will remain in drinkable condition for eight years if stored in a cool, dark place.

In Munich, the Spaten Brewery has seen its world turned upside down. It is famous throughout the world as the site where Gabriel Sedlmayr the Younger developed commercial lager brewing in the nineteenth century. But Spaten's lager beers are now under attack from its wheat beers. Its Franziskaner brands now account for more than half the company's production: the beers even outstrip wheat beer's 30 per cent share of the Bavarian market. The bottle labels show a cheerful monk contemplating a tankard of beer. The original wheat beer brewery, bought by the Sedlmayrs, was the oldest in Munich and once stood next to a Franciscan (Franziskaner) monastery.

The main Spaten wheat beer, Franziskaner Weissbier, 5 per cent alcohol, has an unusually high wheat malt content of 75 per cent to 25 per cent barley malt. The other brands, Hell (light), Dunkel (dark), a filtered Kristall and a strong Bock, are made conventionally from a 50/50 blend of malts. French and German malts are used with a complex and subtle blend of Hallertauer, Tettnanger, Spalt, Perle and Orion hops. Fermentation for the wheat beers is kept

Luitpold's wheat beer is produced in both pale and dark versions.

separate from the lagers to avoid cross-fertilization of the cultures. After primary fermentation, the beer is centrifuged to remove the yeast, then bottled and reseeded with a lager culture for the second fermentation. The beer has a diacetyl rest at 20°C/68°F before moving to a cool storage area.

In the mid-1980s, Crown Prince Luitpold of Kaltenberg, who brews cold-fermented lager beers in his castle brewery (see section on dark lager) bought a second brewery in the town of Fürstenfeldbruck, close to Munich, to make wheat beer. The plant is known as the Martha Brewery as it was founded by a woman of that name in 1573. It was bought by Sebastien Müller, who died without children, and the brewery passed into the safe keeping of the church until Luitpold acquired it. Behind a strictly functional and utilitarian frontage there is a fine brewing plant with gleaming copper mashing and boiling vessels that feed open stainless-steel tanks in blue-tiled surrounds for primary fermentation. The brewery produces both dark and pale wheat beers to feed an insatiable thirst for the style in Bavaria, which accounts for around 30 per cent of all beer sales.

Open fermenters at the Martha brewery: a fresh yeast culture is used for each brew.

'Few wheat beer brewers produce a proper bottle-conditioned beer,' the prince said. 'We produce a fresh yeast culture for each brew.' He laughed and added: 'The English use the same yeast for 200 years but we produce a fresh culture for each brew. If you use the same yeast from the normal run there will be some dead cells present. One hundred per cent fresh yeast gives greater stability and freshness to the bottle: remember, 40 per cent of the flavour of beer comes from the yeast.' A fruity warm-fermenting yeast is used for primary fermentation, a lager working culture for secondary. The bottles are warm conditioned for two weeks, longer in cold weather, to encourage a powerful secondary surge, and is then cold conditioned. Pale and Munich malts are used with Hersbrucker, Perle and Tettnanger hops, which produce 12–13 units of bitterness.

I drank the beers in the rustic tavern attached to the brewery. The Dunkel Weisse is packed with delicious chocolate flavours from the dark malt, with some earthy hop character and a hint of sourness. The light or Helles is a classic of the style, with a fruity, spicy and peppery aroma, with more fruit and spices in the mouth, followed by a long citric fruit finish. The tavern, which serves Bavarian dishes accompanied by Weisse beer, has a traditional Stammtisch, a large table reserved for locals: woe betide you if you occupy their hallowed places.

The imposing bulk of the Maisel brewery in Bayreuth where a strong Bock wheat beer augments a traditional unfiltered one.

The wheat beers of Berlin, unlike their Bavarian counterparts, are in serious decline. At one time there were seven hundred Weissbier brewers in the Berlin area; now there are two. Berliner Weiss is an acquired taste, closer in style to the sour lambics of Belgium. The popularity of both lambics and Bavarian wheat beers makes the decline of the Berlin style all the more puzzling. As well as an early addiction to Pilsner beers, Berliners may have lost interest in their local and remarkable style as a result of the long, cruel division of the city, with one wheat beer brewery almost lost from view on the 'wrong' side of the wall. Reunification may have come too late to revive the fortunes of Berliner Weiss.

The beers are made by a type of lactic fermentation. The origins of the style, which dates from at least the early seventeenth century, are obscure. One suggestion is that Protestant Huguenots, driven out of France and other Catholic countries, settled in Berlin and Brandenburg and brought with them a method of brewing using spontaneous fermentation which they had picked up in Flanders as they travelled north east. The beer was once celebrated. Napoleon's troops, when they were stationed in Berlin, described Berliner Weiss as 'the Champagne of the North'. It is a remarkably accurate description, for the grapes of the Champagne region around Rheims produce such a tart wine that it becomes acceptable only after a long, slow ageing that produces a sparkling version and which involves some lactic activity. The wheat beers of Berlin, like Champagne, quickly lose their head as a result of their acidity. They are low in alcohol (around 3 per cent volume), are extremely pale in colour, have a light fruitiness and little hop aroma. Unlike lambic, the beers are fermented with a conventional warm-fermenting yeast strain but it is used in concert with a lactic culture. The lactic culture was first isolated early in the twentieth century by scientists who created Berlin's renowned university research and brewing school, the VLB (Versuchs und Lehranstalt für Brauerei). The culture is called *Lactobacillus delbrücki* in honour of Professor Max Delbrück, who led the research team at VLB.

The Berliner Kindl Brauerei, the bigger of the two producers, had to rebuild its brewhouse in the 1950s. The original vessels were confiscated by the Russians

when they marched into the city at the end of World War II. Commendably, Kindl designed the new brewhouse in the 1930s Bauhaus style, still using copper. The well water is softened. The wheat malt percentage is thought to be around 30 per cent and the finished alcohol is a modest 2.5 per cent. The hops are the Northern Brewer variety and bitterness units measure 10. After mashing and boiling, the lactobacillus is added first to start acidification, followed by the ale yeast. Fermentation lasts a week, followed by several days of cold conditioning. The beer is then filtered and bottled with conventional yeast and some kräusen (unfermented wort).

Schultheiss, the other Berliner Weiss

Drinkers in the tavern next to the Martha brewery sit at a Stammtisch, a table reserved for regular customers.

brewery, had breweries on both sides of the wall but the one in the east, at Pankow, became government-controlled. After the collapse of communism, Schultheiss regained control of the site only to close it. Its remaining brewery is actually on two neighbouring sites: a large brewery in Kreuzberg that produces Pilsner and other conventional beers and a smaller plant, the Schoneberg. The brewery blends equal amounts of wheat and barley malt in the mash to produce a 3 per cent beer. Hallertauer hops achieve just 4-8 units of

Berlin wheat beer is brewed with a lactic yeast culture that gives it a tart, sour flavour.

Berlin to add a dose of either woodruff, a herbal essence, or raspberry syrup: the first turns the beer green, the second a pale, peachy red. The syrups cut the acidity of the beer and add a touch of sweetness.

Perhaps Berliner Weisse needs the kind of inspiration that has revived the fortunes of wheat beer in Belgium. The Belgian version is mainly associated with the region of Brabant and the university city of Leuven with its brewing school. The rich soil is ideal for growing barley, oats and wheat. Monks were brewing there from the fifteenth century and turned to the grains from the surrounding fields for their raw materials. Before the hop was in universal use, the monks added herbs and spices to balance the malt and give tartness to the finished beer. When the region was part of the Netherlands, brewers used the many exotic spices, herbs and rare fruits that Dutch traders brought back from the East: the 'white beers' of Brabant became renowned for their use of such ingredients as coriander and Curaçao orange peel. The term 'white beer' (*bière blanche* in French, *witbier* in Flemish) was used to distinguish the style from darker beers made solely from barley malt and identify the dense head of white foam created when the beer is poured. The development of pale ales and Pilsner-type lagers in the twentieth century bit deep into sales of wheat beer. The area around the small town of Hoegaarden had thirty wheat beer breweries in the nineteenth century but they had all disappeared by the 1950s.

The style was revived in the 1960s by Pierre Celis (pronounced 'Sellis') who had

bitterness. Top fermenting yeast and lacto-bacilli are blended together with wort that is between three and six months old to encourage a lively fermentation which lasts for just three or four days. The beer is warm conditioned for three to six months and is then kräusened and lactobacillus added for bottling. The result is an astonishingly complex, fruity, sour and quenching drink. Both Kindl and Schultheiss wheat beers are bottle conditioned and will improve and become more complex with age. The beers are so sharp, tart and acidic – like drinking pure lemon juice – that it is the habit in

Schultheiss survived the communist period and still brews a 'Champagne of the North'.

Hoegaarden. . .the pace-setter in the revial of Belgian wheat beers.

lived next door to the last wheat beer brewery in Hoegaarden. Celis worked in the brewery as a young man and studied the techniques of making the style. When he opened his own brewery in the village, he called it De Kluis, the Cloister, in honour of the local monastery that started the white beer tradition centuries before. The grist is divided equally between malted barley and unmalted wheat. Hops are East Kent Goldings for aroma and Czech Saaz for gentle bitterness. Bitterness units are around 20: the brewer is not aiming for a big hop bitterness. Milled coriander seeds and orange peel are added during the copper boil with hops. Following fermentation, the beer is warm conditioned for up to a month and then given a dosage of sugary wort and reseeded with yeast before bottling or kegging. The beer is 4.8 per cent alcohol. It has an appealing spicy nose with clear evidence of the sharp, tangy orange peel. It is tart and refreshing in the mouth with a big citric fruit character, while the finish is bitter-sweet, tart, spicy and clean.

Hoegaarden White is now a massive international brand. Pierre Celis sold the business to Interbrew, the Belgian giant that owns Stella Artois, and some drinkers feel the beer has lost a little of its character since the change of owner.

Hoegaarden has spawned a growing number of competitors: Steendonks Witbier and Haecht Tarwebier from two other Brabant breweries; Riva's Dentergems apple-fruity Witbier; the dry and spicy Blanche de Namur from du Bocq; De Gouden Boom's lemony Brugs Tarwebier/Blanche de Bruges; an uncompromisingly tart and spicy Titje from the Silly Brewery near Tournai; and Oudenaards Wit Tarwebier from Clarysse.

The style has seeped over the border into the Netherlands. Heineken's De Ridder brewery in Maastricht brews a 5 per cent Wieckse Witte with lots of tart, lemony, spicy character. In Amsterdam the Maximiliaan brew-pub, which with a nice touch of irony, is based in a former convent on the edge of the city's red light district (6/8 Kloveniersburgwal), makes a tangy, spicy Waags Wit. The sizeable independent Arcen Brewery makes a 5 per cent Arcener Tarwe while the De Drie Horne makes a darker, fruity and sweet Wit. De Leeuw's Witbier (4.8 per cent) is packed with spices and tart fruit.

Pierre Celis, aged 65 when he sold De Kluis to Interbrew, was determined to stay in brewing and he was keen to settle in Texas in the United States. By 1992, with his daughter Christine, he had opened the first new brewery in Austin since 1907. He

Superb copper kettles at Hoegaarden: a more functional new brewhouse has been added to cope with demand.

imported hand-hammered copper vessels made in Belgium in the 1930s that had once brewed both Pilsner and pale ale. The brewing liquor comes from limestone wells. Texas winter wheat grown in Luckenback is blended with barley malt imported from Belgium. Celis uses American-grown Cascade and Willamette hops. Celis White (3.9 per cent weight/4.8 volume) is modelled on the original Hoegaarden brew and is spiced with coriander and Curaçao orange peel. It blossoms with rich fruit and herbal aromas and flavours. It has won the gold medal for American wheat beers four years running at the Great American Beer Festival held in Denver, Colorado and it has seen one of the most spectacular growths in sales of any new beer launched in the US, with production reaching 40,000 barrels in 1996. In 1995 Miller, through its subsidiary Craft Brewing Co., took a majority stake in the Celis Brewery. At present Celis and his daughter remain in charge of day-to-day control of the company.

The De Ridder brewery in Maastricht brews a wheat beer with a lemony, spicy character. Wieckse comes from the same root as 'wick', an Anglised version of an old Saxon word for a settlement.

Wheat beer brewing in the United States owes much to the Pyramid Breweries group based in Washington state and California. Founders Beth Hartwell and Tom Baune launched the company as a micro in Kalama, Washington in 1984 and their Chaucerian-sounding Wheaten Ale quickly became one of their leading brands. They sold the company, which has expanded with a brew-pub in Seattle and a new plant in Berkeley, California that opened in January 1997. Wheaten Ale has been replaced by Pyramid Hefeweizen. In spite of the Germanic name, the company claims it is the definitive example of American wheat beer, a style that disappeared during Prohibition. It has a high malted wheat content of 59.5 per cent with 39.5 per cent malt from two-row barley and 1 per cent caramalt. The hops are American Liberty and Nugget. The yeast strain is a Bavarian cold-fermenting culture that is used at an ale temperature. The beer is 4.1 per cent weight/5.1 volume and has a perfumy aroma, is tart and spicy in the mouth with a clean, quenching and aromatically fruity finish.

On the other side of the Cascade mountains in Yakima, Bert Grant of Scotch Ale and Imperial Stout added a HefeWeizen to his range in 1997. Knowing his humour, he will no doubt claim that it is a perfect example of a genuine Scottish wheat beer.

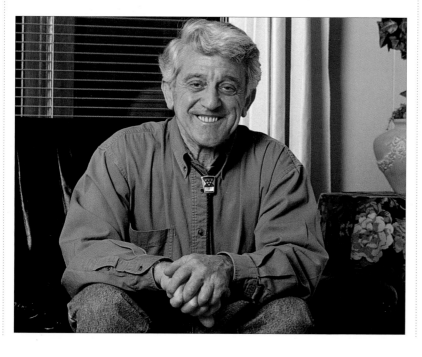

Pierre Celis revived 'white beer' in Belgium and then moved to Austin to introduce Texans to the pleasures of the style.

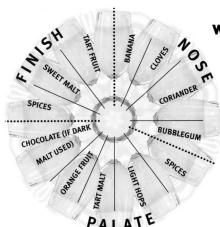

WHEAT BEER STYLE
Apples, cloves and even a hint of banana dominate Bavarian-style wheat beers while the Belgian versions tend to be spicy and lemony.

Celis White has won the Gold Medal for its class four years running at the Great American Beer Festival.

Pyramid in Seattle calls its wheat beer Hefeweizen in the German fashion but it is based on an American recipe that disappeared during Prohibition.

WHEAT BEER BREWERS

Arcense Stoombrouwerij
Kruisweg 44, 5944 EN Arcen, Netherlands

Berliner Kindl Brauerei
50 Werbellin-strasse, Neu Kölln, 1000 Berlin 44

Brasserie Du Bocq
rue de la Brasserie 4, 5191 Purnode, Belgium

Brasserie de Silly
Ville Bass A141, 7830 Silly, Belgium

Bierbrowerij De Drie Horne
Berndijksestraat 63, 5171 BB Kaatsheuvel, Belgium

Brouhuis Maximiliaan
Kloveniersburgwal 6-8, Amsterdam

Brouwerij De Ridder, BV
Oeverwal 3-9, 6221 EN Maastricht, Netherlands

Celis Brewery
2431 Forbes Drive, Austin, Texas 78754

Clarysse Brouwerij
Krekelput 16-18, 9700 Oudenaarde, Belgium

De Gouden Boom Brouwerij
Langestraat 45, 8000 Bruges, Belgium

Grant's Yakima Brewing Co.
1803 Presson Place, Yakima, Washington 98903

Haacht Brouwerij
Provinciesteenweg 28, 3190 Boortsmeerbeek, Belgium

Hoegaarden, De Kluis Brouwerij
Stoopkenstraat 46, 3320 Hoegaarden Belgium

Weissbrauerei Hans Hopf
Schützenstrasse 10, 83714 Miesbach, Germany

Kaltenberg Marthabräu
Augsburger-strasse 41, 82256 Fürstenfeldbruck, Germany

Palm Brouerij
Steenhuffeldorp 3, 1840 Steenhuffel, Belgium

Pyramid Ales
91 South Royal Brougham Way, Seattle, Washington 98134

Riva Brouwerij
Wontergemstraat 42, 8720 Dentergem, Belgium

G Schneider & Sohn
1-5 Emil Ott-strasse, 8420 Kelheim, Germany

Schultheiss Brauerei,
28-48 Methfessel-strasse, Kreuzberg, 1000 Berlin 61

Spaten-Frankiskaner-Bräu
Mars-strasse, 8000 Munich

ALT

Alt means old in German and the beers brewed and drunk in and around the great industrial city of Düsseldorf are known as Altbier. As with the wheat beers of Bavaria, Altbier is seen not as something old fashioned but a distinctive, flavoursome beer made by the old, pre-lager method of warm fermentation. Düsseldorf was once a major coal-mining area and this may explain some similarity between the Alt beers of the city and the bières de garde of northern France; they were made to refresh working people after a hard day's labour. Düsseldorf is close to the Dutch border and Maastricht, where warm-fermenting ales also survive; the two cities may have encouraged one another to remain true to older brewing techniques.

With their burnished copper colour from the blending of darker malts with pale malt, Altbiers are also not dissimilar to English bitters, though the similarities should not be exaggerated. Either empirically or learning from modern brewing techniques, Altbiers are warm fermented in the ale fashion but are then cold conditioned (lagered) for several weeks. The result is beer with a smoothness and rounded character quite different from the more robust aromas and flavours of an English pale ale or bitter.

The most characterful Altbiers are found in the famous brewing taverns of the city's Alt Stadt, the charming Old Town with its cobbled streets and gas lamps. Enormous amounts of beer are knocked back in small glasses not much bigger than a chaser, accompanied by heaped plates of local food. Im Füchschen, the Little Fox, in Ratinger-strasse, is a large rambling building with tiled walls, red-tiled floors and wooden benches. The house beer is tapped from wooden casks on the bar; as one cask is

At the Little Fox tavern in Düsseldorf casks of Altbier are delivered on tracks to the bar and whisked away as soon as they are drained.

emptied it is whisked away and replaced with a fresh cask. The beer has a toasted malt palate and a sweet, fruity finish.

Zum Uerige in Berger-strasse means 'At the Place of the Cranky Fellow'. The house beer is brewed in gleaming copper kettles in full view of the crowds that pack the maze of rooms in this early nineteenth-century building. The Alt is 4.6 per cent alcohol, is brewed from three malts and Spalt hops with around 50 units of bitterness. It is dry hopped and the initial roasty maltiness is offset by a good developing hop bitterness.

Zum Schlüssel, the Key, is in Bolker Strasse, birthplace of the poet Heinrich Heine. It is a less frenetic place than Zum

Uerige, light and airy, with a tiled floor, long tables for diners and copper brewing kettles seen through a window at the rear. The beer has an appealing perfumy hop aroma, a bitter-sweet palate and a dry finish. A local at the bar told me, 'After the fifth one you start to taste it.' He was doing his best to prove the point.

The biggest commercial brewer of Alt is Diebels, a family-owned company set up by Joseph Diebels in 1878 in the hamlet of Issum, a few miles outside Düsseldorf. It has been in the family for four generations and is now run by Dr Paul Bösken-Diebel who is chairman and chief executive. In a country best known for its lager beers, Diebels is the sixth biggest brewing group in Germany, producing around two million hectolitres (44 million gallons) a year.

Diebels Alt is 4.8 per cent alcohol, copper coloured with a pronounced peppery hop aroma balanced by rich malt. It is bitter in the mouth and has a dry and nutty finish with a hint of orange fruit. Pale Pilsner malt makes up 98 per cent of the grist, with 2 per cent roasted malt, a nice 'Scottish' touch. (Other Alt brewers use a dash of Vienna or black malt for colour and body.) Hops are Northern Brewer for bitterness and Perle for aroma, producing 32 units of bitterness. Brewing liquor from the company's own wells has calcium hydroxide ('lime milk') added to soften it. The modern Steinecker brewhouse has tiled walls with a striking mosaic showing the old brewery at the turn of the century. Four mash kettles feed four wort kettles, where the hops are added in one addition. Mashing uses the decoction method. The fifty-year-old yeast strain is an ale culture but it is cropped from the bottom of conical fermenters. It is noticeably less fruity than a typical British ale yeast and it fully attenuates the wort, turning most sugars to alcohol. (A Diebel's brewer earnestly wrote in my notebook that he used *Sacccharomces cerevisiae* 'unlike you British who use Brettanomyces'. No self-respecting British brewer would let a wild yeast such as

The copper brewing kettles at Zum Uerige are on full view to drinkers. The house beer has a pronounced roast malt character balanced by a good hop bitterness.

Brettanomyces near his beer, and I can only assume that the Diebel's brewer must have been served a vinegary pint in London.) Primary fermentation lasts just two days. The green beer has a short diacetyl rest and is then stored or lagered at a cold temperature in tanks for between ten days in summer and three weeks in winter.

As a result of Düsseldorf's proximity to the Netherlands, it is not surprising that a few Dutch brewers have added an Alt to their repertoire. In the town of Budel in Dutch Brabant, Budels Alt is less restrained than the German versions. At 5.5 per cent alcohol it has a massive peppery hop aroma, dark chocolate and malt in the mouth and a

long, dry and intensely bitter finish with hints of fruit and coffee. It is brewed from pale and dark malts and hopped with German varieties. Arcense makes an amber-coloured 5 per cent Altforster Alt with a malty and slightly roasty aroma and palate. De Leeuw (The Lion) Brewery is based in Valkenberg near Maastricht and has the closest links with Düsseldorf. Its Venloosch Alt (4.5 per cent) is packed with dark and roasted malt character. Grolsch, the Netherlands' major independent brewer, best known for its Pilsner in the snap-lock bottle, has added an Alt to its range. Based in Gelderland in the east of the country, Grolsch is also close to Alt territory, and its

The modern brewhouse at Diebels, the biggest of the Altbier brewers. The beer has a small proportion of roast barley added for colour and flavour.

Amber (the English word is used on the label) is a true warm-fermenting beer, though a second yeast culture is added late in fermentation for a period of cold maturation. It is an all-malt beer with a small amount of wheat malt blended with pale and coloured barley malts. German hop varieties create 40 units of bitterness: in the true Alt fashion, a rich, biscuity malt nose and palate give way to a big, dry, bitter finish. It is a beer of considerable complexity and character.

In the United States, with a large sector of the population descended from German immigrants, it is not surprising that Alt has become a popular style for several craft brewers. The Stanislaus Brewing Company in Modesto, California is based in a German community, and all its main products are in the Alt tradition and are labelled 'Alt biers' to emphasize the Germanic roots. The brewery was founded in the early 1980s by Gareth Helm and his German-born wife Romy Graf. They began by brewing on their farm in converted dairy vessels but now have a fully fledged brewery, bar and

St Stan's is based in California but brews a range of Altbiers to emphasize the German origins of the style.

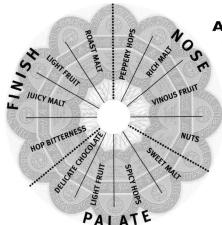

ALT BEER STYLE

Warm fermented, Alt beers have a gently fruity flavour with body and roundness provided by dark malts. Hop bitterness is high but does not overpower the biscuity richness of the malt.

restaurant. The main product is St Stan's Amber Alt (4.5 per cent weight/5.6 volume). The label shows a monk with a huge foaming tankard of beer and the marketing line 'Conceived in heaven, brewed in California'. It is an all-malt brew with a dark fruit and bready start, a rich malty-fruity palate and a lingering bitter-sweet finish with a gentle touch of hop bitterness. St Stan's Dark (4.8/6 per cent) is a malty beer with overtones of coffee and chocolate.

The most northerly brewer of Alt in the world is the Alaskan Brewing Company in

Juneau, best known for its multi-award winning Smoked Porter. Founders Geoff and Marcy Larson discovered that a German immigrant brewer had made Altbier in Juneau early in the century. To recreate a genuine German Alt they use pale and caramel malts with American Cascades and Czech Saaz hops. They chose a yeast strain with enormous care in order to achieve the right balance of flavours. The beer (4.2/5.25 per cent) has a big malt and light fruit bouquet and palate with hops dominating the smooth finish.

ALT BEER BREWERS

Alaskan Brewing Company
5429 Shaune Drive,
Juneau, Alaska 99801

Arcense Bierbrouwerij BV
Kruisweg 44, 5944 EN Arcen,
Netherlands

Budelse Brouwerij
Niewstraat 9, 6021 HP Budel,
Netherlands

Privatbrauerei Diebels GMBH
Brauerei-Diebels-strasse 1, Issum 1,
Düsseldorf

Im Füchschen
Ratlinger-strasse, Düsseldorf 1

De Leeuw Bierbrouwerij
Pater Beatrixsingel 2,
63012 VI Valkenberg an den Geul,
Netherlands

Grolsche Bierbrouwerij
Eibergseweg 10, 7141 CE Groenlo,
Netherlands

Zum Eurige Obergarige
Hausbrauerei, 1 Berger-strasse,
Düsseldorf 1

Zum Schlüssel, Bolker-strasse
Düsseldorf 1

Stanislaus Brewing Company
821 L Street, Modesto, California 95354

KÖLSCH

Cologne has a closely guarded secret: it has the biggest number of breweries of any city in either Germany or the rest of the world. The number is twenty and the fact that their unique style is not better known is due to the fact that it is protected by the equivalent of a French *appellation contrôlée*. Brewers who are not covered by the ordinance can neither brew nor call their beers by the name of Kölsch, which comes from the German name for the city, Köln.

Cologne, the capital of the Rhineland, has been a major brewing city since it was under Roman occupation. The manufacture of alcohol, whether beer, mead or cider, flourished during that period, and by the early Middle Ages beer was brewed and controlled by monasteries. A brewers' guild was established in 1396 and is the oldest traders' guild in the city. As monastic power waned, commercial breweries, mainly attached to taverns, developed at a fast pace.

The tradition continued into the twentieth century. Until World War I, most beer was produced in taverns. It was a warm-fermenting style and, in common with the Altbiers of Düsseldorf and the ales of the Low Countries, was consumed in large quantities by people engaged in heavy manual labour. At a time when the younger generation revered their elders, Kölsch was a family beer, not one to be disowned by teenagers determined to debunk the habits of their parents. As a result, the habit of drinking the local beer was deeply engrained in the people of Cologne. Nevertheless, the Kölsch style could easily have disappeared under the lager juggernaut but for the determination of the local brewers to defend it through their Association of Brewers. They have had to make some compromises: the beer is now paler and it has a period of cold conditioning

ing or lagering following fermentation. But it remains a genuine warm-fermenting beer.

In the 1960s the brewers laid down ground rules for Kölsch and attempted to define the style. In the 1970s they engaged in several court cases against brewers outside the Cologne region who called their

Kölsch beer waiters are all called 'Kobes', a diminutive of Jakob. They wear blue uniforms and serve at great speed.

beers Kölsch. All this activity culminated in 1985 in the signing of a convention drawn up by the brewers and the Federal

Government's department of fair trading. The convention is made of parchment and the seals and signatures of all Kölsch producers are attached. It is a source of enormous pride to producers who have struggled for so long to protect their beer.

The style is often known as 'Wiess', a Cologne rendering of Weiss or white. The name refers to the colour, as Kölsch is not a wheat beer in the Bavarian manner, though a proportion of wheat malt is sometimes blended with pale barley malt. The average strength is around 5 per cent. Hallertauer and Tettnanger hops produce bitterness units in the high twenties: extreme bitterness is avoided. The character varies from producer to producer, but in general Kölsch has a malty aroma with some light fruit, is soft in the mouth from the local water and has a delicate perfumy hop character. Yeast

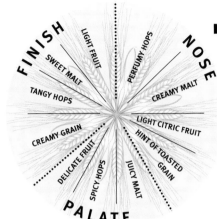

KÖLSCH BEER STYLE

A malty aroma, a soft, dry palate from local water and delicate, perfumy hops with some light fruit are the signature of a beer protected by German law.

strains attack the malt sugars with great enthusiasm, producing a dry, fully attenuated beer.

The biggest producer of Kölsch today is the Küppers Brewery. It was founded little more than twenty years ago and, in a

conservative area, is still looked upon as something of an upstart. It has built market

Herr Schenzer, the production director of Früh in Cologne, in his brewhouse. He supplies the best-known Kölsch tavern in the city.

share through adroit advertising but its beer is easy-drinking and unexceptional. An unfiltered version called Wiess has a more distinctively fruity and hoppy character. The best known of the taverns serving Kölsch is P.J. Früh in the Am Hof near the great cathedral. The beer used to be brewed on the premises but a new brewery has been built outside the city centre. Früh's is a classic beer tavern: there are large rooms set aside for eating as well as drinking, but the serious connoisseurs stand in an area jocularly called the Schwemme or swimming pool. Waiters in traditional blue uniforms and leather aprons hurtle among the customers, carrying trays packed with small glasses of beer. The waiters are all addressed as 'Kobes', a diminutive of Jakob:

The logo for a Cologne brewery uses the symbol of the Kobes waiter and even explains that the beer is warm or top fermented – Obergärung.

Früh's beer is available in the Am Hof near Cologne's cathedral. Serious drinkers gather in a part of the bar known as the 'swimming pool'.

the same nickname is used for waiters in Alt beer taverns in nearby Düsseldorf. Casks of beer are raised from cellar to bar by dumb waiter and drained in the twinkling of a glass. Früh's Kölsch is an all-barley malt beer with delicate fruit on the nose and light, tart hops in the finish. Gaffel in the Old Town has a nutty, spritzy version of the style that throws a big, fluffy head when poured. The Heller brew-pub in Roon-strasse has a fine vaulted cellar bar with stained-glass windows. The beer comes in two versions: a malty, sweetish Kölsch and an unfiltered, slightly acidic Ur-Wiess. The beer is brewed

from organic barley and Hersbrucker hops, a thoughtful touch from careful brewers.

They would not approve of a Dutch 'Kölsch' except on the grounds that imitation is the sincerest form of flattery. The Arcense Brewery in Arcen, which has a strong predeliction to brew just about any style of beer in the world, produces a 5 per cent Stoom (Steam) Beer which is warm fermenting, with a blend of barley and wheat malts and Northern Brewer and Hersbrucker hops. It has 22 units of bitterness and has a fruity aroma with good peppery hop character.

KÖLSCH BEER BREWERS

P.J. Früh
Cölner Hofbräu, 12–14 Am Hof, 5000 Cologne

Privat Brauerei Gaffel-Becker
41 Eigelstein, 5000 Cologne

Brauhaus Heller
33 Roon-strasse, 5000 Cologne

Küppers Kölsch Brauerei
145–155 Altebruger-strasse, 5000 Cologne

Brauerei Schwarz
6 Heumarkt, 5000 Cologne.

Gebrüder Päffgen
Obergarige Hausbrauerei,
64 Friesen-strasse, 5000 Cologne

TRAPPIST

In the summer of 1997, when monks from the Sint Sixtus Trappist monastery of Westvleteren in Belgium held talks with the commercial brewers of St Bernardus in neighbouring Watou, they had a simple request: 'Please take the image of a monk off the labels of your beers'. St Bernardus had been licensed in 1946 by the abbot at Westvleteren, Father Gerardus, to brew their beers under licence and to promote them commercially. The monks restricted their own production to 3500 hectolitres (76,989 gallons) a year for consumption within their community and in a café opposite the entrance to the monastery. Confusion followed, for the monks' beers were brewed to exactly the same strengths and recipes as the St Bernardus products, which carried the word 'Sixtus' on the labels. The monks had granted a licence to St Bernardus as they shrank from overt commercial activity. The presence of commercial versions in the wider market place undoubtedly helped boost the image of Westvleteren, but the monks

became uneasy at this too-evident connection with Mammon. The licence to brew by St Bernardus expired in 1992 and 'Sixtus' disappeared from the labels. But five years later the monks approached the

A panoply of Belgian Trappist ales. The monks have joined forces to stop their tradition being engulfed by commercial Abbey beers.

Left: There is a monk on the label, a saint in the title and the brewery is based in a road called Trappist Way but St Bernardus is not a Trappist ale.

Right: Chimay is the best known of the Belgian Trappist breweries and produces red, white and blue ales, the names taken from the colour of the caps on the bottles.

138

The range of beers from La Trappe in the Netherlands. The monks have added a fourth beer called Enkel or Single to the portfolio.

trickle and then a flood of commercial 'abbey' beers, which to the gullible and inexperienced appear to be the real thing, served to cause confusion and debase the coinage of the monks' ales. The problem was exacerbated by the fact that a number of religious orders that had stopped brewing (some in the Napoleonic period) licensed commercial brewers to make beers using their monastic names and drew substantial royalties as a result.

In 1997, at the same time as the Westvleteren monks were holding talks with St Bernardus, representatives of all five Belgian Trappist breweries were meeting to discuss how to protect their beers from the ravages of commercialism. In 1998, with

brewery with the request to remove any suggestion that the brewery's beers came from the Trappist tradition.

This concern for upholding and not demeaning the Trappist tradition is shared by the other brewing monks in Belgium. They feel they must protect a way of life built round the making of beer, bread and cheese to sustain them in their work and prayer. When the best-known of the Belgian Trappist breweries, Chimay, started to sell small amounts of beer in the 1920s and on a bigger scale after World War II, the brothers had no idea how a voracious industry, endlessly seeking new brands and flavours to exploit, would endanger and undermine the monastic tradition. As news of the quality of Trappist beers spread, a

Brewing brother. . .Brother Tarcissius helps in the La Trappe brewery, standing in at weekends when the lay workers take time off.

Schaapskooi in the Netherlands, they formed the International Trappist Association to place a common seal, 'Authentic Trappist Product', on their beers as a mark of authenticity. They baulk at any talk of a Trappist 'style': all their beers may be warm fermented and bottle conditioned but the beers from each monastery have evolved and developed in different ways. They are talking of something more profound than 'style'. They are offering an *appellation contrôlée*, a guarantee of origin.

The Trappists took their name from an abbey founded at La Trappe in Normandy in 1664. The French Revolution forced many out of France as their abbeys were sacked and their lands confiscated. They headed north into the Low Countries and settled afresh to live off the produce of the fields. They brewed beer to offer to guests and pilgrims, to drink with their simple

The imposing entrance to the Koningshoeven abbey near Tilburg. The brewery in the grounds is called 'Sheep Fold' but is designed like a railway signal-box.

Koningshoeven was built in severe Gothic style in the 1880s on land donated by the monarch to the monks when they arrived from France.

With a little help from my lay friends...Father Thomas, head brewer at Chimay, is supported by Mark Habran in the modern brewhouse.

back the brewery from Stella. The monks had sensibly stored their brewing equipment and, most important, their ale yeast culture. For many years the brewery produced just one regular beer called Dubbel, but a Tripel and a Quadrupel joined it, followed, somewhat idiosyncratically in 1995, by the lowest-strength beer of the range, Enkel or Single. Dubbel, the main brand, is 6.5 per cent and is brewed from pale, Munich and other coloured malts and hopped with Northern Brewer from the German Hallertau. It is tawny coloured with an orange Muscat aroma and palate overlain by peppery hops. The 8 per cent bronze Tripel bursts with Goldings hops and spicy fruit. The 10 per cent Quadrupel was first brewed in 1992 as an autumn beer and now appears as an annual vintage. It is reddish in colour and has a deceptively smooth palate

vegetarian meals, and to sustain them during Lent. The tree-girt and lake-fronted abbey of Koningshoeven was built in severe Gothic style in the 1880s close to the town of Tilburg in the ancient region of Brabant that is now divided by the border with Belgium. The abbey was built on land donated by the king to the monks when they arrived from France: *Koningshoeven* means 'the King's Gardens'. The adjacent brewery was built first, between 1884 and 1885, to help finance the construction of the abbey. It has the charming rustic name of Schaapskooi, which means the 'sheep fold', though from the outside it looks remarkably like a railway signal-box, the first-floor entrance reached by an iron staircase. Brewing now takes place in a modern stainless-steel plant that includes the lauter tuns

more commonly associated with lager brewing. The brewhouse is illustrated with photographs of the earlier and more conventional vessels while a jocular inscription says 'There is no beer in heaven, so we drink it here', disappointing news for those who believe in an after-life.

After World War II the brewery was bought by the Belgian Stella Artois group, which wanted to build a bridgehead in the Netherlands. It produced an unlikely 'Trappist Pils' and installed a small lager plant. The lager was not a success and the monks raised the necessary funds to buy

Father Mattias at the Sint Sixtus abbey in Westvleteren. Ales from the smallest of the Trappist breweries are sold in a café across the road from the abbey.

with delicate fruit and a deep spicy-fruity finish. Enkel, 5.5 per cent, is pale, dry, hoppy and quenching. All the beers are sold under the La Trappe name.

It was monks from Westvleteren, now the smallest of the Trappist breweries, who founded the Abbaye de Notre Dame de Scourmont ten miles from the small town of Forges-les-Chimay in the Hainaut region. Chimay is now the biggest of the Trappist breweries and the best known internationally. In 1850 seventeen monks from Westvleteren were given permission by their abbot to leave the monastery and build a new one on forest land donated by the Prince of Chimay. The monastery was completed in 1864. A small brewery had been finished two years earlier, constructed to provide sustenance for the monks and to raise funds for the abbey. The beer became available in bottled form from 1885, and in 1925 the prior, Emmanuel le Bail, allowed wider distribution, with the image of the abbey on the label and the legend 'ADS',

The abbey of Orval is composed of buildings with a striking blend of Romanesque and Burgundian styles with some Art Deco flourishes. The ruins of the former abbey still stand in the grounds.

Lick that...a Belgian postage stamp bears the symbols of all the Trappist breweries.

which stood for Abbaye de Scourmont. Between the two world wars the monks produced just one bottled beer of around 4.5 per cent strength.

The abbey and brewery were occupied by German forces during World War II. After the war, the brewery was rebuilt and the monks embarked on a course of greater commercial distribution to help pay for the construction work on both the abbey and the brewery. The head brewer, Father Théodore, consulted the great brewing scientist Jean De Clerck from Leuven University's brewing faculty. De Clerck advised on the design of the brewhouse, the style of beers and, crucially, isolated a pure

Orval's beer goblet was designed by the architect of the abbey, Henri Vaes.

yeast culture that developed the fruity character of the beers, with their powerful hint of blackcurrant. The yeast works remarkably quickly at a high temperature, with fermentation lasting for only two or three days. When De Clerck died, the monks marked their debt to him by allowing his burial in the abbey grounds, a rare honour for someone from the secular world.

The monks rightly treat their beers as seriously as wine. On my visit, the current head brewer, Father Thomas, led me to a sampling room where we tasted several vintages of his beers. He expounded on the need to allow the 'Grand Cru' versions, sold in Bordeaux-shaped bottles with corks and wire cradles, to breathe when opened in

order to vent off some of the carbon dioxide produced during bottle fermentation. All three beers can be laid down to improve, but Father Thomas believes that after five years the two darker ones will develop a port wine character.

A new brewhouse was installed in 1989. The 1950s brewhouse, with its magnificent copper vessels, has been replaced by stainless-steel ones, with many vessels hidden from view behind tiled walls. Production is now in the region of 110,000 hectolitres (2.4 million gallons) a year. The local water, drawn from the monks' own wells, is soft and remarkably free from agricultural and urban impurities: the water is fundamental in creating the rounded, full-bodied

The brewhouse at Orval is a symphony of burnished copper vessels. The cross on the wall can be seen in all the Trappist breweries.

character of the beers. The monks, in the best Trappist tradition, are somewhat vague and almost silent on the ingredients used but I discovered from lay brewing staff that they prefer winter barley from the French Champagne area. An extremely pale, Pilsner-type malt is blended with caramalt for colour and body. German Hallertauer hops are blended with American varieties from the Yakima Valley.

The beers are known by the colour of their caps. The original is Chimay Red, also known as Première in a corked bottle. It is

7 per cent alcohol and has a fine copper colour with dark fruit on the aroma and palate, and great hop bitterness and nutmeg spice on the finish. Chimay White (8 per cent), introduced in 1968, is a radically different beer from its stablemates. A version of White in a corked bottle was added in 1986: it is called Cinq Cents and marked the 500th anniversary of the town of Chimay. With a fuller attenuation, it is drier than the other Chimay beers. It has an enticing orange-peach colour, is dry, hoppy and spicy with citric fruit on the aroma and finish. Chimay Blue or Grande Réserve in a corked bottle is 9 per cent and has an enormous depth of fruit, giving it a port wine or, according to Father Thomas, a Zinfandel character. There is plenty of spice from hops and yeast. Each year's Blue is vintage dated and will improve in bottle after two years and will stay in condition for five, as will Red and White. All three beers are given a dosage of priming sugar and yeast for bottle conditioning. Chimay Blue is the ideal companion for blue cheese or the soft cheeses made by the monks, one of which has beer blended with it. The monks plead with drinkers not to chill their sublime beers and to serve them at room temperature.

The Abbaye Notre Dame d'Orval is a place of breathtaking beauty and great tranquillity. The tranquillity belies a turbulent history that has seen the buildings destroyed by fire and, when rebuilt, destroyed again during the French Revolution. The present complex of buildings surrounds the preserved ruins of the former abbey. The abbey is in densely wooded countryside in the Ardennes, and stands on a sharp bend in the old Roman road that runs from Trier in

Father Antoine at work in his brewhouse at Rochefort abbey. The notice in the foreground warns 'Don't touch the vessels with the hands!'

The staffs of life...the brewing monks at Orval make bread and cheese as well as beer to sustain them in their simple way of life in the Golden Valley.

Germany to Rheims in France.

The name Orval is a reworking of the French 'Val d'Or' or Golden Valley. According to a charming legend, the feudal overlord of the region, Countess Matilda, the Duchess of Tuscany, came to the valley in 1076 to visit a small group of Benedictine monks who had made the arduous journey from Calabria in Italy to build an abbey there. As she sat by the edge of a spring in the abbey grounds, she accidentally dropped her wedding ring into the water. She was still in mourning following the death of her husband and was overcome with grief at the loss of the ring he had given her. She prayed that it would be returned to her, at which moment a trout rose to the surface of the spring with the ring in its mouth. 'This is truly a golden valley!' the duchess exclaimed and gave a generous endowment to the monks, who were able to extend the size of the abbey. The image of a trout with a ring in its mouth is used on beer labels and in promotions.

The monastery was rebuilt in the twelfth century by Cistercian monks from the Champagne region. It was burnt down soon afterwards and rebuilt. For centuries it played an important role in the political and spiritual life of the region. The monastery was sacked following an artillery barrage in 1793 by French revolutionaries who came over the border in the mistaken belief that the deposed Louis XV was hiding there. The present buildings were constructed over a long period extending from 1926 to 1948, with monks from as far away as Brazil answering a call to settle at Orval and recreate a place of great serenity dedicated to worship and charitable work in the community. The abbey was designed by the architect Henri Vaes, a great admirer of Cistercian buildings. His stunning creation is a remarkable blend of Romanesque and Burgundian styles with some startling blunt 1920s touches. Vaes even designed the brewery's beer glass, which looks like a medieval goblet.

The brewery was built in 1931 with the aim of providing sustenance for the monks (they call the beer 'liquid bread') and generating finance for the construction and maintenance of the monastery. The formula for the beer was devised by a German brewer named Pappenheimer. He may have perferred to make lager but he worked to the monks' specification, which includes the English system of 'dry hopping', which means that a handful of hops are added to the finished beer for extra bitterness and aroma. There are thirty monks left at Orval to run a vast estate and to do charitable work in the community. Father Lode is in charge of brewing but much of the work is delegated to lay people. Father Lode greeted me warmly but declined to be photographed in his brewhouse in case people thought Orval was too commercial. It is, first and foremost, a place for retreat.

I was shown round by François de Harenne, the commercial director, whose family has been associated with Orval for many years. 'We do not want too malty a beer,' he told me as we entered the brewhouse. 'We want a discreet malt taste.' The result is a beer that positively explodes with hop character and measures 40 units of bitterness. Nevertheless, the monks do not stint on the malts they use, choosing four to five English, Dutch, French and German spring barleys. A touch of caramalt, similar to English crystal malt, gives the beer its

The brewery at Westmalle was expanded in the 1860s to help finance a Trappist colony in the Belgian Congo. In 1932 the abbot designated the ales 'Trappistenbeer', which helped give the monks' products greater recognition.

orange-peach colour. Pure white candy sugar is added during the copper boil for flavour and to encourage a powerful primary fermentation. The copper hops are German Hallertauer and Styrian Goldings. East Kent Goldings from England are used for dry hopping, chosen for their resiny, piny aromas. Brewing liquor is drawn from the well that gave rise to the legend of Orval.

Orval enjoys three fermentations. Primary fermentation is with a conventional ale yeast. The unfinished 'green' beer is pumped to conditioning tanks where four to five more yeast strains are added. One of these is a wild yeast, a member of the Brettanomyces family used in lambic brewing. It has been carefully cultured in the monastery laboratory. As it can attack the dextrins as well as maltose sugars in the wort, the result is a beer with a high level of attenuation, strong in alcohol, with virtually no sugars left.

The beer is bottled with a dosage of the first yeast and some candy sugar, which encourages a third fermentation. The beer is stored in the brewery for six weeks. It is declared at 6.2 per cent alcohol but will reach close to 7 per cent as a result of

bottle fermentation. This bone-dry beer has an aroma of peppery hops and tart fruit, the palate is dominated by gooseberry fruit, and the finish is long, intensely bitter and with a hint of herbs and lactic sourness from the action of the wild yeast. The acidity of the beer, especially when it is aged for months or a few years, makes it the perfect aperitif. It should be stored upright (the bottles are not corked) at a cellar temperature of 12°C/54°F. The abbey shop sells the beer and also the bread and the cheese made by the monks. The monks make some 38,000 hectolitres (835,883 gallons) of beer a year, of which around ten per cent is exported. The L'Ange Gardien (Guardian Angel) restaurant is a few minutes' walk from the abbey and offers rustic dishes cooked in Orval.

The Abbey Notre-Dame de Saint-Remy is another settlement in the wooded Ardennes region. It is close to the small town of Rochefort, and the name features on the labels of the monks' beers. The abbey is reached up a narrow, wooded road. It was founded as a convent in 1230 by Gilles de Walcourt, the Count of Rochefort. The hard climate and grinding poverty proved too much for the nuns and they were replaced

146

by monks in 1464. Documents show that a small brewery existed from around 1595 to provide beer for the community, using barley and hops grown in the grounds.

The monks were forced to abandon the abbey during the French Revolution, when scant attention was paid to the border between France and the Low Countries. The abbey was rebuilt in 1887 by Trappists from the Abbey d'Achel and a brewery was opened two years later. The present brewhouse dates mainly from the 1960s, with some additions in the 1970s, and produces around 15,000 hectolitres (329,954 gallons) a year. It is a symphony of burnished copper set amid tiled walls, the sunlight pouring through stained-glass windows and glinting on the mash vessels and coppers. One tun carries the warning '*Ne pas toucher les cuivres avec les mains!*' – 'Don't touch the vessels with the hands!'

The head brewer, Brother Antoine, favours barley from France, Belgium and the Netherlands in the form of pale Pilsner malt and darker Munich malt. Dark candy sugar is used in the copper along with German Hallertauer and Styrian Goldings hop varieties. Two strains of yeast are used for both primary fermentation and bottle conditioning: the beer is given a dosage of white sugar for fermentation in the bottle. The three beers have red, green and black crown caps and are labelled Six, Eight and Ten from an old and now defunct Belgian method of indicating strength. Rochefort Six is 7.5 per cent alcohol in modern terms. It has a pale brown colour with a gentle, fruity and slightly herbal palate. Rochefort Eight (9.2 per cent) is a beer big in aroma and body, copper-brown with a rich fruity nose and palate reminiscent of raisins and dates. Rochefort Ten (11.3 per cent) has enormous depth as the strength suggests. Gentle hops blend with dark fruit, nuts and

chocolate. Brother Antoine says the character of his ales was determined by their original use as 'liquid bread' during periods of fasting.

The two remaining Belgian Trappist breweries are in Flemish-speaking areas and in more rugged countryside. Westmalle's official name is the Abbey of Our Lady of the Sacred Heart but is usually known as the Trappist Abbey of Westmalle. Paradoxically, given the antipathy between the monks and French revolutionaries, the abbey was founded at the height of the revolution. Three Trappist brothers had escaped from France to Switzerland and planned to go to Amsterdam and from there sail to safety in Canada. But French revolutionaries were active in the Low Countries and their close links with fellow revolutionaries in America meant that a sea journey to Canada would be fraught with danger. The monks accepted an invitation from the Bishop of Antwerp

to establish a religious community in his region. In 1794 a rich farmer at Westmalle donated some of his land to the brothers. They were joined by other refugee Trappists and a dozen monks set to work to build an abbey in flat, wind-swept land. The beautiful mellow stone abbey, set behind walls and guarded by avenues of elm trees, was completed in 1804. A brewery was not added until 1836 and supplied only the monks' daily needs. In 1865 a brewing monk of Prussian origin, Ignatius Van Ham, extended the brewery to sell beer to finance the creation of a Trappist community in the Congo. Sales were restricted to the surrounding area and it was not until the 1920s that they were sold more widely.

In 1932 the Abbot of Westmalle, Edmond Ooms, gave his beers the appellation 'Trappistenbeer' and two years later commissioned a secular architect to design a new and larger brewhouse. Classic copper vessels are set on tiled floors in a powerful 1930s design that has clear Art Deco influences. The brew kettle is fired by direct gas flame, a system that gives a defining burnt malt, toffee character to the beers as some of the malt sugars are caremelized during the boil with hops. The brewing liquor is hard, and the monks use French and Bavarian summer barleys which are kilned to produce extremely pale Pilsner-style malts. Whole hop flowers are used: the brothers are somewhat reticent about naming all the varieties but will admit to putting Styrian Goldings, Tettnanger from Bavaria and Czech Saaz in the kettle in three stages. Candy sugar is also added during the boil phase.

Westmalle is the second biggest of the Trappist breweries, producing more than 100,000 hectolitres (2.2 million gallons) a year. It has given the designations 'Dubbel' and 'Trippel' to Belgian beer, terms now widely used by other brewers. They are not so much indications of strength, though a Triple is stronger than a Double, but are taken to mean that the Double is darkish and malty while the Triple is pale, hoppy and tangy-fruity. Westmalle Dubbel, 6 per cent alcohol, is russet coloured due to the use of some dark malt and dark candy sugar. It is chocolatey, fruity and spicy: the fruitiness is complex with suggestions of guava and other tropical produce. The Tripel is 9 per cent and has just 13 units of colour, almost as pale as a Pilsner. Bitterness units are 35 to 38. This is a classic beer. It throws a dense head in the glass and has a profound orange-citric fruit aroma and palate, with a rounded, warming alcohol and a good underpinning of resiny hops and a tantalizing herbal note. White candy sugar is added during the boil. Both Dubbel and Tripel enjoy slow secondary fermentations in tanks – three weeks for Dubbel, five for Tripel – at 8–10°C (46–50°F). The beers are then bottled with priming sugar and reseeded with the same yeast culture used for primary fermentation: the bottles are warm conditioned for two to three weeks.

The Abbey of Sint Sixtus was founded in 1831 in the hamlet of Westvleteren in flat Flanders countryside that was the scene of dreadful carnage in World War I. Westvleteren is close to the town of Poperinge, capital of the Belgian hop-growing region. A small brewery was added to the abbey in 1838 solely to provide sustenance for the monks. In the 1920s the Abbot Dom Bonaventure De Groote renovated the brewery in local Flemish artisan style, with brewing vessels set in tiled

surrounds. The extension of the brewery led to a deep theological debate within the community about becoming too dependent on commercial activity. At the end of World War II it was decided to restrict production to around 3500 hectolitres (76,989 gallons) a year for the monks and a handful of local cafés. It was at this point that the monks gave a licence to the nearby St Bernardus Brewery in Watou to produce St Sixtus beers for wider commercial scale.

On my only visit to St Sixtus on a rainy, blustery autumn day, cowled monks hurried out and emphatically pulled the main gates of the abbey shut. I was able, though, to speak at a side entrance to a friendly monk, Brother Mattias. Fortunately, the monks' ales can be sampled immediately opposite the abbey in the comfortable and homely Café de Vrede. The brewery does not operate every day and

TRAPPIST STYLE

Not so much a style, more a tradition, with highly individualistic renditions from each abbey. Look for ripe fruit, spices, a big perfumy and bitter hop character, and chocolate and coffee notes in darker ales. All the beers will improve with age.

when news of a new batch of beer is heard over the bush telegraph, café owners and beer lovers arrive with vans, cars and even on bikes to take away cases.

The beers are designated by the colour of their crown corks and are notably malty and spicy. The range begins with a green-capped Double (4 per cent), followed by a Red (6.2 per cent) with dark fruit and peppery hops, and a Blue Extra (8.4 per cent) with an enormous attack of tart fruit and alcohol. The top of the range Abbot (10.6 per cent) has an explosion of fruit (raspberries and strawberries) and malt allied to a soft, silky and alluring creaminess. The St Sixtus beers are described as 'Flemish Burgundy' and a sign in the Café Vrede, written by a monk thirty years ago, says 'The Good Lord has changed water into wine so how can drinking beer be a sin?' It is, of course, a rhetorical question.

TRAPPIST BREWERIES	
Abbaye de Notre-Dame d'Orval 6823 Villers-devant-Orval	**Abdij Koningshoeven** Trappistenbierbrouwerij de Schaapskooi, Eindhovensweg 3, 5056 TP Berkel-Eschot
Abbaye de Notre-Dame de St Rémy Rue de l'Abbaye 8, 5430 Rochefort	**Abdij Trappisten van Westmalle** Antwerpsesteenweg 496, 2140 Malle
Abbaye de Notre-Dame de Scourmont Rue de la Trappe, 294, 6438 Forges-les-Chimay	**Abdij Sint Sixtus** Donkerstraat 12, 8983 Westvleteren

ABBEY BEERS

The proliferation of abbey beers over the past few years may cause confusion and weaken the appreciation of true Trappist ales, but it cannot be denied that some of the older versions do have some lineage and history connected to religious establishments. It is the proliferation of new beers with quasi-religious names and only the most tenuous links with religious communities that are the main cause for concern.

The monks of both Leffe and Grimbergen allowed commercial brewers to produce beers under their names in order to raise funds for their religious work. Both communities come from the Norbertine tradition, one which the monks are anxious to defend. At the same time as the Trappist brewers were meeting in 1997 to discuss how best to sustain and protect their brewing tradition, the abbot at Grimbergen was instructing a distributor of the beers brewed in the monastery's name to remove a label showing a monk in a brown habit: Norbertines wear snow-white robes.

The brands produced under the Leffe and Grimbergen names are far and away the biggest of the abbey beers, a result of their ownership by the brewing giants Interbrew and Alken-Maes. The Abbaye Notre-Dame de Leffe was founded in 1152 close to the banks of the River Meuse at its confluence with the smaller River Leffe. The community has had a tumultuous history: flooded by the Meuse, ransacked by soldiers during the struggle for control of the Low Countries, destroyed by French revolutionaries, rebuilt and then bombed during World War I. A small brewery is thought to have been built on the site in the thirteenth century and supplied ale for the local monks and their parishioners. A new brewery was installed when the monastery was rebuilt in the eighteenth century but the monks

Leffe is the biggest of the abbey brands, now owned by Interbrew. The abbey at Leffe stopped brewing during the French Revolution.

ceased to brew their own ale when their community was destroyed during the French Revolution.

During the 1950s the abbey faced severe financial difficulties and a local brewer, Albert Lootvoet, suggested to the abbot that he should produce beers using the Leffe name and pay the monks a royalty for the use of their name. The brewery was subsequently taken over and the Leffe brands were transferred to the Mont St-Guibert Brewery in the town of the same name south of Brussels. The company was

Leffe's glass…the image of a stained-glass window masks the fact this a strictly commercial brew.

bought by Stella Artois of Leuven, which was later to form Interbrew when it merged with Jupiler of Jupille-sur-Meuse. Production of the Leffe brands and a pale ale called Vieux Temps was transferred to the main Stella Artois plant in Leuven. The only exception was the best beer in the range, Leffe Tripel (8 per cent), which is bottle conditioned and brewed at Interbrew's De Kluis plant in Hoegaarden. It has a golden colour and a dominating citric hop aroma and palate, with hints of oak and vanilla. Leffe Blonde (6.3 per cent) is the main brand, and is heavily promoted by Interbrew in France and Britain. It has some peppery hop on the aroma and a dry and bitter finish. A dark version of the beer

is called Brune. Other beers in the range include Radieuse (8.2 per cent), a malty, rich ale, and Vieille Cuvée (8.2 per cent), a full-bodied brown beer with rich malt and roasted grain dominating the aroma and palate, and with a hint of herbal spiciness in the finish.

The symbol of the Abbaye de Grimbergen is a phoenix, and the symbol is also used on the labels of the beers that bear the abbey's name. Grimbergen has been sacked and pillaged on a regular basis, rising phoenix-like from the flames on every occasion. A bar close to the abbey is called the Fenixhof.

The abbey was founded in 1128 by St Norbert in the village of Grimbergen in

Brabant in what is now virtually a suburb of Brussels: it is a rare example of an abbey built by the founder of an order, and not by his followers. The abbey was severely damaged on many occasions during the many conflicts that raged over the Low Countries. When it was substantially rebuilt in 1629, the monks added a brewery, their labours aided by the presence of a *'hoplochting'*, Brabant dialect for a hop garden. The brewery was dismantled during the French Revolution and the brewing vessels were sold. In 1840 the

Maredsous is a Benedictine abbey near Namur. The beer that carries its name is brewed by Moortgat of Breendonk.

A powerful ecclesiastic image is used to promote Steenbrugge which comes from a small brewery based in the medieval city of Bruges.

monks licensed the Janssens and Peeters Brewery to make beers under their direction, and this relationship continued until 1958 when the rights were given to the large brewery group Maes. Maes has since merged with the Alken group and Alken-Maes is now owned by BSN of Strasbourg, producers of Kronenbourg. The Grimbergen beers are brewed in Alken-Maes' Brasserie Union in Jumet near Charleroi, which specializes in warm-fermented ales. Disappointingly, the beers are now pasteurized, robbing them of much of their complexities of aroma and flavour.

Perhaps it is because St Norbert came from the Rheims area of France that the beers licensed by his followers have a rich, winey and almost liqueur-like fruitiness. The 6.2 per cent Dubbel is dark brown in colour with a chocolate and sultana palate and a finish full of warming alcohol. Tripel (8.1 per cent) is a blond beer with a good peppery-spicy hop aroma, a full malty body, and a winey-fruity finish balanced by citric hop flavours. The powerful 10 per cent Optimo Bruno is claimed to derive from an original recipe supposedly discovered in the monastery. It is amber-coloured with a massive kick of vinous fruit and alcohol, earthy hops and the typical rich, warm Grimbergen finish. No doubt aware of the success of the paler Trappist beers as well as Leffe Blonde, Alken-Maes has introduced Grimbergen Blonde (6.5 per cent) principally for the French market.

Other major abbey beers include Affligem (from a Benedictine monastery founded in 1074), brewed by De Smedt; Corsendonk (an Augustinian priory),

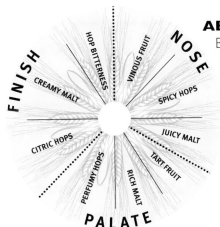

FINISH — NOSE — PALATE

HOP BITTERNESS · VINOUS FRUIT · SPICY HOPS · JUICY MALT · TART FRUIT · RICH MALT · PERFUMY HOPS · CITRIC HOPS · CREAMY MALT

ABBEY BEER STYLE

Big malty, winey aromas and palates, spices and deep hop bitterness are typical of Abbey beers though aromas and flavours are often diminished by pasteurization.

Moortgat's Maredsous comes in a handsome bottle with a cork and wire cradle.

brewed by Bios and Du Bocq; Maredsous (a Benedictine abbey near Namur), brewed by Moortgat; and Tongerlo (a Norbertine abbey between Antwerp and Hasselt) brewed by Haacht. In the rush to capture a slice of the abbey beer market, brewers have used the names of abbeys which have long since disappeared, mainly during the French Revolution. These include Abbaye d'Aulne, Abbaye de Cambron and Abbaye des Rocs. When genuine names cannot be found, we enter the world of illusion and possibly delusion with the likes of Moinette (Little Monk), Divine (Brasserie Silly), Triple Moine (Du BocQ), and Pater Lieven (Van den Bossche). Where it will all end, heaven alone knows.

The growing number of abbey beers,

often with rich aromas and flavours, undoubtedly increases choice and diversity for drinkers. But it would be tragic if the often misplaced emphasis on the religious roots of these beers detracted from the role and influence of genuine Trappist ales, one of the most fascinating but endangered traditions in the world of beer. Even Belgians, great beer connoisseurs that they are, are confused. It is surely time for the Belgian government to end the confusion by insisting that the labels for abbey ales do not mislead consumers into thinking they are buying into heritage and tradition; all too often consumers are the victims of subtle commericalism and clever advertising in a market that is increasingly competitive.

SELECTED ABBEY BREWERIES

Affligem
Brouwerij de Smedt, Ringlaan 18,
1890 Opwijk

Corsendonk
Brasserie Du Bocq, rue de la Brasserie 4,
5530 Purnode

Grimbergen
Brasserie Union,
rue Derbeque 7,
6040 Jumet

Leffe
Brasserie St Guibert,
rue de Riquau 1,
1435 Mont St Guibert

Maredsous
Moortgat Brouwerij, Breendonkdorp 58,
2659, Breendonk

Tongerlo
Brouwerij Haacht, Provinciesteenweg 28,
3190 Boortmeerbek

BELGIAN PALE AND GOLDEN ALES

The English term 'ale' is widely used and understood in Belgium. As the modern nation of Belgium was carved out of the Low Countries principally by British diplomats in the nineteenth century, there have been close links between the two countries ever since. These links were heightened by the deep affection felt by Belgians for the British forces which helped liberate them in both world wars. At the end of World War II, the now extinct Lootvoet brewery in Overijse in Flemish Brabant brewed an ale called RAF Spéciale to mark the efforts of the British Royal Air Force in defeating the German Luftwaffe. As a result of this hands-across-the-North-Sea friendship, imported English and Scotch ales became popular and Belgian brewers responded with their own versions: Scotch ales, both imported and home-brewed, are highly prized, to such an extent that both Scottish Courage and Whitbread have brewed beers exclusively for the Belgian market. Palm, the leading pale ale brewer in Belgium, produces John Martin's Pale Ale under licence for a large company in Antwerp: the beer is based on a superbly hoppy-spicy Courage pale ale known as Bulldog in its home market.

In the early part of the twentieth century, before Pilsner brewing took off in Belgium, the consumption of ale was boosted by a form of prohibition that banned strong distilled spirits, gin in particular, from sale in bars and cafés. Brewers responded by producing strong pale and golden ales with strengths often as high as 8 per cent by volume. With the arrival of Pilsner in the 1920s, ale brewers dubbed their products either 'Belge' or 'Spéciales Belges'.

The Palm Brewery, the biggest producer of Belgian ale, lies in the shadow of the church of Steenhuffel but in every

other way dominates the village as its major employer. Steenhuffel stands on land reclaimed from the sea and protected by dykes. Visitors can visit the brewery and also the nearby restored feudal château of Diepensteyn where Brabant draught horses are reared, a brewery museum is housed and sumptuous meals based on cuisine artisanale are served, each dish accompanied by a Palm beer.

Palm began life as a small brewery attached to a tavern called De Hoorn (The Cornet) in 1747. In 1908 it was bought by Arthur Van Roy who developed the brewery commercially but stayed true to ales at a time when Pilsner-style lagers were becoming popular. His plans were disrupted by World War I. The brewery was badly damaged and Van Roy and his staff built a new plant and launched Spéciale Palm, an ale that used the palm as a symbol of the ultimate victory over the upstart lager: the triumph of hope over experience, as Dr

Gambrinus, the legendary Duke of Brabant, inspired brewers and drinkers with his toping.

Kwak Pauwel with licorice in the recipe is served in a glass with a stand.

Samuel Johnson said in a different context. The beer and the brewery prospered. When Spéciale Palm won the top prize in the 'Ancienne Belgique' class at Expo '58, it became a household name throughout the country. Sales rose still further from the 1970s with the revival of Belgian speciality beers, which now account for 20 per cent of the market. The company, renamed Palm in 1975 to signify the importance of the main brand, which accounts for 92 per cent of production, is still run by descendants of the Van Roy family. Palm produces 600,000 hectolitres (13.2 million gallons) a year, making it the sixth biggest Belgian brewery. Brabant draught horses are featured strongly on labels and posters as their cinnamon-coloured bodies and white manes are thought to resemble a glass of Palm beer.

General manager Jan Toye, a member of the ruling family on the distaff side, showed me round his gleaming copper-vesselled brewery with enormous pride. A 1970s brewhouse was joined by a second one built in 1989: production is based on a double decoction system, with portions of the mash heated to a higher temperature, pumped back to the first vessel and finally filtered and clarified in a lauter tun or mash filter. Pale malt for Spéciale Palm comes from two-row maritime spring barley varieties, including Alexis and Triumph grown in England, France and the Netherlands. It is blended with a darker malt similar to English crystal, with 15 per cent maize and 2 per cent sugar. Palm has a love affair with the Golding hop: East Kent Goldings and Whitbread Goldings Variety are used in the copper boil while Styrian Goldings are used for dry hopping after fermentation. Brewing liquor comes from the brewery's own well and minerals are added to Burtonise it. A multi-strain yeast attacks malt sugars at

Palm D'Or...the brewhouse at Palm in Steenhuffel has some fine copper mash tuns and kettles. The main brand accounts for 92 per cent of production and was given the name Palm to signify ale's ultimate victory over lager.

different stages of primary fermentation, which lasts for a week in vessels behind tiled walls and visible only through portholes. Sugar is added to encourage a strong secondary fermentation in conical vessels. The finished beer appears with 5 per cent alcohol, 24 units of colour and 20 units of bitterness. It has an appealing light chestnut colour, a dense, rocky head, a rich orange-citric aroma balanced by spicy hops, a pronounced orange jelly palate, and a long dry, fruity and hoppy finish. A 5.5 per cent version called Dobbel Palm is produced for the Christmas season.

It is surprising to find that such a great trading city as Antwerp has only one brewery left. As De Koninck means 'The King',

you might expect a touch of almost supercilious hauteur among the brewery's ruling family. But Modeste Van den Bogaert, as his first name indicates, is not given to boasting. Does he use a single or multi-strain yeast? 'Perhaps,' he said with a heave of his heavy Flemish shoulders and offered me another beer in a glass known as a 'bolleke', which to an English-speaker with a grasp of the vernacular could be taken as another terse form of reply. Fortunately his son Dominique and brewery spokesman Guy Van Keel were rather more forthcoming as we toured the brewery.

De Koninck is remarkable for being a one-beer brewery. Like Mr Van den Bogaert, the company has shrugged its collective shoulders at the twentieth century, ignored the lager explosion and gone on brewing what it knows best, a warm-fermented ale. The brewery started life in 1833 as a small brewhouse attached to a tavern called The Hand on the Mechelsesteenweg, a road that once marked the boundary of Antwerp. The brew-pub was owned by Joseph Henricus De Koninck, and his family controlled it until 1919. Behind the imposing Art Deco façade of the current brewery, a techno-logical revolution has taken place. A typically Flemish brewhouse with brick-clad kettles was replaced in 1995 by a spacious, lofty plant that looks more like the deck of the Star Ship Enterprise than a beer production unit. The system is based on a mash tun, mash filter (lauter tun) and brew kettles. The 5 per cent beer is made from a blend of two pale Pilsner malts with a darker Vienna 'red' malt. De Koninck rightly prides itself on using no cheaper cereal adjuncts or brewing sugars: it is an all-malt beer. The local water is softened for brewing. Whole flower hops, stored in a room known as the 'treasure house', are exclusively of the Saaz variety, mainly from the Czech Republic with some from Belgian fields. Primary fermentation, using a single strain yeast, lasts a week in open vessels. Attenuation is around 83 per cent, leaving some malt sugars behind for body and full-ness in the finished beer. The beer is then stored and conditioned in conical vessels for a further week at a cold temperature to allow a second fermentation. The draught version accounts for 65 per cent of production and is simply rough filtered and unpasteurized. The bottled version is only pasteurized in summer to avoid spoilage from high temperatures.

In the comfortable, wood-panelled reception room, the Van den Bogaerts père and fils poured generous bollekes of De

Dominique Van den Bogaerts pours a glass of De Koninck in the Antwerp brewery. The beer uses no cheap cereal 'adjuncts'.

The De Koninck glass is known as a Bolleke, which amuses British visitors. In the Café Pelgrim over the road from the brewery drinkers are offered a shot of yeast to go with the beer.

Koninck: bolleke means 'little goblet'. It is a brilliant ale in every way, from its thick collar of foam that leaves a generous 'lace-work' inside the glass as the beer is consumed, through its tempting pellucid russet colour, its peppery-spicy aroma and orange citric fruit palate, to the long, fruity-hoppy finish, all overlain by a delicious toasted maltiness. Having said that, De Koninck is a one-beer brewery, a stronger, 8 per cent version of the standard ale was added in 1993 to celebrate Antwerp's status as Cultural Capital of Europe. It was called Cuvée Antwerpen '93 and proved so popular that is now a regular beer, renamed Cuvée De Koninck. It has a pronounced dark sultana fruit and malt character, balanced by spicy hops.

In the side street opposite the brewery's delivery bays, the Café Pelgrim offers some of the finest draught De Koninck in Antwerp. Regulars there like to add a shot glass of yeast to their beer, and the brewery sends over supplies in a bucket every day. The yeast, addicts say, adds a spicy note to the beer and has medicinal properties.

How do you distinguish a golden ale from a pale ale? Neither De Koninck nor Palm are especially pale due to the use of such darker malts as crystal and Vienna red. To the eye they are amber, chestnut, copper or russet in appearance and they are sharply different from one of the best-known Belgian ales. As a result of its complexity of production, its seductive aromas and flavours, and its alluring burnished gold colour, Duvel is a world classic. It is also a beer that creates confusion. As a result of the colour – seven to eight on the international brewers' chart and only fractionally darker than a Pilsner – many people assume it is a lager, whereas it is fermented with a top-working yeast. The beer outside Belgium is universally called 'Du-velle' on

Duvel, Belgium's most famous golden ale, has a special glass designed to retain the beer's vast head of foam.

the assumption that the word is French. In fact, it is Flemish. It means 'Devil' and is pronounced with heavy emphasis on the first syllable: Doo-vul.

The Moortgat Brewery in Breendonk, north of Brussels and on the road to Mechelen, was founded in 1871, though Johannes-Petrus Moortgat was brewing in nearby Steenhuffel in the early part of the nineteenth century. Jan-Leonard Moortgat built the reputation of the Breendonck brewery by personally delivering supplies of beer by horse and cart to Brussels 30 kilo-metres (19 miles) away. Breendonk made dark ales and it produced one that was initially called Victory Ale to mark the end of World War I in 1918. According to a

brewery legend, a friend of the Moortgat family said: 'When I drink this beer I feel I have the devil in me'. It was too good a name to pass up and the beer was renamed Duvel but remained a brown ale. Between the two World Wars, when imported Scotch ales had become a cult drink in Belgium, Albert Moortgat of the ruling family visited Britain to study ale brewing and returned with some bottles of McEwan's Scotch from Edinburgh, then a bottle-conditioned beer. Moortgat called in the legendary brewing scientist Jean De Clerck from the Faculty of Brewing at Leuven University. De Clerck studied the McEwan's yeast under a micro-scope and found it was multi-strain, with between 10 and 20 strains. He isolated the three most efficient strains, including one that is resistant to high temperatures: fermentation can rise to 30°C/86°F during the summer. Another sticks like glue to the bottom of the bottle and is ideal for bottle conditioning. Using the new yeasts, Duvel was relaunched in the 1930s but remained dark until the 1970s. The seemingly inexorable rise of lager brewing and con-sumption in Belgium led to Moortgat bottling Danish Tuborg in the 1960s. This forced the company to invest in a modern bottling line, while the income from Tuborg enabled the site to be expanded. The Moortgat family decided it had to produce a pale beer of its own but resisted the move to lager. With the help of Jean De Clerck, a golden version of Duvel was formulated around a mashing, boiling and fermentation regime of enormous complexity that prevents any darkening of the malt sugars.

Mashing is the classic infusion method used primarily in Britain, with lightly kilned Pilsner malt from Belgian and French two-row summer barleys. Hops are Saaz and Styrian Goldings added in three stages during the copper boil, creating 30 units of

*The noses have it...
tasters at work at
Duvel to ensure that
each batch has the
right balance of aromas
and flavours.*

bitterness. Fermentation is partly in conicals, the rest by what Moortgat calls 'classical fermentation' in seventeen open vessels. It was like walking into an orchard in the rooms with the open vessels, the air heavy with the unmistakable aroma of pears: the signature of Duvel is the rich, perfumy bouquet of Poire William. Primary fermentation lasts for just four to five days. The 'green' or unfinished beers are blended at the end of the primary stage. The blended beer is fermented for a second time in conicals, cooled, passed through a centrifuge to remove the yeast, and cold conditioned (the brewery calls it lagering) for three weeks. The beer is bottled with a dosage of yeast and liquid brewing sugar. The bottles are stored for two weeks at 25°C/77°F to allow a third fermentation to take place and then moved to a cold area for two to three months at 5°C/41°F. While Duvel begins

with a gravity of 1056°, which would normally produce a beer of around 5.5 to 6 per cent alcohol, the three fermentations and the addition of sugar in the copper and the bottle means the finished product is a formidable 8.5 per cent: it is a fully

attenuated beer, with nearly all the malt sugars turned to alcohol.

A well-matured Duvel throws such a vast fluffy head of foam when poured that the brewery provides special glasses to contain both beer and collar. The elegant

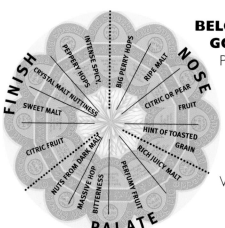

BELGIAN PALE AND GOLDEN ALE STYLE

Perfumy hops, a deep bitterness, juicy and sometimes slightly toasted malt epitomize the style. Fruitiness is tart and citric or, in the case of Duvel, has a pronounced Poire William note.

glass looks like a large brandy balloon. This is fitting as the beer's sublime aroma is similar to a fine Cognac or, given its fruitiness, perhaps Calvados is a better comparison. It is not a beer to be rushed: good café owners store the bottles (there is no draught version) for a further three months before serving it. In the comfortable tasting room in the brewery, where stained-glass windows depict the generations of Moortgats who have run the company, I was treated to a tasting of Duvels of different ages. A young one, just a few weeks old, was yeasty and 'green' and the head died quickly in the glass. A year-old version was superb, with the classic Duvel attributes: a lilting aroma of pears and gentle hops in the mouth and a bitter-sweet finish dominated by more perfumy 'noble' hop character. An eighteen-month Duvel had muted fruit on the aroma and palate and the finish drier.

In spite of the fact that Duvel is an ale, many Belgian cafés treat it like a lager, serving it cold and keeping the glasses in a fridge. Should you chill the Devil? In this form it makes a fine refresher or even an aperitif. But to enjoy it to the full and savour its depth and complexity of aromas and flavours, Duvel should be served cool at around 11°C/52°F. It is perfect with fish, white meat, pasta and spicy dishes or, served in that splendid glass, makes the ideal digestif. Moortgat produces 265,000 hectolitres (5.8 million gallons) a year, of which Duvel accounts for three-quarters. The brewery also makes a small amount of Pils, the abbey beers Maredsous and the wheat beer brewed in collaboration with Palm.

There are now, inevitably, several competitors to Duvel, with such knavish names as Du Bocq's Deugniet (Rascal), Judas from Alkes-Maes, and Sloeber (Joker) from Roman. But where golden ales are concerned, the Duvel has all the best tunes.

The Full Sail craft brewery in Portland, Oregon, has been influenced by the Belgian tradition in formulating its golden ale.

The Devil comes in many forms...Satan is just one of many Belgian brews that attempts to cash in on the popularity of Duvel.

BELGIAN PALE AND GOLDEN ALE BREWERS

Brouwerij De Koninck
Mechelsesteenweg 291, 2018 Antwerp 1

Brouwerij Lamot
Van Beethovenstraat 10, 2800 Mechelen

Palm Brouwerij
Steenhuffeldorp 3, 2901 Steenhuffel

Moortat Brouwerij
Breendonkdorp 58, 2659 Breendonk

BELGIAN BROWN ALES

The southern border of the region of East Flanders marks the gateway to Wallonia and the French-speaking areas of Belgium. It may be a powerful linguistic dividing point but there is a strong affinity between the Saisons of French Hainaut and the 'oud bruin' or provision beers of the Flemish area. The affinity is underscored by the fact that Oudenaarde, capital of East Flanders, was briefly the capital of the whole of Flanders, a role also undertaken by Lille. Oudenaarde, on the banks of the Scheldt, was an important centre of textile manufacture, and is home to the world's best-known example of cuisine à la bière, carbonade flamande, a beef and onion stew cooked with beer.

The complexity of the beer, its spicy, vinous and resiny hop character overlain by a delectable hint of sourness, makes it the ideal companion for a dish that would overwhelm a more subtle brew. The richness and full-bodied nature of the beer style is heightened by the use of dark malts and even roasted barley. Recalling the oldest days of beer making, some Flemish brown ales have fruit added to them to give an extra dimension. The term 'oud bruin' means old brown. The beers date from a time when work was largely agricultural and brewing was confined to the winter and spring; as with the Saisons of Hainaut, they are provision beers, vital parts of the food and diet of the common people.

The best-known producer of old brown is Liefmans of Oudenaarde. The brewery was founded in 1679 and its fortunes were revived, after years of slow decline, in the 1970s by the remarkable figure of Rose Blancquaert, a former ballet dancer who became the owner's secretary and took over when he died. In her younger days, Madame Rose, as she is known, would recall her years as a ballerina by leaping into

empty copper vessels to perform pirouettes. With the aid of her son Olav, who served his apprenticeship at another brewery, she restored the fortunes and fame of Liefman's beers. Madame Rose now runs a restaurant in Oudenaarde called De Mouterij, The Maltings, where she naturally serves the best carbonade flamande in the region, cooked in Liefman's beer.

The 5 per cent alcohol Oud Bruin is made from a blend of Pilsner malt (from Gatinais and Triumph varieties) with Munich caramalt, Vienna red malt and roasted barley. Whitbread Goldings Variety are used as a bittering hop with aroma provided by Czech Saaz and Bavarian

Liefmans of Oudenaarde is the best-known producer of Oud Bruin or Old Brown ale. Bottles come wrapped in tissue paper, the colour denoting the particular style of beer.

Tettnanger: the hops produce 20 units of bitterness. The hopped wort is fermented for at least eight days (two Sabbaths) in open copper vessels using a multi-strain yeast culture that originated in the famous Rodenbach 'sour red beer' brewery in West Flanders. After primary fermentation the beer is matured for four months in the brewery. It emerges with a fascinating sweet-and-sour aroma and palate, raisin-like fruit and a good spicy hop note. A stronger version,

Flanders ales such as Liefmans have a close affinity with the Saisons of French-speaking Belgium.

a genuine provision ale, is the result of blending Oud Bruin with beer that has been matured in the brewery for six to eight months. The blend is centrifuged, primed with sugar, reseeded with yeast and stored for three months. The 6 per cent beer is called Goudenband – Gold Ribbon. This silkily alluring beer with its fruity and vinous nose and palate, and sherry-like finish underpinned by delicate hop notes will improve with cellar conditioning: the brewery recommends three to five years.

Once a year Liefmans makes cherry and raspberry beers using the stronger of the two ales that form Goudenband. A further fermentation and conditioning lasts for six to eight weeks. The kriek has a strength of 7.1 per cent and the fruit is tart, pungent and wonderfully refreshing. The frambozen version is 5.1 per cent, is sweeter than a lambic raspberry but nevertheless has a magnificent aroma and tingling palate.

There has been some concern for the future of Liefmans since it was taken over in 1990 by the Riva group in Dentergem. Riva claimed the mashing and boiling vessels at Oudenaarde were worn out and had to be replaced. Since 1992, the Liefman's beers have been mashed and boiled at Dentergem, the wort then transported in tankers to Oudenaarde for fermentation and storage. Riva says it will restore full production to the Liefman site. Riva nevertheless enjoys a good reputation for investing in old brewers. It has a stake in the historic Het Anker (Anchor) company in Mechelen. This important old trading city is just over the border in Antwerp province but has been an important centre for brown-ale brewing from at least the sixteenth century. Het

Anker is a delightful site based round a large cobbled courtyard: customers can enjoy beer and food in the open air in warm weather or just inside in a large rustic restaurant. The site was originally a *béguinage*, old French for a convent run by a sect, the Béguin, founded in Liège in the twelfth century (St Paul said that 'faith was the anchor of the soul'). The brewery is large and rambling, with some ancient vessels that are in the course of being replaced. Het Anker makes a pleasant, chocolatey Bruynen but is most famous for Gouden Carolus, named after a gold coin minted in honour of the emperor Charles Quint (Charles V) who was educated in Mechelen.

Gouden Carolus takes its name from a gold coin minted in honour of Charles V.

Almer Mater...the Roman brewery in Mater brews several bottle-conditioned brown ales including a dark and malty Doubbelen Brunen.

The remarkably deep and complex 7.8 per cent bottle-conditioned beer is a blend of pale and dark malts and has chocolate and burnt fruit notes on the aroma and palate. It is the perfect nightcap.

Back in East Flanders, the ancient Roman brewery in the village of Mater dates from 1545 and brews a chocolatey 5 per cent Oudenaarde and a big 8 per cent Doubbelen Bruinen (double brown) that is packed with dark malt and hop flavours. The beers are brewed with pale, Munich and caramalts, and candy sugar is added to the copper boil with Saaz and Hallertauer hops. The beers are bottle conditioned. In Oudenaarde, the small Clarysse brewery makes Felix, a robust oud bruin with a big peppery and spicy hop character. Cnudde, a tiny brewery in Eine, started life in 1919 and almost closed in 1992 but was kept going by the owner's three sons. The 4.7 per cent Cnudde Bruin is fruity and distinctive and hard to find. Cnudde also makes a very occasional Kriek.

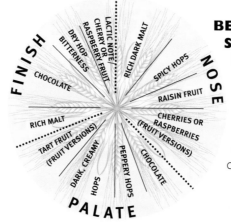

FINISH — DRY HOP BITTERNESS / CHOCOLATE
LACTIC NOTE / CHERRY OR RASPBERRY FRUIT / RICH DARK MALT
NOSE — SPICY HOPS / RAISIN FRUIT / CHERRIES OR RASPBERRIES (FRUIT VERSIONS)
PALATE — RICH MALT / TART FRUIT (FRUIT VERSIONS) / DARK CREAMY HOPS / PEPPERY HOPS / CHOCOLATE

BELGIAN BROWN ALE STYLE

Fruity, a hint of sourness, big hop bouquets and chocolate maltiness spotlight the Old Brown ales. Some even have cherries and raspberries added and several are bottle conditioned.

BELGIAN BROWN ALE BREWERS

Clarysse Brouwerij
Krekelput 16-18, 9700 Oudenaarde

Cnudde Brouwerij
Fabriekstraat 8, 9700 Eine.
Het Anker Brouwerij
Guido Gezellaan 49, 2800 Mechelen

Liefman's Brouwerij
Aalstraat 200,
9700 Oudenaarde

Roman Brouwerij
Hauwaert 61,
9700 Mater

BELGIAN SOUR RED

When asked what the early London porters of the eighteenth and nineteenth centuries tasted like, in particular the well-matured old or 'stale' element in those beers, my advice is to go to West Flanders in Belgium and sample the sour red beers of that region; there is a powerful connection between this singular style of beer and the one that revolutionized brewing in England three centuries ago.

The leading brewer of sour red beer is Rodenbach in Roeselare. The beer is the result of long maturation in unlined oak tuns where it is allowed to stale from the action of wild yeasts and other microorganisms. The result is an exceptional beer, acidic, tannic, wonderfully refreshing and a great restorative. I approached my first-ever glass of Rodenbach in a restaurant in Ostend with great caution but was immediately captivated by its tart and quenching character. Now, despite the wealth of beer available in Belgium, I tend to choose a Rodenbach from a beer menu as the ideal way to begin a tasting or a meal.

The Rodenbachs are a remarkable family who came from Coblenz in Germany. In the eighteenth century Ferdinand Rodenbach was stationed in the Low Countries as a military surgeon when the region was under Austrian rule. He married a local girl in 1748 and decided to settle among the Flemish. His descendants threw themselves with impressive energy into all aspects of Belgian life, including the struggle for linguistic, cultural and political independence from the Dutch. In 1820 Alexander Rodenbach bought a small brewery in Roeselare, a remarkable business venture as he was blind. The brewery prospered following an extensive visit to England in the 1860s by Eugeen Rodenbach to study brewing techniques. His

experience encouraged him to develop the stale, aged beer that is the hallmark of the company today.

There has been considerable speculation concerning the breweries Eugeen visited in England. Some writers have suggested, without any historical support, that he must have gone to Greene King in Bury St

Copper brew kettles at Rodenbach where local Belgian hops from Poperinge are used for aroma: the brewer does not want too much bitterness.

The tiled tun is found in older breweries in the Low Countries. The taps allow the brewer to test the conversion of starch to sugar.

Open fermenters at Rodenbach. The brewery
will eventually carry out all fermentation in
enclosed conical vessels.

probably visited the brewery run by John
Barras, which was founded in Gateshead in
1770 and moved to Newcastle in 1860.
Barras, which later became part of the
Newcastle Breweries group, produced a
renowned porter that was stored for a full
twelve months in wooden tuns to ripen. As
the early porters were tawny or brown
rather than black, there is a possibility the
inspiration for Rodenbach's beer was
English porter.

An old malt kiln in the grounds has
become a fascinating museum, packed with
artefacts about brewing. Well water comes
from underground springs beneath a lake
on the other side of a road called
Spanjestraat, which means Spain Street,
emphasizing another link with the
complicated colonial past of the Low
Countries. The brewery's general manager
lives in some style in a château by the lake.

The brewhouse dates from the 1920s and
1930s: it had to be rebuilt after World War
I as the German army stripped the plant of
copper. It has some delightful Art Deco
flourishes and brass-railed staircases lead
from one level to another, taking in mash
kettles, lauter tuns amd brew kettles.
Rodenbach's beers are made from a blend of
pale malts, both spring and winter varieties,
and a darker Vienna 'red', similar to English
crystal malt, that gives them their distinctive reddish hue. The malts make up 88 per
cent of the grist, the rest coming from maize
grits: the maize reduces haze in the beer,
helps break down the starch in the malt and

Edmunds in Suffolk as eastern England and
West Flanders are geographically close and
the English company makes a Strong Suffolk
Ale that is a blend of two beers, one of
which is stored in unlined oak vats. But storing beers in this way was common in
England in the 1870s and Greene King has
no knowledge of a visit from Rodenbach.

After some prompting, the Rodenbach
Brewery looked into its records and told me
it thought Eugeen had gone not to Suffolk
but much further north 'near the border
between England and Scotland, where he
came across a brewing process that had a
third fermentation in which two beers were
blended'. My research suggests that he

Sweet and sour. . . beer is aged for at least 18
months in ten halls holding 300 giant, red-
hooped tuns.

The old malt house at Rodenbach is now used as a small museum.

at least eighteen months and as often for as long as two years.

The maturation halls are one of the wonders of the brewing world. There are more than ten halls housing 300 giant, red-hooped tuns that stand on raised brick bases. The smallest holds 120 hectolitres (2640 gallons), the biggest 600 (13,198 gallons). The staves of each tun are numbered and coopers are kept busy repairing the vessels. No nails are used and cracks in the wood are filled with wheat and beeswax. Some alcohol escapes through the wood. The insides of the tuns are regularly scraped to keep the correct balance of tannins and caramels in the oak. The scraping is carried out only when the deposit of micro-flora is enough to affect the taste of the beer. During the long rest in wood, lactobacilli and acetobacters are busy adding a sour, lactic quality to the beer. The regular beer, known as Classic (5 per cent alcohol), is a blend of young beer from the metal tanks and aged beer. It has a sour, winey aroma, is tart and quenching in the mouth, with more sour fruit in the finish. Grand Cru is 6.5 per cent alcohol and is bottled straight from the wooden tuns. It is bigger in all respects: oaky, tannic, sour and tartly fruity with a dash of iron in the finish. It is also a deeper

encourages a good fermentation. A decoction mashing regime is used, with portions of the mash pumped to a cooker where the temperature is raised to break down the starch and encourage conversion to maltose. Local hops from Poperinge are employed primarily for aroma: bitterness units are 12–16. The brewery does not want too high a level of bitterness, which would not marry well with the tartness of the beer. In this respect, the beers are at odds with English porter and old ale, which were highly hopped. A multi-strain, warm-fermenting yeast culture is used. It was thought to contain three strains but analysis at Leuven University's beer faculty revealed it contained as many as twenty.

Primary fermentation lasts for seven days in open, copper-lined vessels, followed by a second fermentation in metal tanks.

Conical fermenters are being introduced and will eventually be used for all primary fermentation. The beer destined to become the regular Rodenbach is ready to be bottled after six weeks, but the beer for ageing is stored in ceiling-high oak tuns for

BELGIAN SOUR RED STYLE

Sour, smoky, tannic and tartly fruity, with gentle hop bitterness, Sour Red ales are highly complex and vinous, and marvellously refreshing.

red in colour. Both beers have a curious note of nicotine on the nose while Grand Cru develops a smoky aroma as it warms up. The beers have some sugar added to take the extreme edge off the sourness. To mark 150 years of brewing, a version of Grand Cru was made with a dash of cherry essence to give the beer a delightfully tart and fruity character. It is labelled Alexander Rodenbach and is now produced on a regular basis. All the beers are flash pasteurized. The method of brewing and the enormous care and concern that goes into the long maturation make them world classics. But many devotees of the style would like the brewery to make a version of Grand Cru that is bottle conditioned and without sweetening.

The beers are not only superb companions for food but also make a formidable contribution to cooking. I had a memorable meal in Roeselare at the restaurant Den Haselt (Zuidstraat 19; tel 225240), which

Tuns of work…the inside of an oak vessel that is being cleaned and repaired. The tuns are regularly scraped to keep the correct levels of tannin and caramel in the wood.

Grand Cru is the finest beer from Rodenbach and is bottled straight from the wooden tuns.

specializes in cuisine à la bière and where every course is cooked with a version of Rodenbach. I was greeted with a Rodenbach cocktail and a starter of winkles and quiche. This was followed by salmon marinaded in Alexander, which was the accompanying beer. The main course was Dover sole with Grand Cru and a side dish of onions marinaded in Classic. For pudding I had strawberries and peach sorbet with Alexander and mint.

Rodenbach accounts for around 84 per cent of the sour red beer market. There is a handful of other red beer brewers in the region, though not all mature in wood. The Bavik-De Brabandere Brewery still has wood tuns and makes Petrus, while Bockor's Ouden Tripel also enjoys some time in wood.

WEST FLANDERS SOUR RED BREWERS

Bavik-De Brabandere
Rijksweg 16a, 8752 Bavikhove

Bockor Brouwerij
Kwabrugestraat 5, 8540 Bellegem

Leroy Brouwerij
Diksmuidesweg 406,
8930 Boezinge

Rodenbach Brouwerij
Spanjestraat 133, 880 Roeselare

Strubbe Brouwerij
Markt 1, 8270 Ichtegem

Van Honsebrouck Brouwerij
Oostrozebekestraat 43, 8770,
Ingelmunster

BIERE DE GARDE AND SAISON

The official name for the most northern area of France is the Nord-Pas de Calais but to the locals it is 'French Flanders'. Flanders may no longer exist officially but its name, history and heraldry maintain a powerful hold. There is a style of beer that crosses the notional border between French Flanders and Belgium, a style known as 'bière de garde' in France and 'saison' in Belgian Wallonia. They share a common root: beer brewed seasonally (*saison*) and to be kept or stored (*de garde*). They are warm-fermented ales and their origins are on farms in flatlands of rich, dark soil.

Farmers brewed their ales from locally grown cereals and hops. They were made in the winter for consumption during the summer when brewing was impossible and farm labourers needed refreshment as they engaged in the heavy work of the harvest. But they were drunk, too, by coal-miners in the pits around Lille in France (the ancient capital of Flanders) and the Borinage of Belgium. As the aim of the beer style was to restore lost energy, they tend to be full-bodied, mashed at high temperatures to leave unfermentable sugars in the brew and warm conditioned. They are often amber or copper coloured but there are paler interpretations as well. While they are brewed in French Flanders, neighbouring Artois and Picardy, they are almost unknown in Belgian Flanders: in Belgium they are restricted to the Hainaut area and other parts of Wallonia. They are brewed exclusively in French-speaking areas, though East Flanders has a similar style known as 'old brown' or 'provision beer' (see section on Belgian Brown Ales).

Every summer when the people of Douai stage a street festival, they celebrate with local beers. The two giant figures that lead the procession are called '*Les Enfants de*

A suitable beer. . .an ancient truck used to deliver and promote Ch'ti beers. The name is Picardian dialect and means 'c'est toi' – 'it suits you'.

Copper brewing vessels at the Castelain brewery are visible from the street in a small town once in the heart of the French mining industry.

Gayant' (the Giant's Children) and the name has been adopted by the local brewery, which brews a beer for the occasion called Gayant. Festivals in Douai, Lille and other towns and cities of the region have aroused considerable interest in local food and drink. When beers use local malts and hops they are allowed to use the appellation Pas-de-Calais/Région du Nord on their labels. An ancient hop-growing area straddles the French/Belgian border and is centred on Poperinge and Ypres.

The beer credited with reviving interest in bières de garde is Jenlain, brewed in a hamlet of the same name south-east of Valenciennes. The brewery started life on a farm. When sales of beer prospered, the farmer became a commercial brewer. Félix Duyck took over in 1922 and today Brasserie Duyck is run by his son Robert and grandson Raymond. Jenlain is sold in nine countries and production has grown from 20,000 to 90,000 hectolitres (439,994 to almost 2 million gallons) a year. It is a cult beer among the young in Lille, to such an extent that Duyck has bought its own specialist bar in the city, selling its full range of beers, at 43 Place de Rihour.

In spite of this considerable success, brewing remains firmly traditional, with mashing and boiling carried out in copper vessels. Malts from Flanders, Champagne and Burgundy are used along with four hop varieties from Belgium, France, Germany and Slovenia. Jenlain, 6.5 per cent, is a russet-coloured, spicy, malty ale of great depth with a long bitter-sweet finish. Some versions come in Champagne-style bottles with corks and wire cradles. Like most bières de gardes, Jenlain is now brewed all year round, but Duyck and several other brewers in the region have diversified into seasonal ales. Bière de Noël (6.8 per cent) is a malt-accented Christmas beer, while Printemps (6.5 per cent) is brewed in December and stored until March. Duyck has added a pale ale called Sebourg (6 per cent), named after a village whose brewery ceased production in the 1930s. The beers are stored for at least a month.

March or spring beers (*mars* or *printemps*) recall an ancient style that heralded the end of winter and the rebirth of the soil and its provender. Responsibility for recreating spring beers lies with the Ricour family who run the St-Sylvestre Brewery in the village of St-Sylvestre-Cappel between Steenvorde and Hazebrouck. In 1984, Pierre Ricour and his sons Serge and Christophe introduced a spring beer as an experiment. It has spawned dozens of similar ales throughout the region: it is now a familiar sight in the region to see the sign '*La bière de mars est arrivée*' — a playful leg-pull of the better-known annual arrival of Beaujolais Nouveau. The St-Sylvestre version is now called Bière Nouvelle, to signify the renewal of the spring. It is 6.5 per cent alcohol, is warm fermented and brewed from pale and Munich malts with the addition of 25 per cent wheat. It has a booming hop quality and enjoys a second fermentation in the bottle.

St-Sylvestre is best known today for 3 Monts. It was introduced a year after Bière Nouvelle when Serge and Christophe took full control of the plant, with its magnificent copper vessels, from their father. The beer

THE DOUAI GIANT

Gayant is a dialect word for giant: there are some 150 towns and villages in French Flanders that have giants, symbols of history, culture and industry. The Douai giant, dressed in a knight's military uniform, weighs 370 kilos (815 pounds) and is carried by six people. His wife is called Marie Cagenon and they have three children, Jacquot, Fillon and Bin-Bin. The giant was built in the sixteenth century to celebrate a victory over the French who had invaded Flanders. The natives of the Frisian islands in northern Germany claim that the famous King of Beer, Gambrinus, was the son of two giants who led an army of giant knights over the sea on dragons to Flanders where they overthrew the French to establish the Flemish kingdom. In fact, Flanders was created in the ninth century by Charles II, the Holy Roman Emperor, known as Charles the Bald.

The giants of Douai on parade during the town's annual festival.

celebrates three nearby hills, Mont Cassel, Mont des Cats and Mont Recollets. The golden ale is made from Pilsner-style pale malt and some brewing sugar with local Brewers Gold and German Tettnanger hops. It is fruity, clean and quenching, with a hint of sourness from the house yeast (each beer has a different yeast culture) and a stunning hop aroma and finish. It is filtered but not pasteurized. The brewery's standard and long-running 4 per cent ale is called Hop Country. The Ricours brothers have added a Christmas beer, malty and big-bodied, at 8 per cent, Bière des Templiers, a bottle-fermented, 8.5 per cent abbey-style ale, and La Gavroche, named after a character in Victor Hugo's *Les Miserables*. It is a bière rouge, between amber and brown in colour, is also 8.5 per cent and is bottle fermented.

These joyous ales can be drunk in L'Etoile du Jour in the village and in the fine restaurant Le Petit Bruxelles in nearby Cassel.

Brasserie Castelain at Bénefontaine, near Lens, is best known for its Ch'ti range of bières de garde. The name is Picardy dialect for '*c'est toi*' and means literally 'it suits you'. The brewery is part of a farm built in 1926 and was bought by the Castelain family in 1966. It is run with great enthusiasm today by Yves Castelain, who has had to find new markets for his beers following the decline of the local mining industry. The brewery, with gleaming copper vessels visible from the street, produces around 30,000 hecto-litres (659,908 gallons) a year. Yves Castelain uses Flemish and Gatinais barleys and has developed his own recipes for pale and amber versions of Ch'ti as well as Jade,

A serious beer with a gentle joke on the label: hills are rare in French Flanders.

The De Clerck brewery in Péronne has a long history dating back to 1774. The beers are based on old family recipes, and locally grown barley and hops add distinctive Flanders flavours.

brewed from organic malt and hops, Christmas and March beers, and an abbey-style, bottle-conditioned Sint Arnoldus, named after the patron saint of Flemish brewers. True to style, M. Castelain teases out malty and fruity aromas and flavours from his beers, while hops from Flanders and Bavaria are used with restraint. Around 10 per cent brewing sugar is added during the copper boil with hops. He uses a lager yeast but he ferments at an ale temperature of 15°C/59°F: lager yeast gives him greater control over production, he says. The beers are fermented for ten to twelve days and are then stored and conditioned for up to two months. The beers are filtered but not pasteurized. Ch'ti Blonde is made from four malts, the Brune from eight, including Munich, cara-Munich (a partially caramelized version), and torrefied or scorched malt. Both beers are 6.5 per cent alcohol: the blonde has a sweet, perfumy

Gone fishing...Colvert is the French for mallard and the pale and perfumy beer is popular with fishermen along the Somme.

malt character overlain by gentle citric fruit from the hops, while the Brune is rich, complex and biscuity with a powerful hint of raisins on the palate. The 4.6 per cent organic Jade has a good earthy and perfumy hop aroma, with sweet malt in the mouth and a fruity finish that becomes dry.

De Clerck has a long brewing record. Joannes De Clerck built a small brewhouse next to his farm in the village of Hendeghen, near Hazebrouck, in 1774. Members of the family moved to Peronne in 1928. As breweries in French Flanders were swallowed and closed by international giants, Michel De Clerck decided in the 1980s that survival lay in brewing distinctive traditional Flemish beers. He ransacked old family recipe books and used as far as possible locally grown barley and hops to make his full-flavoured and distinctive brands.

The small, cramped brewery, producing around 8000 hectolitres (175,975 gallons) a year, is in an old maltings, with ceilings so low that old copper kettles project through two floors. The beer that helped rebuild De Clerck's reputation is Pot Flamand, which means Flemish Jar or Mug. The 7 per cent amber beer is made from pale and darker Picardy malts with Belgian, Czech and French hop varieties. After primary fermentation, with a bottom-working yeast, the beer enjoys eight weeks' conditioning, known as *le temps de garde*. It is then filtered and bottled in wired and corked Champagne bottles. Pot Flamand is also sold under the name La Belle Siska: *siska* is a dialect word that stems from the Latin-derived *cervoise*, French for ale. De Clerck's biggest-selling brand is another 7 per cent bière de garde, a blonde Colvert made with pale malts and a big perfumy hop character from Czech Saaz. 'Colvert' is French for mallard and the label shows a duck and a fisherman, making it a popular beer among the

De Clerck's La Fanette has a bucolic label that recalls the time when bières de garde were brewed to refresh agricultural labourers.

It chimes with the times …L'Angelus from Brasserie d'Annouellin is a wheat beer with a massive tangerine aroma and flavour from hops and the house yeast.

fanatical fisherfolk who line the banks of the River Somme.

The connection between farming and brewing is exemplified by Brasserie d'Annouellin, where the beers are fermented in horizontal tanks in cellars that were once used as cattle byres. The small, spick-and-span town of Annouellin lies between Lens and Lille and its farm-brewery, with its own hop garden, was founded in 1905 by the Lepers family. The present fifth-generation owner of the brewery, Bertrand Lepers, is married to Yvonne, who comes from a farm-brewery at Flers. In the small brewhouse the mash tun doubles as the copper, a typical feature of brewing in French Flanders and Wallonia; after the wort has been clarified it is pumped back to the kettle for boiling with hops. Primary fermentation lasts a week, followed by two weeks of conditioning. M. Lepers gets fresh supplies of bottom-working yeast every week from the large commercial Jean d'Arc brewery. Local malts and hops are used: the

hops no longer come from the brewery's own bines. The beers are dry to taste, mirroring M. Lepers' own humour, best seen in the original label for his bière de garde, Pastor Ale, which carried the tag line '*C'est une symphonie*'. But commercial overuse of Beethoven's music, in particular the crude rendition of the *Ode to Joy* as the anthem of the European Union, made the beery joke seem stale and it was dropped. Pastor Ale nevertheless remains a most

harmonious beer, an ode to joyous drinking. It is 6.5 per cent alcohol and is brewed using just pale malt: M. Lepers avoids brewing sugar. The beer has a burnished gold colour, pronounced orange fruit and spicy hops on the nose, more tangy fruit in the mouth and a big, dry, fruity and hoppy finish. Flemish hops are used for bitterness, Czech Saaz for aroma. A 7.3 per cent L'Angelus, with a painting by Millais on the label, is even more outstanding. It is a wheat bière de garde (bière de froment) and uses 30 per cent buck wheat in flour form. L'Angelus is bronze coloured and has a powerful citric tangerine aroma backed by spicy hops, with more tart fruit in the mouth and a long, bitter-sweet finish. With its pronounced orange fruit character, it is the Grand Marnier of the beer world. The beers are filtered but not pasteurized.

Any marginal difference between Wallonian Saisons and French/Flemish bières de garde disappears at the Café Restaurant au Baron in Gussignies.

Rakes inside the mash tun at d'Annouellin. The vessel also acts as the copper.

Gussignies is in Hainaut, but it is French Hainaut, hard by the Belgian border. The Bailleux family who own the restaurant and bar (open only at weekends) also brew on the premises and it stresses its proximity to the border by producing beers called both bière de garde and Saison. The beers are brewed by Roger Bailleux, who worked for a large brewing group before building his own small plant in 1989. He uses four malts with Flemish Brewers Gold hops augmented by such Bavarian varieties as Hallertauer, Hersbrucker and Spalt. When I first met M. Bailleux at a presentation in Lille, I was intrigued by his delightful golden bière de garde called Cuvée de Jonquilles. The 7 per cent beer is both flowery and fruity but, despite its name, it is not brewed using daffodils. It is a spring beer and the flowering of the daffodil is a potent symbol of the annual renewal as winter fades. Saison Saint Médard, also 7 per cent, has a rich cherry colour and a fruity aroma not unlike a Belgian kriek but without the lambic sourness. There is full-bodied malt in the mouth and the finish is tart, fruity and dry. Cuvée de Noël started life as a Christmas beer but is now available all year round. It has a delightful spicy, chocolate character from hops and malt. The beers are unfiltered and bottle conditioned and will improve with cellar ageing. M. Bailleux uses true top-working yeasts: it is sad to find so many brewers of bières de garde using lager yeasts, albeit while fermenting at ale temperatures.

The relative obscurity of Wallonian Saisons compared to Franco-Flemish bières de garde has encouraged the practitioners of the style to remain true to tradition. These are more bucolic and less commercial beers, often made in rustic brewhouses. There is no tinkering with lager yeasts: these are true ales made by warm fermentation and top-working yeasts. When farmer-brewers were

Above: Les Brasseurs in Lille is a brew-pub that offers a wide range of warm-fermenting ales.

Below: Border-line case...Bailleux's beers are called both bière de garde and Saisons.

172

a more powerful force in Wallonia, they produced a wide range of Saisons, including weak beer for children and family beers. Sometimes a double mashing at two temperatures and multi-strain yeasts that did not convert all malt sugars to alcohol led to full-bodied and full-flavoured ales that enjoyed a second fermentation either in cask or bottle. Often spices and other cereals such as oats and wheat were used. Today's Saisons are more refined but they are liberally hopped, warm fermented and bottle conditioned.

The classic Saison brewer today is Dupont, based on a farm with its own spring at Tourpes, about twenty minutes' drive from Tournai. The brewery was founded in 1850 and has been run by the Duponts since the 1920s. Marc Rosier, grandson of the original Duponts, is now in charge with his sisters. The small, charming, steam-filled brewhouse, with the mash tun doubling as the copper, produces 5–6000 hectolitres (110–132,000 gallons) a year. Pale and caramalts with Kent Goldings and Styrian hops are used. The 6.5 per cent Saison is

The art of the brewer for the pleasure of the gourmand, says the label from Lille's brew-pub.

called Vieille Provision: 'Old Provision' is a term that dates from the time when stored seasonal beers were an important part of the nutrition and diet of farmers, their families and workers. The beer has an intense peppery hoppiness from the generous use of East Kent Goldings, a hazy golden colour and a dense head when poured. Avec Les Bons Voeux de la Brasseries is quite a mouthful: it gives you the best wishes of the brewery. It is a 9.2 per cent Christmas ale

bursting with hops and citric fruit. Dupont also produces beers under the Moinette label. The name comes from Marc Rosier's own farm on the site of a former abbey. '*Moine*' is French for monk and the 'little monk' beers are both 8.5 per cent, a blonde and a brune. The pale version is hoppy, aromatic, the brown fruity and sweet. There are also organic versions of some of the beers: Moinette Biologique and Saison Dupont Biologique.

La Brasserie à Vapeur, the Steam Brewery, in the village of Pipaix, dates from 1785 and uses equipment from the 1920s, though much of the original copper was stripped by German forces during World War II. In a large building that looks more like a farm outhouse than a brewery, the antiquated brewing vessels are on two floors, with a cast-iron mash tun with a wooden surround and coppers also made of cast iron. The plant is powered by a coal-fired steam engine. The brewery closed in 1984 and was reopened by two local schoolteachers, Jean-Louis and Anne-Marie Dits, who started brewing as much out of their fascination with Wallonian

At Les Brasseurs customers can get a sample tray holding small tasting glasses with the full range of the house beers.

Hard-nosed, not daft...the Silly Brewery
promotes its beers with the aid of old
trucks and vans.

industrial archaeology as beer. Anne-Marie was killed in an accident in the brewery but Jean-Louis has soldiered on, brewing only at weekends. He makes a 6.5 per cent Saison de Pipaix spiced with anis, black pepper, medicinal lichen and other 'botanicals'. The beer is spicy with a pronounced orange fruitiness. There are also two 8 per cent beers, Vapeur Rouge and Vapeur en Folie. After fermentation, the beers are conditioned for three weeks, then primed with sugar in the bottle and warm conditioned for up to a month. The Rousse, which includes ginger, has a russet colour, a hoppy, orange fruit aroma, and is tart, slightly vinous and sour in the mouth.

The Silly Brewery causes amusement to English speakers but it merely takes its name from the village in which it stands, which in turn is named after the local river, the Sil. It is a farm-brewery dating from the 1850s. It was founded by Nicholas Meynsbrughen and is still owned by his descendants. Saison Silly is brewed from French malts with Belgian caramalt for colour, and English Goldings hops. In the cramped brewhouse the mash tun also acts as a hop back: the wort is pumped back to the tun for filtration after the copper boil. Fermentation lasts for a slow fifteen days in small conical vessels using an ale yeast, and the beers are then conditioned in tanks for two weeks. The Saison is copper-coloured with peppery hops and winey fruit on the nose, dark fruits in the mouth and a dry and hoppy finish. Silly also brews pale and brown saisons under the name of Double Enghien, a Silly Scotch in the style of Scotch ales exported to Belgium, and a well-named Divine (9.5 per cent), described as an 'artisanal beer' with a big peppery hop aroma, hops and dark fruit in the mouth and a bitter fruit and hops finish.

The Du Bocq brewery in the village of Purnode, near Namur, brews a highly regarded 6.1 per cent Saison Regal. La Binchoise is a new micro-brewery in the old

La Binchoise in the old
walled town of Binche
brews a honey beer
that uses 60 kilos (132
pounds) of honey for
each brew.

walled town of Binche near the industrial city of Charleroi. It does not claim to brew a Saison but several of its products are strictly-seasonal, including a 9 per cent Christmas Beer, with a vast spicy hop aroma with orange fruit in the mouth and on the finish, a 5 per cent festival beer, an 8.5 per cent honey beer (Bière au Miel) with 60 kilos (132 pounds) of honey per brew after the boil. The 9 per cent Marie is named in honour of Marie de Hongrie (Hungary), sister of Charles V, the sixteenth-century Holy Roman Emperor who was also king of Burgundy and the Low Countries.

The strongest beer in the whole of Belgium comes from Wallonia. The Bush Brewery is in Pipaix, in the heart of the Saison brewing area. It is a former farm, its attractive green-shuttered buildings fronting the main road to Mons. Bush Beer is a mighty 12 per cent alcohol: it would be classified as a barley wine in Britain, and while it is not labelled as a Saison its origins are rooted in the style. The brewery is owned by the Dubuisson family: *buisson* is French for bush. The brewery was founded in 1769 and the name of the beer was anglicized in 1933 as a result of the popularity of English ales at the time in Belgium. Annual production today is around 15,000 hectolitres (329,954 gallons). The amber-coloured, warm-fermented beer is made from pale and caramalts with Styrian and Kent Goldings hops. The Goldings dominate aroma and palate along with delicious vinous fruit, and nuts from the darker malt. Bush Beer has 42 units of bitterness. Primary fermentation lasts a week in enclosed vessels and the beer is then cold conditioned for four to six weeks. Dubuisson also brews a darker version for Christmas with an aroma like Dundee cake, with rich sultana fruit in the mouth and a big winey finish.

The attractive façade of Dubuisson, brewers of Bush Beer, another brewery that started life on a farm.

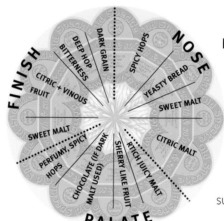

BIERE DE GARDE AND SAISON STYLE

Rich malt, perfumy hops, tart fruit, and chocolate and nuts from darker malt are the highlights of a style fermented at a warm temperature to leave some unfermented sugars in the brew.

BIERE DE GARDE AND SAISON BREWERS

Brasserie d'Annouellin
4 Place du Général de Gaulle,
59112 Annouellin, France

Brasserie Bailleux
Café-Restaurant Au Baron,
Place de Fond des Rocs, Gussignies,
59570 Bavay, France

Brasserie Castelain
13 rue Louis Pasteur, Bénefontaine,
62410 Wingles, France

Brasserie Dubuissomn
Chaussée de Mons 28, 7904
Pipaix, Belgium

Brasserie Dupont
Rue Basse 5, 7911 Tourpes-Leuze, Belgium

Brasserie Duyck
113 rue Nationale, 59144 Jenlian, France

Brasserie Saint Sylvestre
1 rue de la Chappelle, 59114
Saint-Sylvestre-Cappel, France

Brasserie de Silly
Ville Bass A141, 7830 Silly, Belgium

Brasserie à Vapeur
Rue de Marechal 1,
7904 Pipaix, Belgium

LAGER BREWING

The word 'lager' is German and means 'to store' or a storage place. In German-speaking countries or those, such as the Czech Republic, where German was once widely used, lager is a term in the brewing process, the period of cold conditioning and maturation. The word is not used to describe a style, and the results of cold fermentation are sold as beer, bier, bière or, in the Slavic languages, variations on the word *pivo*.

To watch classic lager brewing at first hand, I went to the Staropramen (Old Spring) Brewery in Prague. Since the fall of communism, the British brewing group Bass has bought a large stake in the brewery and has declared its intention to remain true to

traditional brewing methods. A new brewhouse was added in 1997 but it was modelled along the lines of the two existing brewhouses. Staropramen was built in the 1870s and the two older brewhouses were designed in 1930 and 1968. The brewing regime remains unchanged and, crucially, lagering will continue to be in horizontal vessels to maintain the full, rich, bitter-sweet character of the beer.

Mashing is a double decoction system. This method is traditionally used in Germany and central Europe because in the last century the quality of barley was poorer than in Britain and maritime Europe. A longer and more exhaustive mashing regime countered quality problems, in

A classic lager brewery in Alloa, Scotland, modelled on the Dutch style.

particular high levels of nitrogen in the barley that would cause the finished beer to be cloudy. Lager malt is also less 'modified': this means the conversion of starch to fermentable sugar has not progressed as far during the malting stage as in malt prepared for ale brewing. The decoction system gives the enzymes a better opportunity to continue starch conversion; in effect, it completes the malting process.

At Staropramen the malt grist is mixed with soft brewing liquor in a mash kettle at 32°C/90°F. The temperature is raised to 52°C/125°F, at which temperature protein in the cereal starts to break down. A third of the mash is then pumped to a second vessel called the mash cooker. The temperature is raised to 65°C/149°F: this is the temperature, whether in infusion or decoction mashing, at which saccharification takes place, the final conversion of starch to sugar. The temperature is held at 65°C/149°F to allow conversion, then it is raised to 70°C/158°F, which is too high for the enzymes to work and saccharification stops. This portion of the mash is then boiled to remove fatty acids and is returned to the original kettle where it raises the temperature of the whole mash to 65°C/149°F. Starch conversion now proceeds in the kettle. Another third of the mash is pumped to the cooker and goes through the same procedure before being returned to the kettle. The final third of the mash doesn't leave the kettle and is therefore not boiled; this helps to give fullness and sweetness to the beer, a hallmark of Czech brewing.

The entire mashing regime lasts for four hours. Each time the temperature of the mash is raised, it remains at that level for twenty minutes. These 'stand times' help to remove nitrogen from the mash. Finally, the entire mash is pumped to yet another vessel, the lauter tun, which has revolving rakes and a slotted base. The mash is clarified as the sugar-rich liquid, now known as wort, percolates out through the base through the spent grains. The wort is pumped to the brew kettles where it is boiled with Saaz whole flower hops for two hours. The hops are added in three stages, the final one at the end of the boil.

The hopped wort is cooled in heat-exchange units and pumped to open square fermenting vessels. Staropramen has a total of 140 such vessels. The yeast is pitched when the temperature of the wort is 8°C/46°F. During fermentation, it rises to

Original mashing and boiling vessels at Staropramen in Prague. An exhaustive decoction mashing regime is used to ensure there is a full conversion of malt starches to fermentable sugar. The system involves mash kettles, mash tuns and lauter tuns and takes up to four hours. The sweet extract is then boiled for two hours with Saaz whole cone hops.

11.5°C/52°F after three days. To prevent off
flavours developing if the temperature is too
high, the wort is cooled by cold (2°C/35°F)
water running though coils inside the
fermenters. The temperature is maintained
at 4°C/39°F for seven days and then transferred to the lager cellars.

Staropramen has 700 lagering tanks. The
premium beer, called 12 degrees, using the
Czech Balling system of measuring the
strength of alcohol, is lagered for seventy-
five days at 2°C/35°F. During this period, a
slow second fermentation takes place, with
the yeast turning most of the remaining sugars into alcohol and carbon dioxide. The
production of CO_2 is important: during the
first couple of weeks in the lager tanks some
of the CO_2 is allowed to escape, taking with
it unwanted rough flavours and chemical
esters known as volatiles. For the remainder
of the lagering period, the CO_2 is retained
within the tanks to condition the beer.
When the second fermentation is finished,
the beer then matures, with the yeast and
protein settling to the bottom of the tanks.
If the brewer is not satisfied that a sufficiently vigorous second fermentation is
taking place, he will kräusen the beer: this
is a German expression and means adding
some sugar-rich, partially fermented wort
to the lager tanks for the yeast to feed on.

In the manner of traditional Bavarian and
Bohemian lager breweries, the lagering tanks
at Staropramen are placed horizontally. In
most modern breweries it is now the custom
to ferment and lager in upright conical

*Left: the new brewhouse at Staropramen, built in
1997 uses the same process as the older
brewhouses. No corners are cut to ensure
consistency of flavour in the finished beer.*

Horizontal fermentation vessels at Staropramen …the brewers say the position is vital to ensure a slow second fermentation that leaves some sugars in the beer for 'body' and flavour.

vessels. The difference is crucial to the character of the finished beer. Steve Denny, a micro-biologist from Bass who has been seconded to Staropramen, told me that in horizontal vessels the second fermentation is slow and not all the sugars are turned to alcohol, which leaves fullness, body and some sweetness in the beer. In conical vessels, the yeast is caught up in currents that rise and fall, temperature is less stable, secondary fermentation is faster and more of the sugars turn to alcohol. The beer is 'fully attenuated'. Staropramen, by its attention to detail and dedication to traditional methods, is determined to maintain the true aroma and flavour of Czech beer.

Branik, with Staropramen, is a member of the Prague Breweries group. Its 10 degree beer is typical of everyday, quaffing lagers. Premium beers are stronger at 12 degrees.

PILSNER

n February 1838 thirty-six barrels of beer were poured down the drain in the main square of Pilsen, the great industrial powerhouse of Bohemia. The beer had been declared unfit for consumption and its public despatch heralded changes in brewing in Pilsen that were to reverberate around the world. Tavern owners banded together to build a new brewery, one that would embrace the new technologies developed in Munich in neighbouring Bavaria.

The Burghers' Brewery, as it was first known, was built in the suburb of Bubenc, which had a good supply of soft spring water, and sandstone foundations ideal for digging cellars in which to store beer. The raw ingredients were readily available: fine malting barley from Bohemia and Moravia with aromatic hops from the Zatec region. The burghers employed one of the leading architects of the day, Martin Stelzer, to design their new brewery. He may have played a major role in the style of beer that emerged from the brewery in 1842 and was first sold at the Martinmas Fair on 11 November. Stelzer visited several breweries at the forefront of new brewing technology and steam power in other European countries and based his Pilsen plant on the results of his research. He also brought back to Pilsen with him Joseph Groll, a young but experienced brewer from Vilshofen in Bavaria who was well versed in the skills of lager brewing.

Groll was a rough, ill-mannered man but he could brew good beer. His instructions from his new employers in Pilsen were simple: brew beer by the new lager method, ensure it was of sound quality and make it as different as possible from the popular Bavarian lagers. What he produced in 1842 astonished and delighted drinkers in Pilsen.

It was a golden beer, the first such type ever seen, for the lagers brewed in Munich were deep brown in colour. The theory in Pilsen is that the wrong sort of malt was supplied to Groll but this seems fantastic: if an experienced brewer does not like the malt he is given, he will change it. It is much more likely that Groll deliberately set out to brew a paler beer than the Bavarian style. To achieve that aim he would have needed a malt kiln fired by coke rather than wood to dry and cure his malt. The only known country to use coke-fired kilns by the 1830s and 1840s was England, which had pioneered the production of pale beer with India Pale Ale. Did Martin Stelzer import a coke-fired kiln from England for the Burghers' Brewery that produced a far paler malt than Groll was used to, enabling him to meet his employers' request for a distinctive new beer? He would have been helped

The Burghers' Brewery in Pilsen shortly after it was opened in the 1840s. It is possible that the pale gold of its beer was achieved by using coke-fired malt kilns in the English style.

by the high quality of Moravian malt, which is low in nitrates and thus helps the clarity of the beer, the extremely soft water of Pilsen and generous levels of Zatec hops. At the Pilsner Urquell Brewery they point out that Pilsner malt is kilned at 82–84°C (179–183°F), while traditionally the malts for pale lagers in Munich and Vienna are cured at a slightly higher temperature,

resulting in beers that are bronze or amber.

The beer from the Burghers' Brewery was a sensation. It coincided with mass-produced glass that encouraged a demand from drinkers for clear beers rather than the cloudy ones hidden inside pewter or leather tankards. The clarity of the beer from Pilsen was the result of the long and careful extraction of sugars from the malt, and the yeast

The entrance to the Burghers' Brewery in Pilsen ...triumphal Napoleonic arches typify the pride and pomp of the mid-nineteenth century.

used for fermentation, presumably brought by Groll from Vilshofen. The cleanness, refreshing nature and clarity of the beer entranced drinkers while its deep complexity – malty, hoppy and bitter-sweet –

appealed to a wider audience than those reached by darker beers. Its reputation spread like a bush fire and supplies were soon leaving by canal boats and the new railway network to all areas of the Austro-Hungarian Empire, of which Bohemia at the time was a part. A Pilsner Beer Train left every day for Vienna. The beer became a cult drink in Berlin and Paris, and it reached Hamburg and the other cities of northern Germany via the River Elbe. By 1874 Pilsner beer had arrived in the US and lager brewing began to challenge the hegemony of ale introduced by the Founding Fathers.

It was the Austrian connection and the widespread use of German in Bohemia that gave the beer its name. Pilsner means 'from Pilsen', just as a Frankfurter comes from Frankfurt, a Hamburger from Hamburg and a Budweiser beer from Budweis. In the Czech Republic the term Pilsner can, logically, apply only to beer brewed in its town of origin: it is an appellation. But the rest of the world was not so meticulous. Brewers, encouraged by public demand, rushed to make pale lagers which they called Pilsner, more usually Pilsener, or just Pils for short. In 1898 the Burghers' Brewery registered the name of its beer as Pilsner Urquell, meaning 'Original Source Pilsner' in German (the Czech rendition is Plzensky Prazdroj). The documents referred to the 'absurdity and illogicality of using the word "Pilsner" for beers brewed in towns outside of Pilsen'. The neighbouring Germans played fair, developed often brilliant interpretations of the style and included the town of origin on their labels: hence Bitburger, Krombacher and Warsteiner Pils. These brewers shortened Pilsner to Pils to avoid any suggestion their beers came from Pilsen. But in most parts of the world, Pilsner became a bowdlerized beer, often low in alcohol, brewed with inferior ingredients such as corn and

rice, and with low levels of hops. They say in Pilsen today, 'We are the only brewers of Pilsners – others brew pale lagers'. The Burghers' Brewery became the biggest brewery in the Austro-Hungarian Empire. In 1913 it brewed more than 1 million hectolitres (220,000 gallons).

In 1868 a second brewery had been built in the city. The engineering company Skoda was one of the main investors in what was

called the First Shareholders' Brewery, later changed to Gambrinus. It was followed by the Pilsen Corporate Brewery in 1892 (later Prior), and finally the Czech Pilsen Brewery was opened in 1910. Mergers led to the eventual closure of the last two companies. The Burghers' Brewery and Gambrinus

An early manual machine for filling bottles in Pilsen.

themselves merged in 1935 and are now part of the same privatized group following the end of communism. In spite of the fame of the brand, the Burghers' Brewery did not formally change the company name to Pilsner Urquell until the 1950s. By 1996 the company was brewing more than 4 million hectolitres (880,000 gallons) and exporting to 58 countries.

When I first visited Pilsner Urquell in the mid-1980s, I was immediately aware that this was a rare place, with nineteenth-century bourgeois pride and pomp uncontained by the drabness of communism. I entered through the great Napoleonic triumphal arches of the main gate. At the end of the long thoroughfare beyond the gate stood a glass-covered building reminiscent of a British railway terminus. Beyond that was a water-tower almost Moorish in design as if calling the bibulous to prayer; it was built in the 1920s and modelled on a Dutch watch-tower. The most fascinating sight, however, was the giant oak lagering casks in the brewery courtyard. In strict rotation, the casks were brought up from deep sandstone cellars that stretched for six miles beneath Pilsen to be relined with pitch. The brewery had 3500 lagering casks, each holding between 30 to 35 hectolitres (660 to 770 gallons). The pitch sealed the wood and ensured that wild yeasts did not infect the beer. The richness, the mellowness, the dash of wood and vanilla in the finished beer owed something to being stored in oak for seventy days.

Since proper records started to be kept in 1927, Pilsner Urquell has not changed its colour rating, bitterness, pH or level of attenuation, according to the brewery. But the fermentation process has changed out

of all recognition in the 1990s, and some lovers of the beer feel it has been diminished as a result. The mashing regime, however, is unaltered. Pilsner Urquell uses the most exhaustive system known, a triple decoction mash. There are two rows of polished copper kettles and lauter tuns. Pilsner malt is poorly modified. It is boiled three times at progressively higher temperatures, with the mash pumped from one cooker to another. This allows the enzymes in the malt the opportunity to attack the starch and turn it into fermentable sugar. The company believes the method of mashing to be

An Art Deco touch was used to promote Pilsen's most famous beer in the 1920s.

A steam engine once used to power the brewery is still on view at Pilsner Urquell.

inextricably linked to the taste of the beer and imparts a slight hint of toasted grain. The sweet wort that results from the long mashing procedure is clarified in a lauter tun, then boiled three times with Zatec hops. The copper boil lasts for around two and a half hours: most breweries consider ninety minutes sufficient but at Pilsner Urquell they consider the length of the boil aids the clarity of the beer and wards off infection. In the old days the hopped wort was then pumped to small open fermenting vessels made of Bavarian oak. Astonishingly, the brewery used five variations of its yeast strain, each one employed in different vessels, their contents later blended. Primary fermentation, in a vast, dimly lit room, was at 4–6°C (39–43°F). The unfinished beer was then transferred to the sandstone lagering cellars and matured there for seventy days at 0–3°C (32–37°F). The beer that emerged from this long and painstaking process was without question one of the great classics of world brewing. It was 4.4 per cent alcohol by volume, with 40 units of bitterness, high by lager standards. But the rich juicy malt and buttery aroma and palate of the beer countered the extreme bitterness of the hops, though it finally became dry in the finish.

Pilsner Urquell had remained true to methods of brewing that some might call quaint as a result of the long years of benign neglect by the communist regime. Once the free market replaced communism, feverish activity transformed the Pilsen brewery. Since 1993, 3.6 billion Czech crowns, raised mainly from banks, has been pumped into the brewery. The aim has been to produce more beer and to speed up fermentation, the first a laudable aim, the second one more dubious. The wooden vessels have been sidelined and both primary fermentation and lagering now take place in upright

Bring your prayer mats. . .the water tower at Pilsner Urquell is based on a Dutch design but looks almost Moorish in character. It provides soft liquor that is a vital element in the taste.

One of the brewhouses at Pilsner Urquell. The triple decoction mashing regime is one of the most exhaustive in the world of lager brewing.

Old oak vessels that were used for primary fermentation at Pilsner Urquell. They have been sidelined in favour of conical stainless-steel vessels.

conical vessels made of stainless steel. There are 104 fermentation tanks in a new complex at the brewery. Those used for primary fermentation hold 1800 hectolitres (39,594 gallons) of beer each while the lagering vessels each contain 3300 hectolitres (72,590 gallons). Fermentation is faster: primary lasts twelve days and lagering twelve weeks maximum, less in summer when demand for beer is greater.

As Pilsner Urquell acknowledges, fermentation is faster in upright vessels than horizontal ones. In traditional horizontal tanks, the yeast slowly nibbles away at the remaining sugars, turning them into alcohol, while the beer purges itself of rough, unwanted flavours. There is far greater activity in a conical vessel, with beer and yeast caught in great surges and currents of activity. The yeast hungrily attacks malt sugars, resulting in a higher level of attenuation, more alcohol and a dryer and more bitter beer. The brewery has had to tinker with hop levels to avoid the beer becoming too bitter and controls the level of attenuation with temperature adjustments to the fermenting vessels. Only two of the five yeast strains are now used.

No brewery can remain in a time warp. But change must go arm-in-arm with traditional values. Pilsner Urquell claims that it spent a year matching the flavour of the beer before going over to full conical production. The beer is still magnificent, a joy to drink. But a lot of the complexity has gone. It is more austere, firm-bodied, with greater hop aroma and flavour. Some of the softness of the malt has disappeared, making it more Germanic than Czech in character. At the brewery they proudly call Pilsner Urquell the Champagne of the beer world; the worry is that it could become yet another Sauvignon Blanc or Chardonnay of the beer world.

It's that duke again….…Gambrinus from Brabant graces the label of Pilsen's other brewery.

GAMBRINUS

The First Shareholders' Brewery in Pilsen changed its name to Gambrinus to distinguish itself from neighbouring Pilsner Urquell. The name Gambrinus is used by several breweries world-wide and is a corruption of Jan Primus, the legendary Duke Jean I of Brabant in the thirteenth century, whose prodigious drinking bouts earned him the title of 'King of Beer'.

Gambrinus of Pilsen never brewed in wood. The original brewhouse used cream-painted cast-iron kettles. Fermentation was in open cast-iron vessels and lagering in horizontal tanks. In the 1980s the copper vessels were replaced by stainless steel but now the entire Gambrinus brewing operation has been closed following its merger with Pilsner Urquell and the symbolic dismantling of the wall that separated the two breweries.

Gambrinus beers are now produced in the Pilsner Urquell plant, with a double decoction mash rather than the triple used for its former rival, with fermentation and lagering in the new conicals. Malt and hops are identical to Urquell's: local Bohemian and Moravian malts and Zatec hops. The Gambrinus yeast strain has been retained to ensure the same taste characteristics. Gambrinus 12 degree beer is 4.5 per cent alcohol by volume and has 33 units of bitterness. It has a delightful aroma reminiscent of fresh-mown grass, a more delicate bitterness than Pilsner Urquell's and a malty/hoppy finish that becomes dry. Twelve degree beers in the Czech Republic indicate both premium quality and strength; they are all-malt beers that can be sold in Germany as they meet the Reinheitsgebot or Purity Laws.

PILSNER STYLE

Complex aromas of sweet, slightly toasted malt, aromatic hops, a quenching palate and a long, lingering finish packed with malt and bitter hops personify the classic beers of Pilsen.

PILSNER AND PRAGUE BREWERS	
Pilsner Urquell/Gambrinus U Prazdroje 7, 30497 Pilsen, Czech Republic	**Prague Breweries (Staropramen)** Nazdrazni 84, 150 54 Prague 5-Smichov
Pilsen is rendered 'Plzen' in Czech.	

BUDWEISER

I made my first pilgrimage to Czechoslovakia in the mid-1980s in search of some of the world's most revered lager beers. However, the Czech communist authorities were not enamoured with the description of 'journalist' on my visa application. As a result, the much delayed visa was granted just in time for a desperate dash to the airport. I was delayed at Prague airport and my travails were not over when I rang the bell at the Branik brewery – I was chased away by a guard with a machine gun. Eventually things did improve and I went to Pilsner Urquell in Prague where I interviewed a nervous manager and was escorted round the brewery and its lagering cellars. But I did not get to see the Budweiser Budvar brewery. It was off limits, closed to the public, a state secret. It brewed beer but most of it, as the Minister for Overseas Trade told me, was for export, in order to earn the people's republic much needed hard western currency. I was determined to unravel the mystery and history of Budweiser beer and learn why an American beer of the same name dominated world sales.

Anheuser-Busch, the American brewer of Budweiser, claims in advertisements and promotions that its beer is the original. Yet long before it was first brewed in St Louis, Missouri, in 1876, Budweiser had become an appellation for beers brewed in and around Ceské Budejovice, a town best known by its old German name of Budweis. The south Bohemian town close to the Austrian border was founded in 1265 by Otakar II. Soft water from a deep underground lake, sweet Moravian malt and aromatic Zatec hops combined to make beers of exceptional quality in the town. By the fifteenth century there were forty-four breweries in Budweis. In 1547 King Ferdinand I summoned a Budweis brewer

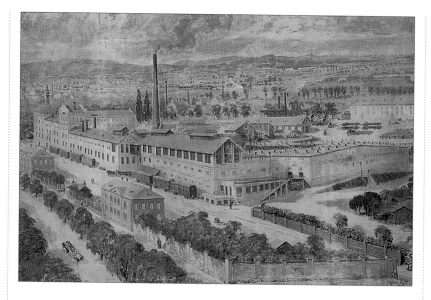

to make beer for him, allowing the brewer to call his company the Royal Court Brewery of Bohemia and enabling all brewers in the town to bask in the shadow of 'the beer of kings'. When Bohemia became part of the Austro-Hungarian empire, beers from the town were given the generic name of 'Budweiser'.

By the time of the Industrial Revolution,

Budweis, now Ceské Budejovice, home to the Budejovicky Pivovary, shortened to Budvar, seen here at the turn of the century.

Beer mornings...the soft velvety and vanilla character of Budvar made it popular with women drinkers.

most of the small house breweries in Budweis had disappeared, replaced by larger concerns that had embraced refrigeration and cold fermentation. Two breweries came to dominate the town, a reflection of ethnic rivalry between Czech- and German-speakers. In 1795 the Velky (Great) and Maly (Small) breweries merged and became known as the Citizens' Brewery. It came under the control of German-speakers, who translated Citizens' Brewery into Bürgerbräu, and moved to a new site in 1847. According to a history of Czech breweries published in Brno in 1994:

'The Citizens' Brewery ranked from the outset among the foremost breweries and exported beer not only to a number of European countries but also to America. The quality of the "Budweiser" beer brewed and exported is attested by numerous awards at exhibitions at home and abroad. In 1882 the brewery had several trade marks registered.

A brewer at the Samson Brewery in Ceské Budejovice tests the quality of the sweet extract from the mash tuns. Samson was originally called the Citizens' Brewery and labelled its beers 'Budweiser'.

"Budweiser Export Lager Bier" and "Budweiser Export Bier", with the commercial appellation Budweiser Bürgerbräu, may be regarded as the most important.'

It was the considerable success in domestic and world markets by the Citizens' Brewery and its Budweiser beers that prompted a group of Czech-speaking businessmen to launch a rival brewery in the town in 1895. It was called the Budejovicky

Lift that bail...the beers from Budweis were not just meant for townees but also refreshed rural workers who harvested the grain essential for beer making.

Pivovary – literally, the Budweis Brewery. The beer was sold simply as 'Budvar', a contraction of the commercial name, for domestic sales, but exports were more firmly labelled 'Budweiser Budvar' to stress the historic link with the great brewing town. The label on Budvar exported to the United States early this century and distributed by Paul Ostruk of 120 West 42nd Street, New York City, declared it was 'Imported Original Bohemian Budweiser Beer from Budweis City'.

As the century progressed and animosity grew between Czech- and German-speakers in the new Czechoslovak Republic, the Citizens' Brewery changed its name to Samson and used that name for its beers. Budvar became the sole user of the term Budweiser. Under communism, Budvar was a remarkably spick-and-span plant compared to other run-down and under-capitalized breweries in old Czechoslovakia. The reason was simple if cynical: in order to win export sales and hard currency, the communist government had invested considerable sums in Budvar to allow it to expand. In the late 1980s it was producing around 250,000 barrels a year: capacity has more than doubled since then.

The brewhouse is magnificent, with polished copper kettles standing on tiled floors. A double decoction mash is used. Primary fermentation is in traditional open tiled squares, lagering is in horizontal tanks for the premium 12 degree beer. Conicals are used for the 10 degree domestic beer. The 12 degree beer is lagered for a full three months, one of the longest periods in the world. It is all-malt, which has helped it become a cult beer in purity-conscious

Point taken…a 1920s promotion for Budvar stressed its home-town base that gave a generic title to the beers from Budweis.

Germany. The hops come from Zatec. The beer has a starting gravity of 1049° and is fully attenuated, with a finished strength of 5 per cent alcohol by volume. It has 20 units of bitterness compared to around 40 in Pilsner Urquell. It has a rich, slightly toasted malt aroma with a dash of vanilla and aromatic hops, it is rich and rounded in the mouth, with a great juicy malt attack and a gentle hop bitterness, while the finish has a near-perfect balance of malt and hops with a delicate note of apple from the house yeast.

The centre of Ceské Budejovice has a large square surrounded by imposing buildings, an arcaded shopping mall, and is dominated by a fountain topped by a statue of Samson, the mythical strong man. It was the statue of Samson that prompted the old Bürgerbräu Brewery to change its

name to another symbol redolent of history and strength. Mashing and boiling takes place in cast-iron vessels. Primary fermentation is in open squares, lagering in horizontal vessels. Conicals were planned for the 10 degree beers but the management assured me the 12 degree would stay in traditional tanks to avoid any flavour changes. The 12 degree beer is a typical Budweis product, with a rich malt character, some delicate citric fruit from the hops and a well-balanced finish. Samson also produces a dark lager.

THE BATTLE OF THE BUDWEISERS

For most of the twentieth century, a battle has raged between Anheuser-Busch in the US and the Budvar Brewery in the Czech Republic over who has the right to the title of Budweiser. One result of endless court

battles has been that Budweiser Budvar is no longer sold in the US.

Anheuser-Busch, the world's biggest brewing corporation, has the muscle to get its version of Budweiser into most countries in the world. But it has been frustrated by the fact that it cannot use the full title in countries where Budvar has registered its title first and the American beer's label name has to be reduced to 'Bud'. Even before the fall of communism, Anheuser-Busch visited Czechoslovakia and offered to help develop Budvar's international sales in return for a settlement of the trade mark dispute, which meant in effect Budvar dropping the name Budweiser from its labels. The communists refused. Since the change of regime, Anheuser-Busch has stepped up its 'hearts and minds' campaign

in the new Czech Republic. It has offered to inject capital into the brewery in return for a 34 per cent stake. The Czechs are unimpressed and the government has told Anheuser-Busch that when Budvar is privatized it will seek new partners. Budvar has made it clear that Anheuser-Busch is not high on the list of potential partners.

Stung by these rebuffs, Anheuser-Busch has launched legal suits in countries such as Vietnam, where Budvar has registered its title first, in an attempt to overturn the registration. In 1997, when the Assistant Registrar of Trade Marks in London ruled that both brewing companies could use the name Budweiser in Britain, Anheuser-Busch stepped up its campaign with a double-page advertisement in the trade press. The heading said: 'You can be the genuine article – or

Topping up ceremony... the gleaming chrome beer engine in the Little Bears tavern in Prague dispenses Budvar beer with a heavy collar of foam.

you can wish you were'. Underneath was a series of Budweiser labels from 1876 to the present day with a solitary bottle of the Czech beer and the caption: '1895 Budweiser Budvar first brewed in Bohemia'.

Anheuser-Busch's claim to own the original Budweiser is at odds with the fact that the term was for centuries both a generic title and an appellation for beers brewed in and around the town of Budweis. As we have seen, the Citizens' Brewery in Budweis was brewing beers under the name of Budweiser from at least the 1880s and was doing so as part of the heritage of the town,

not because a beer of the same name had appeared in St Louis, Missouri, of which the Czechs were almost certainly unaware. The claim to own the original Budweiser is also belied by the history of the Anheuser-Busch company itself and its own statements in the last century.

Eberhard Anheuser and Adolphus Busch were Germans from the Rhineland and Hesse respectively who emigrated to the United States. Anheuser bought the Bavarian Brewery in St Louis, Missouri, from another German, George Schneider. Anheuser was joined by his son-in-law

Busch in 1864. Busch had a genius for marketing beer and he decided the company had to move away from dark Bavarian lagers aimed solely at German-Americans and brew a beer style with greater sales potential. He travelled widely in Europe to study new beer styles and technology. He saw at first hand the brewing revolution in Pilsen, and Anheuser-Busch did launch a St Louis White Label Pilsener Exquisite. But he was equally entranced by the beers of Budweis and returned home fired with determination to make a beer of the Budweiser style. Budweiser was launched in 1876 and by the 1890s took on the subsidiary title of 'the King of Beers', a reworking of the Bohemian title of the 'Beer of Kings' for beers from Budweis. But Busch was willing to acknowledge the source of his inspiration. He testified in a court case in 1898 between Anheuser-Busch and the Fred Miller Brewing Co as follows:

Question: Is it true that Anheuser-Busch manufactures a certain beer known as Budweiser Beer?

Answer: Yes, sir.

Question: Is that beer made according to a particular process; if so, what process?

Answer: The Budweiser Beer is brewed according to the Budweiser Bohemian process.

There is no claim there that his beer is an 'original'. On the contrary, Busch accepted his beer was based on a Bohemian model. Earlier, in a case between Anheuser-Busch

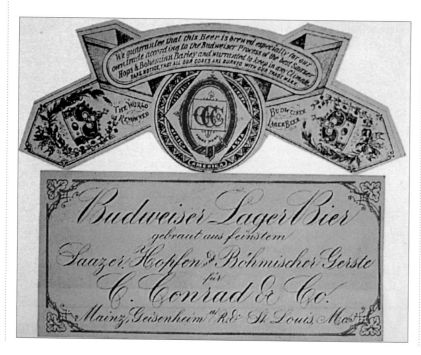

The first label for American Budweiser said, in German, that the beer was made from Saaz hops and Bohemian malt.

'Bud' today lists rice before barley malt on its label and no indication of the origin of the hops is given.

made from 'Saazer Hopfen & Bohmischer Gerste' — Saaz hops and Bohemian malt, Saaz being the German rendition of Czech Zatec hops. By 1908 the label was still in German but by then Saazer hops had been joined by Reis (rice), and Bester Gerste (best malt) had replaced Bohemian malt. In 1917 the label was in English but still claimed to use Saaz hops. But by 1939, following the repeal of Prohibition, when a handful of large brewers had the vast American market to themselves, Budweiser was brewed from 'choicest hops, rice and best barley malt'.

The reason for the introduction of rice was the discovery by American brewers that if they used a native variety of barley called 'six row' they could also blend in cheaper adjuncts such as rice or maize. Six-row malt tends to produce a coarser beer than classic two-row but it contains a high level of natural enzymes that will convert not only its own starches into fermentable sugar but also those in other unmalted cereals.

American Budweiser is 4.8 per cent alcohol by volume, has between 10 and 12 units of bitterness and is lagered for two to three weeks. The use of rice means it fails to meet the strictures of the German Reinheitsgebot or Purity Law. It has come a long way from the 'original' Budweiser brewed in 1876.

and the Joseph Uhrig Brewing Company in 1880, Busch told the court: 'The process I have described is the process by which beer is made in Budweis to my best knowledge'. A short-lived agreement in August 1911 between Anheuser-Busch and Budejovicky Budvar stated: 'The firm Budejovicky Budvar has not surrendered the right to use the word Budweiser. . .to denote the geographical origin of its beer products in the trade. The Anheuser-Busch Brewing Association also in the future marks with

the words Budweiser its products. . .except the word Original or a similar denotation, being liable to mislead the public in the direction that beer products of Anheuser-Busch are manufactured at Budweis, Bohemia.'

Anheuser-Busch today makes quite different claims for its beer, saying it is the original. Yet surely an 'original beer' would remain true to style despite the passage of years? The first label in 1876 was printed in German and said Budweiser Lager Beer was

BUDWEISER STYLE

Sweet, biscuity malt with a touch of vanilla, an aromatic gentle hop bitterness, and a delicate hint of apple fruit in the finish typify the beers from Budweis.

HELLES AND PALE LAGER

The golden beer from Pilsen became widely available due to the adroit use of waterways and new railways. But brewers in countries or regions close to Bohemia were slow to abandon their brown and amber beers. In Bavaria, the switch to cold fermentation pioneered by Sedlmayr in Munich was almost universally adopted by all brewers. But in a vast and mainly rural country, drinkers remained loyal to their dark or Dunkel beers. Sedlmayr's Spaten Brewery did not make a pale lager beer until 1894, more than fifty years after Pilsen's. Paulaner, also of Munich, began to promote Helles or pale lager only in the 1920s.

Change was faster in the Prussian north, where industrialization had come earlier. Brewing and the exporting of beer had been a major activity in Hamburg and the other cities of the Hanseatic League, the federation of trading towns of northern Germany formed in the fourteenth century and at its most powerful in the fifteenth. Hamburg was known as 'the beer house'. A shipping law of 1270 names beer as the most important trading commodity of the city at the mouth of the Elbe.

Pilsner beer reached Hamburg and northern Germany via the Elbe. Even though the golden lager won first prize in a Hamburg trade fair in the 1860s, local brewers did not immediately attempt to replicate the style. Tea, coffee and wine became the preferred drinks. The proximity of Denmark to Hamburg gave brewers in northern Germany easy access to the new pure bottom-fermenting yeast culture perfected by Hansen at Carlsberg of Copenhagen. But when they moved to cold-fermented lager beers, the Prussians at first replicated the popular dark Münchner beers from Bavaria. One of Hamburg's surviving breweries is called Bavaria-St Pauli and was

Lager is thought of as a post-war phenomenon in Britain but Spaten's Munich beers were on sale in London early this century. The term 'lager' was used in English-speaking countries to distinguish it from warm-fermented ale or beer.

New horizons...an early Spaten promotion stressed the world-wide impact made by the new lager method.

created specifically to brew Bavarian-type dark lagers (St Pauli is a Hamburg suburb). The city's best-known brewery, Holsten, opened in 1879 in Altona but is now based in Hamburg. The company name comes from Holstein, as Hamburg was the principal city of the duchy of Schleswig-Holstein. When Holsten built a new site in Hamburg it was designed to use all the new technologies of modern brewing, with copper vessels, decoction mashing and steam engines. It embraced cold fermentation and by the early part of the twentieth century was producing a golden Pilsener, the preferred German spelling.

In a country so densely populated with breweries, it is impossible to say with absolute certainty which company was the

Holsten, one of Germany's best-known brands, takes its name from the old duchy of Schleswig-Holstein.

first to call a golden lager beer 'Pilsener'. But it seems likely that the brewers of Hamburg and other northern cities were beaten by a family-owned concern in the Rhineland. The small town of Bitburg is in the Eifel lake district, close to the border with Luxembourg and the city of Trier, one of the oldest European cities and the birthplace of Karl Marx. Bitburg's brewery started life as a humble farmhouse operation in 1817 owned by the local Simon family: it was known as Simonbräu during the nineteenth and early twentieth centuries before adopting the more familiar German style of Bitburger. It began by making warm-fermented brown beers but, despite its comparative isolation in a rural area, embraced new technology and lagered its beers by using copious amounts of ice from

The original Holsten brewery in the suburb of Altona. The company swiftly embraced the new technologies of the late nineteenth century to brew lager beers.

MUSEUM MARKS EARLY LAGER

The gradual move from Münchner dark lagers to Pilsner-style beers early this century can be seen in the name of a brewery in Lüneburg a short distance from Hamburg: it is the Moravia Brewery, which takes its name from the Bohemian region that produces the finest malting barley for Pilsner beers. Moravia is now owned by Holsten, which has also turned the old Lüneburg Crown Brewery into a museum. The brewery was founded in 1485 and was bought in 1890 by Hermann Müllering, who converted it to lager brewing. The museum offers a fascinating snapshot of the new industrial brewing technology at the end of the last century, with copper mashing and boiling vessels, and fermentation and lagering in wooden casks. The maturing beer was kept cool by ice cut from local rivers in winter. Next door to the brewery museum is the brewer's house with a Renaissance ceiling, baroque stairway and old oak beams, an indication of the wealth as well as the pomp that accompanied brewing in earlier times. The museum at Heiligengeiststrasse 39, D-2120 Lüneburg is open daily from 10am–12noon and 2–5pm. The Moravia Brewery produces a Lüneburger Pilsener in a suitably old-fashioned snap-lock bottle for local consumption only.

The striking gabled façade of the Brewers' House in Lüneburg.

Lüneburg's Moravia Pils pays homage to the region offering the finest malting barley.

Moravia brews a Lüneburger Pilsener in a snap-lock bottle for local consumption.

the surrounding lakes. Its meticulous records report that it brewed the first German Pilsener beer in 1883. The company's fortunes were boosted when a rail line was opened to supply the Prussian army with cannon from the steelworks of Saarbrücken, providing Bitburger with markets in Saarland and to the north. It is possible that it was the arrival of the German Pilsener from the Rhineland that prompted the fiercely proud and competitive brewers of Hamburg, Bremen, Lüneburg and Friesland to produce their own versions.

In 1890 the Simon family, under the direction of Theobald Simon, the driving force behind the development of the company, built a modern and much-admired 'Dampfbierbrauerei', a steam brewery with energy from steam engines and a refrigeration plant modelled on the plants designed by Carl von Linde in Bavaria. A laboratory was added to ensure that a pure strain of yeast was perfected, making use of the pioneering work of Louis Pasteur in France and Emil Christian Hansen in Copenhagen. Theo Simon's watchword was quality for his *untergäriges* (bottom fermenting) beer. When in 1908 the company launched a new beer called Original-Simonbräu-Deutsch-Pilsener, the brewers of Pilsner beer in Bohemia decided it was time to make a stand. In 1912 they started a court action against Simonbräu to prevent it using the term Pilsener. The Simons sprang tigerish-

State of the art new brewery at Bitburger in the Eifel region of the Rhineland.

ly to the defence of their beer. Using expert advice from the brewing faculties of the universities of Berlin and Munich, they argued that their beer used the same raw materials as the Czech brewers while the Eifel brewing water was identical to Pilsen's. There was only one difference: the analysts at VLB in Berlin and Weihenstephan in Munich said the Bitburg beer was better than those brewed in Bohemia. In 1913 a high court in Cologne ruled that while Pilsener should be considered a style rather than an appellation of origin, it requested Simonbräu and other German brewers to

Simonbräu=Deutsch=Pilsene

aus der

Brauerei Th. Simon, Simonbräu Bitburg.

Reichsbank Giro-Konto
Trier.

Fernsprecher No. 2.

Postscheck-Konto Köln
No. 206.

Die Brauerei Th. Simon in Bitburg bringt neben ihrem bekannten „hellen Simonbräu" eine hervorragende Spezialität: Simonbräu=Deutsch=Pilsener" zum Ausstoß, welche sich in Wohlgeschmack und Bekömmlichkeit dem besten Böhmisch-Pilsener voll und ganz an die Seite stellen kann.

Nach den Feststellungen der Versuchs- und Lehranstalt für Brauerei in Berlin vom 12. Januar 1910 lauten
die Analysen von:

Simonbräu=Deutsch=Pilsener:		Original-Pilsener:
Saccharometer-Anzeige (%.B.)	3,58 %	3,58 %
Extrakt	5,18 %	5,18 %
Alkohol	3,51 %	3,51 %
Berechnete Stammwürze	11,99 %	11,25 %
Vergärung, scheinbar	70,2 %	70,2 %
wirklich	56,8 %	56,8 %

Nebenstehende Analyse zeigt die Uebereinstimmung des Simonbräu-Deutsch-Pilsener mit Original-Pilsener in der chemischen Zusammensetzung.

Diese Uebereinstimmung jedoch ist für die Gleichwertigkeit der beiden Biere durchaus nicht allein ausschlaggebend.

Durch die hervorragenden klimatischen, sowie die Höhen- und Wasserverhältnisse Pilsens hat das Böhmisch-Pilsener seinen Weltruf erworben. Diese wichtigen Umstände bestehen aber auch in Bitburg in ungefähr gleichem Maße. Bitburg und Pilsen liegen beide 320 m ü. M. Die reine Eifelhöhenluft wirkt in Verbindung mit der in Bitburg stets vorherrschenden verhältnismäßigen Kühle und den durch die Höhenlage bedingten Luftdruckverhältnissen veredelnd auf die Qualität des Bieres ein und gibt demselben seinen besonderen Charakter. Das beste, dem Pilsener Wasser fast gleiche Brauwasser, allerfeinste, ausgesuchte Saazer Hopfen und erstklassiges Pilsener Malz geben hier bei gleicher Arbeitsweise ein gleichwertiges Produkt.

A promotion for what is thought to be the first German Pilsener. It led to a High Court case brought by the Pilsen brewers. The Czech companies did not win a total victory but the court ruled that German brewers must make clear their golden lagers did not originate in Pilsen.

print the place of origin of their beer on their labels to avoid any suggestion their Pilseners came from Pilsen. The ruling was accepted by German brewers. When Simonbräu became Bitburger it labelled its main product Bitburger-Pilsener. In the course of time many German brewers shortened Pilsener to Pils to remove any last lingering doubt that they were copying the Czech original.

Most German brewers have a Pils in their portfolio today. It will be a beer of around 4.5 to 5 per cent alcohol, well attenuated to produce a dryness of palate and it will have a high level of bitterness. For drinkers who want a slightly fuller and more malt-accented lager with less intense bitterness, brewers offer a beer of only marginally less strength known as a Helles or just Hell. The word means 'pale' and was coined by Bavarian brewers to distinguish it from their Dunkel dark lagers. The term is now widely used throughout Germany and visitors who merely ask for 'a beer' or, worse, 'a lager' will usually be served a Helles. Many brewers will also have a stronger golden lager called Export of around 5.5 per cent alcohol, modelled on the style made famous in Dortmund.

GERMAN PILSENERS

Bitburger, despite its modest size, is the second biggest Pilsener brewer in Germany.

Bitburger's new plant. . .it is linked by underground pipes to the old brewery in the centre of town.

Today it labels its main brands simply 'Pils', and is internationally famous for its catchy slogan 'Bitte ein Bit', meaning 'A Bit please': it is sold in 35 countries. The original copper brewhouse in the centre of Bitburg is open to visitors and is still in use, but brewing in bulk was transferred to a state-of-the-art plant on a greenfield site on the edge of town in the 1980s. Wort is pumped by underground pipes between the two brewhouses. Bitburger Pils is 4.6 per cent alcohol by volume and is brewed from Alexis, Arena and Steiner varieties of spring barley (much of it grown in the Rhineland) with Hersbrucker, Hüller, Perle and Tettnanger hops. All the Siegel variety of hops from the small area of Holsthum near Bitburg are bought by the brewery and used in the beers. Hops are added to the boil three times for Pils, which has 37 to 38 units of bitterness. It has a delightful aroma of rich juicy malt and floral hops with a softly entrancing malty palate, and a long dry but not overly bitter finish with good malt presence and some light citric fruit from the hops. The house yeast has not changed for as long as anyone in the company can recall. The Pils is lagered for a painstaking three months and

the finished beer is not pasteurized: the head brewer says pasteurization would endanger the delicate balance of flavours in the beer. Export beer is sterile filtered.

Other notable Rhineland Pilseners include Warsteiner, the biggest Pils brand in Germany, from Warstein, a town in an area of lakes and woods to the east of the Rhine and the Ruhr. The Pils is 4.8 per cent

Over and under a barrel...brewery workers pose with giant wooden lagering tanks.

alcohol, is brewed from Pils malt and Hallertauer hop varieties and is lagered for two months. It has a light malt and hops bouquet, is rounded and bitter-sweet in the mouth, and has a delicate dry finish with some citric notes from the hops. Herforder

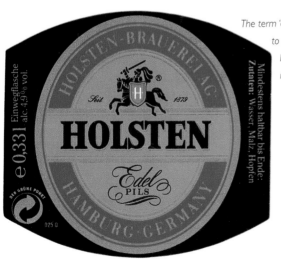

The term 'edel' means noble and refers to the knight on the Holsten label as well as the use of noble hop varieties.

Diät Pils caused confusion in Britain where drinkers thought the beer would help them lose weight.

*A good head for beer
…a familiar sight in
Bavaria, a drinker
dressed in traditional
south German costume
offering 'ein prosit' – a
toast – with a glass
of beer.*

Pils from Brauerei Felsenkeller in Herford is a painstakingly well-crafted beer of 4.8 per cent alcohol and 32 units of bitterness. It is brewed with pale Pilsener malt, 60 per cent Hallertauer Northern Brewer hops for bitterness and 40 per cent Perle and Tettnanger for aroma. The Pils has a rich honeyed malt aroma, rounded malt and hops in the mouth, and a long, dry malty finish with some citric fruit from the hops.

In the north, Holsten is a giant company, with its Pilsener either exported or brewed under licence in many other countries. Holsten and its subsidiaries produce in excess of one million hectolitres (22 million gallons) of beer a year in Germany alone. The Hamburg plant has four separate brewhouses that produce a new brew every hour of every day. To those who know Holsten products only in other countries – especially in Britain where the locally brewed Pils has had its bitterness reduced to around 12 units to attract the 'youth market' – it is a revelation to drink the beers made in Hamburg. The biggest-selling beer is called Edel Pils, 4.9 per cent. Edel means 'noble' and is a reference to both the knight on horseback that is the company symbol and to the noble hop varieties of Bavaria. The 4.8 per cent Premium Pilsener has 24 bitterness units, a fine perfumy hop aroma balanced by slightly toasted malt, with sweet malt in the mouth, and a clean, quenching, dry and hoppy finish with a hint of iodine.

Holsten also produces Diät Pils, 5 per cent, a beer brewed for diabetics in Germany but which has caused considerable misunderstanding in Britain. Holsten opened a distribution plant in London in 1903 and its Diät Pils, in a bottle with a green foil cap, became hugely successful. Advertisements in the 1970s and 1980s informing British drinkers that 'all the sugar turns to alcohol' fuelled the belief that the beer was an aid to slimming or would at least reduce the beer belly to which all drinkers are prone. But a beer low in calories is not necessarily low in carbohydrate, and Holsten has now removed the word 'Diät' from British labels, though it is retained in Germany.

The Jever Brewery in German Friesland was founded in 1848 and was producing a Pilsener before the turn of the century, with

*A Munich beer garden…crowds flock to
them in the summer to drink refreshing
glasses of Helles.*

the aid of extremely soft water from a natural spring that is still used today. Jever Pilsener is not for the faint-hearted. The Frisians have a renowned love of bitter, herby and spicy drinks and make their own liqueurs. The beer has a pronounced dry and bitter hop character that is reflected on the label with the word 'Herb', which means dry. Hallertauer and Tettnanger hops are used in two additions during the copper boil and produce a redoubtable 44 units of bitterness, making it one of the most bitter lager beers in the world. Two-row barleys from Germany, France and the Netherlands are used in an infusion mash system. The beer is lagered for three months and emerges with a tart hoppy aroma balanced by delicate malt, and a fine balance of lightly toasted malt and hops in the mouth. Nothing prepares the uninitiated for the finish: stunningly dry and hoppy with an iron-like intensity.

In the south the closeness of Munich and Pilsen means that the Pilsener beers of the German-speaking city are closer in style to the Czech original, notably full-bodied with greater malt character to balance hop bitterness. As well as Pils, Bavarian brewers also offer Hell, their bread-and-butter, everyday drinking, beer-garden quaffing lagers. Spaten's Hell is 4.8 per cent alcohol and has 22 units of bitterness. It has a superb bitter-sweet, malt and hops aroma with malt dominating the palate and a finish that becomes dry but not bitter. The brewery's Pilsener is 5 per cent alcohol but is more robustly hopped with 38 IBUs, a perfumy hop aroma, a malty middle and a dry finish with a good balance of malt and hops. Augustiner's Hell is 5.2 per cent and is the most popular version of the style in Munich. It has a creamy malt aroma, a malt-dominated palate and a bitter-sweet finish. Hacker-Pschorr's 4.9 per cent Hell is a shade

darker than most examples of the style, with some hop fruitiness on the aroma and palate and a dry finish.

Löwenbräu is the best known of the Munich brewers as a result of its vigorous export policy. The company's 5.3 per cent Hell is strong for the style and is noticeably malty. Its 5.4 per cent Pils is the hoppiest in Munich, with bitterness units in the high 30s from Hallertauer and Saaz varieties. The hops give it a superb citric fruit aroma, there is a good balance of malt and hops on the palate while the finish is shatteringly dry and bursting with hop character.

Paulaner has a mouthful of a beer in

An old storage tank on view in the Spaten Brewery in Munich where commercial lagering was developed.

Original Münchner Hell (4.9 per cent), dry in the mouth and with a hoppy, bitter edge to the finish. Curiously, its Pilsener is a degree weaker at 4.8 per cent and has a big floral hop aroma, a malty middle and a long, dry finish. The brewery labels it, in the manner of German wine makers, as 'Extra Trocken' – Extra Dry.

On the outskirts of Munich, the Weihenstephan University at Freising, famous for its brewing faculty, has a

A right royal offering
...beers from the
Hofbräu or Royal Court
Brewery in Munich.

commercial brewery attached. It makes an Edelpils (4.9 per cent) that is a noble beer indeed, with a fine perfumy hop aroma, a malty body and a dry and bitter finish.

DORTMUNDER EXPORT

Dortmund is Germany's leading brewing city yet ironically its main claim to fame, a beer style known as Export, is little known outside Germany and is even in decline in its heartland of the Ruhr. Yet Dortmund and the university city of Münster in the region of Westphalia have a long and proud record of brewing: the term Export results from Dortmund's vigorous sale of its beers throughout Westphalia, into the neighbouring Low Countries and as far afield as Scandinavia. The history of brewing in Dortmund dates from the thirteenth century when the nobility, as was the custom in central Europe, granted brewing rights to the citizens. In the nineteenth century Dortmund became the powerhouse of Germany, with its great steel and mining industries and a vast and thirsty working class to refresh. Many brewers switched to cold fermentation at an early date once the technique became known to them. Less conservative than the Munich brewers, those in Dortmund began to fashion paler beers

than Münchner Dunkels but ignored the rush to label paler lagers as 'Pilsener'. They named their new golden beers Dortmunder Export, known affectionately in both Germany and the Netherlands as 'Dort' for short. The style is distinctive: a dash of Munich malt gives a polished gold to the colour, water rich in calcium carbonate and sulphate brings out full flavours from malt and hops, and it has a full-bodied maltiness, a delicate hoppiness and a dry but not too bitter finish.

In common with the rest of the industrialized West, Dortmund has witnessed a considerable retraction of its old economic base. With fewer mineworkers and steel-workers to refresh, the city's brewers have sought a new audience for their beers. The Dortmund brewers think Export has a blue-collar image that will deter a younger generation with middle-class aspirations. Export is still made but it now plays second fiddle to the local versions of Pilsener and is often labelled as 'Original'.

The two giants of Dortmund brewing are Dortmunder Actien Brauerei and Dortmunder Union Brauerei, the names shortened to DAB and DUB, making them sound like cuddly figures in a children's television programme. DAB, founded in 1868 as a family-owned company, went public in 1872: Actien means a public company. It was the arrival of DAB that encouraged several smaller Dortmund breweries to merge into a united (Union) company as DUB in 1873. DAB Export (5 per cent ABV) has a sweet malt and cornflour aroma, a full malty body and a bitter-sweet finish with a late burst of hops. DUB has a brewery nobody can miss, with the single letter 'U' blazing out at night from a height of 17 metres (55 feet) on top of a 1920s building. Its 5 per cent Original or Export is a classic beer, with a big malty start balanced by floral hops, a rounded malty middle with more tart hops, and a dry finish dominated by hop bitterness and delicate citric fruit.

The smallest of the Dortmund breweries is Kronen (Crown), though it has grown bigger in the 1990s by merging with former rivals Stiftsbräu and Thier. Its Export is now the biggest-selling version of the style. It can lay claim to being Dortmund's oldest brewery, founded in an inn in the fifteenth century. It was bought by Johann Wenker in 1729 and his descendants, now called Brand, still run the company: they have honoured the memory of their founder with a brew-pub named Wenker in the city. The

Labels from Dortmund's breweries...most are shy of using the term 'Export' these days though it made the city famous.

Dortmunder Union's name was the result of a merger of several of the city' breweries in 1873.

brewery moved to its present site in 1873 in a district called Kronenburg, meaning the crown of a hill: the hill provided deep cellars in which beer was stored before the arrival of refrigeration. The brewery was badly damaged by bombing in World War II and has been largely rebuilt. The beers are unpasteurized and the 4.8 per cent Export, with its burnished gold colour, big malty palate and a bitter-sweet finish that is finally dominated by gentle hoppiness, is a fine beer – if you can find it. Kronen releases no information about it, concentrating on its stronger Pils and Classic. Only Classic is sold in a brewery museum next door.

The beer flag flies more proudly in the old Westphalian university city of Münster where Pinkus Müller has achieved international renown while being little more than

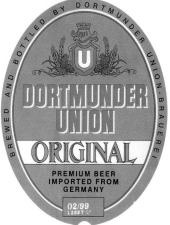

a brew-pub, producing around 10,000 hectolitres (21,996 gallons) a year. Pinkus Müller founded his business as a baker, chocolate maker and brewer in 1816, and it is still run by the large and energetic Müller clan. Beer and food is based in and around the handsome tavern on Kreuz-strasse where

202

hearty local dishes are accompanied by beer. Pinkus Müller's main claim to fame is that it uses only organic malt and hop in its beers. Pinkus Müller makes full use of naturally produced malt and hops in its dry and hoppy Pils while its 5.2 per cent Spezial is close to a Dortmunder Export in style, with a big malty aroma and palate, and hops developing in the dry and refreshing finish, the richness and complexity of the beer accentuated by a long, three-month period of lagering.

BELGIAN AND DUTCH PILS

Stella Artois is now a major international Pils brand but it began life as a humble seasonal beer, brewed for the Christmas period in 1926. Stella is the Latin word for 'star' and was considered a pleasant image for the festive season. It was brewed in Leuven in Belgium by the Artois company: Sebastien Artois bought the Den Horen (The Horns) brew-pub in the university city in 1717, and the business was rapidly expanded by his descendants. Cold fermentation was adopted in the late nineteenth century, and Den Horen Artois became Stella Artois following the success of the 1920s Christmas beer. In the 1980s Stella Artois merged with Jupiler of Jupille-sur-Meuse to form Interbrew. It now owns Labatt of Canada, has breweries in Italy and close links with Whitbread in Britain, and is a major player on the world brewing scene. In spite of the sheer size of the business operation, the 5 per cent Stella Artois brewed in Leuven is made with considerable dedication to traditional methods. It has a six-storey maltings in the city that looks like a multi-storey car-park from outside but which uses highly traditional floor malting techniques inside: the brewers consider that malt spread on heated floors and regularly turned and aerated makes for a cleaner and sweet

sugary extract. In the brewhouse the extract is boiled with Czech Saaz, Northern Brewer and Tettnanger hops from Bavaria, and Styrian Goldings. The finished beer, lagered for two months and with 30 units of bitterness, is dominated by aromatic Saaz hop

Great Lakes of Cleveland proudly proclaims the German city that inspired its Gold lager beer.

Pinkus Müller of Münster uses only organic materials for its beers: a Spezial is close to an Export in style.

character, is firm bodied and malty in the mouth with a dry and hop-accented finish.

Stella's companion, Jupiler, 5 per cent, 25 IBUs, is the biggest-selling Pils in Belgium. Like Stella, it has some heritage on its side. The Piedbouef family founded their brewery in Jupille in 1853 in a town thought to be the birthplace of Charlemagne and with a brewing history dating from the mid-thirteenth century. Jupiler's success is remarkable as it was launched as late as 1966. It is a softly malty beer that lacks the powerful hop character of Stella.

Belgium's second-biggest brewing company is Alken-Maes, a merger of two companies founded respectively in 1881 and 1880. Maes, when independent, survived a period of ownership by the now-defunct Watney group of Britain, and Alken-Maes is now controlled by the vast Danone food and drink empire of France, which also owns the Kronenbourg and Kanterbräu brands in the Strasbourg region.

The Maes plant near Antwerp has a superb, gleaming copper brewhouse visible from the main road. Maes Pils, 5.1 per cent, is lagered for two to three months following a double decoction mash. It is brewed with Czech malt and mainly Saaz hops, and has a crisp hop and juicy malt character. Cristal Alken is the Belgian Pils favoured by connoisseurs. It was designed in 1928 to suit the demands of miners in the Limburg region. As a result it has a more profound hop character than other Belgian versions of Pils. As the village of Alken is close to the German border, there may be some cross-border fertilization of brewing styles (the house yeast came originally from a German brewery) though the brewers who created the style say they were attempting to replicate a true Czech Pilsner. It is 4.8 per cent, the result of a double decoction mash and two to three months' maturation. It has a floral hop

aroma, a creamy malt note in the mouth balanced by tart hops and a long, dry, hoppy finish with hints of juicy malt and citric fruit.

The Pilsener market in the Netherlands is dominated to an awesome extent by Heineken. In common with Carlsberg in Denmark, Heineken so saturated its domestic market that it could grow only by exporting and brewing under licence in other countries. Today Heineken produces more than 60 million hectolitres (1,320 million gallons) of beer a year from its two Dutch plants and around a hundred other breweries world-wide. The giant international group has come a long way from the day in 1863 when the mother of

Gerard Adriaan Heineken bought De Hooiberg (the Haystack) brewery for him in Amsterdam. Gerard was so appalled by the drunkenness and depravity caused by gin drinking in the Dutch capital that he declared he would provide healthy beer for the masses if his mother used her wealth to buy him a brewery. The Haystack was no tiny brew-pub but Amsterdam's biggest brewery dating back to 1592. Heineken busily expanded the business, bought a second plant in the city and by 1873 had a third brewery in Rotterdam.

The company no longer brews in Amsterdam: the Haystack is now a hotel while the second brewery in the city is a museum with fascinating displays and video shows about the history of Heineken and brewing as well as a magnificently preserved brewhouse packed with gleaming copper vessels. Brewing now takes place at Hertogenbosch and Zoeterwoude.

Heineken merged with its local rival Amstel in 1968. Amstel, named after the river that flows through Amsterdam, was founded in 1870 as the Bavarian Brewery, an indication of the awe in which south German beers were held. The two main brands, Heineken and Amstel Bier, both 5 per cent, are typical of the international interpretations of the Pilsner style, though in recent years the Heineken group has attempted to embrace the concerns of both purists and the German market with its pure beer Reinheitsgebot by phasing out brewing sugars and cheaper cereals. Heineken has between 20 and 25 units of bitterness, a delicate hop and malt aroma, a clean palate and some light hop notes in the quenching finish. Amstel has a deeper golden colour and slightly more hop character. In the Dutch market, Amstel 1870, also 5 per cent, has much

Jupiler is Belgium's biggest-selling lager brand. St Christoffel is run by Leo Brand who brews with only barley malt and German hops and refuses to pasteurize his beers.

greater hop character while Amstel Gold (7 per cent) is rich in malt and hops with considerable citric fruit appeal.

Far and away the best Pilsener-style beers brewed within the Heineken group come from Brand of Wijlre, near Maastricht. It is the oldest brewery in the Netherlands and dates from the early fourteenth century. The present site was built in 1743. In the 1970s Brand was appointed the official supplier of beer to the Queen of the Netherlands and has renamed itself the Royal Brand Brewery. It was bought by Heineken in 1989. Brand Pils (sold as Royal Brand Beer in the United States) is yet another 5 per cent Pilsener but is of exceptional quality. Pils is brewed from 90 per cent pale malt from two-row summer barley and 10 per cent maize grits. Bavarian Northern Brewer, Perle and Hersbrucker create 26 to 28 units of bitterness. The beer is lagered for around two months and has a perfumy hop aroma, is malty and hoppy in the mouth, and has a long and lingering hoppy finish. Brand-UP is an even more distinguished beer. The curious name, which sounds like a soft drink, derives from 'Urtyp' (original), shortened to UP. The 5.5 per cent premium Pilsener is all malt, uses Hersbrucker, Spalt and Tettnanger hops, registers 36 to 38 bitterness units and is lagered for 56 days. It has a superb malt, cornflour and hops aroma, has a firm malty middle and a divine finish packed with juicy malt, citric fruit and hops. Both beers are left unpasteurized.

Leo Brand is a member of the same family that runs Brand but he now runs his own brewery, St Christoffel, in Roermond, Dutch Limburg. St Christoffel is the patron saint of Roermond, once a major coal-mining region. Leo Brand trained at Weihenstephan in Munich and worked in several German breweries before building his own plant in 1986: it includes a classic domed, brick-clad copper kettle found in a barn. Christoffel Bier is 5.1 per cent and is made from 100 per cent barley malt and Hallertauer and Hersbrucker hop varieties. With 45 units of bitterness, this stunning beer has an aroma dominated by piney hops, followed by a prickle of hops on the tongue and a dry and bitter finish, overlain and underpinned by a clean, sweet maltiness. Fittingly, it is sub-titled 'Dubbel Hop'. The beer is unpasteurized: 'pasteurization is for the farmyard, not the brewery,' Mr Brand declares.

The country's second-biggest brewer, Grolsch, is also opposed to pasteurization, even for export. The charmingly old-fashioned, 1930s-style snap-lock bottle has helped turn the company's 5 per cent beer into an international cult and it is now sold in forty countries. The beer is labelled Pilsener for the domestic market and Premium Lager abroad. It is brewed with enormous care and dedication, using a blend of spring barley malts from Belgium, England, France and the Netherlands with a small amount of maize (corn). Hops come from the German Hallertau and Czech Zatec regions, with aroma hops added at the end of the copper boil. The beer is lagered for ten weeks and emerges with a distinctive fresh-mown grass aroma, a fine balance of juicy malt and delicate hops in the mouth, and a finish that becomes dominated by delicate hops and light citric fruit.

The closeness of Dortmund to the Netherlands has encouraged the development of bronze-coloured Dutch beers in the style of the German city's Export. Gulpener, from the village of Gulpen near Maastricht, was founded in 1825 and brews a pleasant if unexceptional Pilsener. But its 6.5 per cent Dort, made from pale malt, maize and

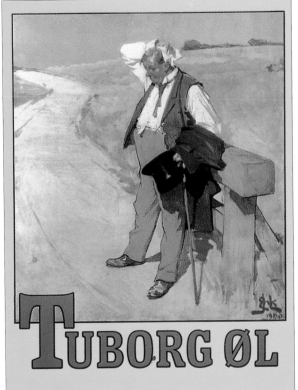

This famous poster for Tuborg is known simply as 'Thirst' and helped build the Danish company's fortune. It merged with Carlsberg to form United Breweries and Tuborg's Copenhagen brewery closed in 1997.

Grolsch is a relatively small Dutch brewing group but its Pilsener in the snap-lock bottle is recognized world-wide.

caramel, with Hallertauer hops, has 20 IBUs and a big malty-hoppy aroma and palate. Alfa's Super-Dortmunder is a powerful 7 per cent and has a big fruity aroma and palate, and a clean, sweet finish. De Ridder in Maastricht, a Heineken subsidiary, makes a Dortmunder Export called Maltezer. The 6.5 per cent beer has a smooth and creamy malt character with good hop presence on the palate and in the finish.

AMERICAN LAGERS

The second wave of immigrants to the United States in the nineteenth century came from central and eastern Europe. Many brought with them not only a passion for good beer but the ability to brew it: there were many skilled brewmasters among those huddled masses seeking jobs and freedom. The newcomers had enjoyed the new lager beers of Europe and soon brewers with such names as Anheuser and Busch, Blatz, Leinenkugel, Pabst, Heileman, Schlitz, Stroh and Yuengling were creating Bocks, Dunkels, Helles, Märzen and Pilseners for large German-speaking communities engaged in such heavy industries as steel and coal.

Many of these beer styles remained unchanged for decades. But as a second generation of German-Americans abandoned bratwurst and lederhosen in order to be accepted into the mainstream of American life, some of the immigrant-owned breweries sought a wider mass market for their beers. They began to adapt their recipes to meet the less meticulous demands of a vast audience unversed in such matters as the true character of a Budweiser or a Pilsener. Bigger brewers found that by using native six-row barley, with its chemically charged enzymic power, they could blend in corn or rice with malt to lower production costs and produce light-tasting lagers that were inoffensive if unexciting.

The course of American brewing changed cataclysmically with the arrival of Prohibition. The Volstead Act, which outlawed the manufacture and sale of alcohol, did not come into full effect until January 1920, but 36 states had already voted for partial or total prohibition from 1916 onwards. The crackdown was a disaster. Bootleg alcohol poured into the US across every available border while illegal beer and moonshine hard liquor were made in millions of illicit stills and baths. Whether imported or home-grown, much of this alcohol came under the control of mobsters.

Prohibition lasted until 1933. When the Volstead Act was repealed, the brewing industry had been changed for ever. Only a

handful of brewers had survived the closedown. Anheuser-Busch, for example, had kept its name in front of the public by converting several of its breweries to ice-cream production, supplying yeast to the baking industry and making malt drinks and alcohol-free 'beers'. In 1900 there had been 4000 breweries in the country. Only a few hundred reappeared in 1933. The Great Depression reduced their number still further, and by the 1980s there were just six national and twenty regional producers left, with a just a handful of the new-wave craft breweries. Mergers and closures means the American market is dominated by three giants: Anheuser-Busch, Coors and Miller. Of the three, A-B continues to gain market share, brews more than 90 million barrels of beer a year and just one brand, Budweiser, accounts for around half of all the beer consumed in the US.

A-B makes a great deal of the fact that Budweiser is 'matured over beechwood chips'. Quite why the company puts such

stress on the process is difficult to comprehend. The use of beechwood in the lagering tank is an old and now virtually extinct Bavarian technique. It adds nothing to the flavour or character of the finished beer, and the wood – in the case of A-B, strips about a foot long and two inches wide – is used solely to attract yeast particles in order to clarify the beer. The beer stays in the lagering tank for just 21 days. It emerges with 4.8 per cent alcohol by volume/3.9 by weight and between 10 and 12 units of bitterness. It is brewed, in twelve giant plants around the US, from a blend of two-row and six-row barley malts and rice: rice is thought to account for around 40 per cent of the grist. Whole flower hops come from the US and the Czech Republic.

The Miller Brewing Company has its roots in Charles Best's Plank Road Brewery in Milwaukee, opened in 1855 and later bought by Frederick Miller. Its main brand for years, Miller High Life (4.6 per cent alcohol by volume/3.6 volume), predates

Prohibition. In 1969 Miller became part of the international Philip Morris tobacco group. Philip Morris busily built its brewing division, leap-frogging it from eleventh place to second in the American brewing league with the help of a new brand Miller Lite (4.1 volume/3.3 weight), one of the first low-calorie beers, described as a 'fine Pilsner beer' but one largely devoid of taste or character. A more recent addition to the range, Genuine Draft (4.6 volume/3.6 weight) is, despite the title, a bottled beer that uses the Japanese system of cold filtering rather than pasteurization, resulting in some pleasant malt and light hops character.

Adolph Coors' brewery at Golden, Colorado, is the single biggest brewing plant in the US, the site chosen in 1873 by Coors as a result of the supplies of pure spring water from the Rocky Mountains. The Golden Brewery produces 20 million barrels a year using ingredients from its own barley fields and hop gardens. In recent years Coors had added Coors Light, Coors Gold and Original Draft to its portfolio as well as a new brewing plant in Virginia. But its main brand by far is labelled simply Coors (5 per cent volume/4 weight) with the subtitle Banquet Beer. Brewed with pale malt and cereal adjuncts with whole flower hops, Coors is the most characterful of the giant national brands, which says more about the opposition than the intrinsic quality of the Colorado product. Nevertheless it has a pleasant malt and cornflour aroma with a quenching palate of sweet malt and delicate hops, and a good light hop note in the bitter-sweet finish.

For a taste of full-flavoured, pre-Prohibition lagers you have to turn to the new breed of small craft brewers. Brooklyn, a suburb of New York City, was once a major American brewing area. The 'broken line' town settled by the Dutch was home to 40

breweries but it lost them all as a result of Prohibition, followed by the Depression, and subsequent mergers and closures in the 1950s. In the 1980s former journalist and home brewer Steve Hindy along with banker Tom Potter revived the Brooklyn tradition with a lager based on a pre-Prohibition recipe devised for them by veteran brewer Bill Moeller, who had once worked for leading regional Rheingold. Brooklyn Lager's rounded, rich malt and hops character has an almost ale-like quality. It is 5.5 per cent volume/4.5 weight and is brewed with a dash of crystal malt alongside the pale. It is dry hopped and has a full-bodied malt, hops and cobnuts aroma and palate with a long finish bursting with juicy malt and tart hops. It is brewed for Brooklyn by F.X. Matt, a large regional of Utica, up-state New York, but Brooklyn now has its own brewing plant where it makes warm-fermented ales.

Jim Koch is a descendant of Bavarian immigrant brewers. He has Anglicized the pronounciation of his name to 'Cook' but in

Above and far left: The Pennsylvania Brewing Company's Allegheny Brewery and pub.

Below: Koching up a fine brew. . . Jim Koch's Boston Lager is in the Munich style..

all other ways has maintained a family tradition that seemed lost when their breweries were closed by mergers in the 1950s. Koch's Boston Brewery is based in another former German brewery, Haffenreffer's, in Boston, though most of his beers are now contract-brewed by other companies throughout the US.

The beers all bear the name and stern portrait of Samuel Adams, a Boston brewer, patriot and revolutionary who played a leading part in the War of Independence and helped to organize the famous Boston Tea Party. Samuel Adams Boston Lager (4.4 per cent volume/3.5 weight) is a superb Munich-style beer, golden, rounded, firm-bodied, brewed from pale and Munich malts and hopped with Hallertauer Mittelfrüh. Koch and his head brewer, Dave Grinnell, tour the Bavarian hop fields every autumn to choose the pick of the crop. The beer has a floral hop aroma, a malty palate and a big

Samuel Adams was a brewer, American revolutionary, organizer of the Boston Tea Party and inspiration for one of the finest revivalist American lagers.

malty-hoppy finish.

You might expect Carol and Ed Stoudt's brewery in Adamstown, Pennsylvania, to make a dark stout but they are of German descent and, unusually for new-wave craft brewers, concentrate on cold-fermented beers. Stoudt's brewing developed out of the restaurant and beer garden opened by Ed Stoudt in the 1960s.

While he ran the business, Carol went on a fact-finding tour of Bavaria, returned to learn brewing skills at the University of California and then started to make beer. Her Export Gold is in the Dortmunder tradition and is brewed from pale, Munich and crystal malts with a complex hop grist made up of Hallertau Mittelfrüh, Tettnanger and Saaz varieties. It has a rich malt and aromatic hop nose, a firm malty palate and a long and lingering malty finish with delicate hop notes.

In California the Gordon Biersch brew-pubs in Palo Alto, San José and San Francisco also specialize in German-style lagers. Master brewer Dan Gordon studied at the Weihenstephan brewing school in Munich and then trained with Spaten before opening brew-pubs with restaurateur Dean Biersch. In spite of Gordon's strong Bavarian pedigree, his flagship beer is a Dortmunder Export (5 per cent volume/4 per cent weight) with around 25 units of bitterness. It has a big malt aroma balanced by tart hops, a rounded palate and a long malty-hoppy finish. The great success of the brew-pubs has led to plans to open a fully fledged commercial brewery in San José.

The Sudwerk Privatbrauerei Hübsch in Davis, California, is emphatically a German-

SAMUEL ADAMS

BREWER • PATRIOT

BOSTON LAGER

BOSTON BEER COMPANY   12 FL.OZ.

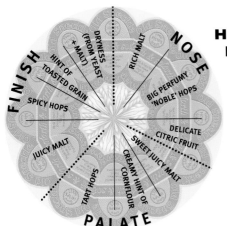

HELLES AND PALE LAGER STYLE

Rich malt, cornflour and noble hops on the aroma, juicy malt and hops in the mouth and a gently bitter, refreshing finish are typical of a German style now copied world-wide.

oriented brewery. Owner Ron Broward borrowed his German mother's maiden name for his company which embraces two brew-pubs and a separate brewery. The brewery was built in the mid-1990s with an imported German Steinecker plant. Hübsch Pilsner (5 per cent volume/4 per cent weight) is outstanding, with a booming 'noble hop' aroma from Hallertauer and Tettnanger varieties, a juicy malt palate balanced by tart hops, and a long creamy, malty, hoppy finish.

PALE LAGER BREWERS

GERMANY
Augustiner Brauerei
Neuhauserstrasse 16, 8000 Munich 1

Bavaria-St Pauli Brauerei AG
Hopfenstrasse 15, Hamburg 4

Bayerische Staatsbrauerei Weihenstephan
Postfach 1155, Freising, Munich

Bitburger Brauerei Theo Simon
Postfach 189, 5520 Bitburg/Eifel

Brauerei Felsenkeller Herford
Postfach 1351, Herford

Dortmunder Actien Brauerei
Steigerstrasse 20, Postfach 105012, Dortmund 1

Dortmunder Kronen GMBH
Märkische-strasse 85, Dortmund 1

Dortmunder Union Brauerei
2 Rheinische-strasse, 4600 Dortmund 1

Hacker-Pschorr Bräu GMBH
Schwanthaler-strasse 113, 8000 Munich 2

Holsten Brauerei AG
Holsten-strasse 224, 22765 Hamburg

Jever/Friesisches Bräuhaus zu Jever
17 Elisabethufer, 2942 Jever

Löwenbräu AG
Nymphenburger-strasse 4, Munich 2

Paulaner-Salvator-Thomasbräu
Hochstrasse 75, Munich 9

Pinkus Müller
4-10 Kreuz-strasse, 4400 Münster

Spaten-Franziskaner-Bräu
Maar-strasse 46-48, Munich 2

Warsteiner Brauerei
Wilhelmstrasse 5, Warstein

BELGIUM
Alken-Maes
Stationstraat 2, 3820 Alken

Maes
Waarloosveld 10, 2571 Kontich-Waarloos

Brasserie Jupiler
Interbrew, rue de Vise 243, 4500 Jupille-sur-Meuse

Stella Artois
Interbrew, Vaartstraat 94, 3000 Leuven

NETHERLANDS
Alfa Bierbrouwerij
Thull 15-19, 6365 AC Schinnen

Koninklijke Brand Bierbrouwerij BV
Brouwerijstraat 2, Posatbus 1, 6300 AA Wijlre

Grolsche Bierbrowerij
Eibergsweg 10, 7141 CE Groenlo/ Fazanstraat 2, 7525 EA Enschede

Gulpener Bierbrouwerij
Rijksweg 16, 6271 AE Gulpen

Heineken Nederland NV
Postbus 28, 1000 Amsterdam

De Ridder Brouwerij BV
Oeverwal 3-9, 6221 EN Maastricht

St Christoffel Bierbrouwerij
Bredeweg 14, 6042 GG, Roermond

UNITED STATES
Anheuser-Busch Inc
1 Busch Place, St Louis, Missouri 63118-1852

Adolph Coors Company
East of Town, Golden, Colorado 80401

Gordon Biersch
2 Harrison Street, San Francisco, California 94105

Boston Beer Company
30 Germania Street, Boston, Massachusetts 02130

Brooklyn Brewery
118 N 11th Street, Brooklyn, New York 11211

F.X. Matt Brewing
811 Edward Street, Utica, New York 13502

Miller Brewing Company
3939 W Highland Bvld, Milwaukee, Wisconsin 53208-2816

Stoudt's Brewing
Route 272, PO Box 880, Adamstown, Pennsylvania 19501

Sudwerk Privatbrauerei Hübsch
2001 Second Street, Davis, California 95616

DUNKEL AND BLACK BEERS

His official title is His Royal Highness Crown Prince Luitpold of Bavaria but his friends call him 'Lui'. And he has many friends, this tall, broad-shouldered man with a wide smile and a warm welcome for all the visitors to Kaltenberg Castle, 48 kilometres (30 miles) west of Munich. He is a member of the Wittelsbach royal family which ruled Bavaria from 1180 until 1918, first as dukes and later as kings. It was an ancestor of Luitpold's, Duke Wilhelm IV, who drew up the terms of the Reinheitsgebot in 1516, the Beer Purity Law that stipulates that only malt, hops, yeast and water can be used to make beer.

Luitpold, like dispossessed monarchs throughout Europe, could have sat around in his castle waiting for the day when he is called back to the throne. But Luitpold says he 'accepts the political and commercial reality' of the times. So what does a Bavarian prince with time on his hands do? He brews beer, of course. In southern Germany he naturally makes a Pils and a wheat beer to satisfy the two main demands of the beer market. But he also brews Dunkel, a dark lager style that seemed on the point of extinction until he revived its fortunes.

Dunkel is made in the small brewery in his castle near Geltendorf: both the 'Kalt' and the 'Gelten' in the names of castle and village are thought to have Celtic associations. There has been a castle on the site since at least the thirteenth century. Before that the Romans built a watchtower there and repulsed the advancing Huns with its aid. The first castle was burnt down during the Thirty Years War with Sweden. It was rebuilt in the sixteenth century and was used by the royal family as a 'grace and favour' home for army officers. In common with all large houses and castles in Bavaria, it had a small brewery but it was used to

Fairy tales can come true...the castle at Geltendorf where the Bavarian style of dark lager known as Dunkel has been revived.

Prince Luitpold in his brewery at Geltendorf has single-handedly saved a beer style from extinction but is not allowed to exhibit at the Munich Oktoberfest.

supply beer only to those living and working in the castle and for taverns in Geltendorf. Kaltenberg's present style, neo-Gothic with Wagnerian flourishes, was the result of work in the 1840s by the same architect who designed Neuschwanstein Castle for 'Mad' King Ludwig II, the castle that was the model for Walt Disney's fairy-tale interpretation.

Luitpold's father, Prince Ludwig, bought Kaltenberg Castle in the 1950s and the brewery came with it. Luitpold, the only son, had read law at Munich University but as the family was short of money he decided to turn the brewery into a commercial venture. It was a typical nineteenth-century house brewery, with small mashing and boiling vessels on the ground floor and wooden

Duke Wilhelm IV who drew up the terms of the
Reinheitsgebot or Pure Beer Law (right) in

1516. The law allows only malted grain, hops,
yeast and water in the brewing process.

lagering tanks deep below ground where the natural temperature allowed the beer to ripen slowly: one room in the cellar can hold 150 cubic metres (196 cubic yards) of ice. The castle brewery has had its capacity boosted from a modest 25,000 hectolitres a year to 120,000 (549,923 to 2.64 million gallons). The ground floor has copper mash and brew kettles in blue-tiled rooms and also houses the stores for hops and malt as well as wooden casks for the finished beer. The

brewery produces all the Kaltenberg beers made by cold fermentation: Dunkel, Helles and Export. A much larger brewery at Fürstenfeldbruck, bought in the mid-1980s, is devoted entirely to warm-fermented wheat beer (see Wheat Beer section).

Luitpold's revival of Dunkel has saved a beer style of historic significance. When commercial lagering of beer was developed in Munich in the last century, Gabriel Sedlmayr and the other great Munich

brewers continued to use brown malt cured over a mix of coal and wood fires in order to meet the demand of drinkers for beers with a burnished russet-brown colour. Barley high in protein and hard brewing water added to the problems of making a pale beer until new technologies helped iron out these little local difficulties. As with the brown ales and milds of England, Dunkel was overtaken in popularity in the 1950s by paler beers that sent it into decline.

Beer mats and labels for König Ludwig Dunkel
feature ancestors of the present Prince Luitpold.

The Bavarian royal family may be history but it
lives on thanks to the revival of dark lager.

The label above features König Ludwig, who was
the last Bavarian monarch.

Kaltenberg's König Ludwig Dunkel, named in honour of the last king of Bavaria, accounts for half the dark beer market in a vast region that houses the world's thirstiest beer drinkers. The beer has a starting gravity of 1055° and is attenuated to close to 80 per cent, leaving some sugars for body and fullness of palate but making it less sweet than other interpretations of the style. At the end of fermentation and storage it emerges with a strength of 5.6 per cent alcohol by volume. The units of bitterness are 20–22, the colour rating is 75 EBC. It is brewed from Pils and Munich dark malts with a touch (0.5 per cent) of roasted barley from which the husk is removed to avoid any astringency in the flavour.

Dunkel has a triple decoction mash and is hopped three times during the boil with Hallertauer-Hersbruck and Tettnanger varieties. Unusually for Germany, the beer is also dry hopped in the lagering tank: most brewers frown on an English method they feel runs the risk of infecting the beer. Prince Luitpold blanches his hops in boiling water before adding them to avoid any possible infection. But he believes the late addition of hops adds an important element of bitterness to the beer and counters any cloying sweetness from the malts.

After primary fermentation with a yeast culture from the Weihenstephan brewing faculty in Munich, the mash is pumped to a tank where it is inoculated with a Delbrücki yeast culture. This is a lactic culture isolated early this century by Professor Max Delbrück in the Berlin Institute of Brewing and used primarily in the production of sour Berlin wheat beer. 'We breed a beer infection,' Prince Luitpold said. 'The sour mash adjusts the pH and

Hearty traditional Bavarian fare is the ideal companion for Dunkel at the dining-table.

A wooden lagering vessel in the cellars of Geltendorf Castle. Fermentation now takes place in small steel tanks.

gives a softer flavour and better head retention to the finished beer. We need no chemicals: it is a biological souring.' The beer is kept for seven days at 10°C/50°F and is then lagered for four to six weeks. The beer is kräusened with sweet wort to encourage a second fermentation and aid carbonation.

The wooden lagering tanks are now kept for display or for storing occasional seasonal beers: the regular beers are lagered in vertical, flat-topped steel tanks. Again, Prince Lutipold controls the technology carefully: 'Fermenters should not be more than twice as high as they are wide. You get

different temperature levels in big conicals which can affect the flavour.'

The beer that emerges from this painstaking process has a superb aroma of juicy malt, chocolate and hops. Malt dominates the palate but the beer becomes dry, bitter and hoppy in the finish, with some of the bitterness coming from the dark malt and roasted barley. It is deliciously refreshing, full flavoured and complex.

Dark lager has survived in the Franconian region of northern Bavaria (Franken in German) in such towns as Bamberg, Bayreuth, Kulmbach and Nuremburg as a result of the comparative isolation of the region until modern times and its wish to retain a distinct identity from the rest of Bavaria. Many of the breweries in the region are tiny, little more than brewpubs. A classic example is the Hausbrauerei Altstadthof in Nuremberg, which means 'the house brewery in the old town'. It is based in sixteenth-century buildings and has copper mashing and boiling vessels with wooden fermenting and lagering tanks. Using organically grown barley and hops,

Prince Luitpold responded to being banned from the Munich Okotberfest by organizing an annual jousting tournament in the grounds of his castle. Vast crowds gather and quaff large quantities of Dunkel. Inspired by Luitpold, there are now many Dunkel beers brewed in Bavaria (below).

Weltenburger comes from a monastery with Kloster or cloister on the label. Kaiserdom has more regal claims and is brewed in Franconia.

It's a cold fermented dark beer but during the communist period the Köstritzer Brewery attempted to export it to Britain as 'stout'. The family doctor figure and the slogan 'Let your daily drink be...' suggests the brewery had heard that stout Is Good For You.

the 4.8 per cent Dunkel is red-brown in colour, has a bready and malty aroma, a creamy palate and malty finish with hints of dark fruit.

In Kulmbach, the Kulmbacher Mönchshof (monks' house) was once a monastery brewery and was secularized at the end of the eighteenth century. Its main brand is Kloster Schwarz Bier (cloister black beer), a 4.7 per cent beer nicknamed 'the black Pils' as a result of its pronounced hop character. It has a malty and yeasty aroma but hops break through on the palate and the finish is dry, quenching and bitter. EKU of Kulmbach is best known for its ferociously strong 13.5 per cent Doppelbock, one of the strongest beers in the world, but it also makes a more modest Rubin (ruby) Dunkel of 4.8 per cent. It is rich and malty with some tart fruit character and a dry finish.

The Klosterbräu Bamberg also has monastic origins: it started life in the sixteenth century when it was owned by a bishop whose monks did the brewing. A dark beer, sold in an adjacent tavern, has the tongue-twisting name of Achd Bambärcha Schwärzla, local dialect for 'real Bamberg black'. The deep brown beer is 5.3 per cent alcohol, has hops on the aroma, with coffee and dark fruit in the mouth and a creamy and bitter-sweet finish.

BLACK BEER OF SAXONY

Shortly after the collapse of communism and the bulldozing of the wall between the two Germanies, I flew to Frankfurt and was then driven by a director of the Bitburger Brewery into Saxony and the region of Thuringia. Bitburger had bought a brewery in Köstritz that made a Saxon speciality known as 'Schwarzbier' or black beer. The black beers of the region are considerably darker than those in Bavaria. Today they are made by cold fermentation, but warm fermentation survived until much later in Saxony and the porter-like intensity of the beers encouraged the main producer, Köstritzer, to export its black beer, even to Britain at one time as 'stout'.

The owner of Bitburger, Dr Axel Simon, a descendant of the founder, grew up in Berlin and remembered as a young child his mother drinking Schwarzbier while she breast-fed him, much as British and Irish mothers once drank stout as a tonic. Axel Simon thinks he may have drunk Schwarzbier as a teenager before his first Pilsener. His affection for the style made him determined to buy the Köstritzer brewery as soon as the two Germanies were reunited. As a state-owned enterprise, the brewhouse had been allowed to fall into disrepair while a new, ugly, functional brewery had been constructed with Eastern bloc vessels that looked, suitably, like army tanks. A jumble of pipes, joined at different angles, had trapped wort and yeast during fermentation, creating frequent infections.

Bitburger, like other west German brewers, could have closed the eastern plant and transferred production to its main brewery in the Eifel. But Axel Simon was determined to make black beer a Thuringian speciality once more. A major investment has dramatically improved the brewery and beer quality, though, sadly, some quaint traditions have disappeared. Older people liked to beat sugar and egg into the beer, but this was frowned upon by the west Germans with their strict adherence to the Reinheitsgebot. Bitburger boosted the strength of the black beer from 3.5 per cent alcohol by volume to 4.6 per cent. It is brewed with 50 per cent pale malt from the Erfurt region, 43 per cent Munich and the rest roasted malt. Hüller hops for bitterness and Hallertauer Mittelfrüh for aroma are used and create 35 units of bitterness. The

beer has an aroma of dark fruit, malt loaf and bitter chocolate, followed by a creamy palate and a long finish with more dark fruit, coffee and chocolate, underpinned by hops.

CZECH DARK LAGERS

When I first visited the U Fleku brew-pub in Prague in the mid-1980s it was a haunt of East German tourists who packed every bench in the warren of rooms and in the rear beer garden; for them it was a Stasi-free zone. Today, U Fleku is on the international tourist trail and you are as likely to hear American and Australian accents as German. The owners even charge an entrance fee; it is a modest 40 pence or 60 cents but it is enough to deter the cash-strapped Czechs. Beer has been brewed at U Fleku in Prague since at least 1499. A large wall-clock juts out over the pavement and marks the entrance which leads into the maze of wood-panelled rooms with benches and settles. In warm weather, drinkers spill out into the spacious beer garden overlooked by the brewhouse. The tavern's name stems from 1762 when it was bought by Jakub Flekovsky and his wife. In the Czech style, it was known as U

With help from its owner Bitburger, Köstritzer is now promoting its dark beer with some elan.

Bitburger has poured million of marks into the Köstritzer brewery.

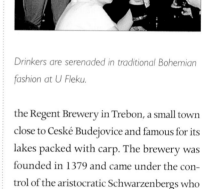

Flekovsky, shortened over time to U Fleku: 'U' serves the same role as 'chez' in French and means 'at the house of'.

The small brewhouse has a capacity of 6000 hectolitres (131,982 gallons). It is sufficient for the needs of the owners, because U Fleku's beer is not available outside the tavern. Fermentation begins in an open 'cool ship' vessel, a large, shallow pan covering an entire floor. A new brewhouse with polished copper kettles was installed in the 1980s. The 13 degree dark lager (4.5 per cent alcohol by volume) is made from Pilsner (50 per cent), Munich (30 per cent),

A large clock greets visitors to the U Fleku brew-pub in Prague.

caramalt (15 per cent) and roasted malt (5 per cent). Zatec hops are added three times during the copper boil. The finished beer has a pronounced house yeast character with roasted malt, chocolate, coffee and licorice notes, an underpinning of hops and a smooth, creamy and malty-juicy finish.

One of the best brewers of dark lager is

The beer garden behind U Fleku; drinkers come from all over Europe and North America.

Drinkers are serenaded in traditional Bohemian fashion at U Fleku.

the Regent Brewery in Trebon, a small town close to Ceské Budejovice and famous for its lakes packed with carp. The brewery was founded in 1379 and came under the control of the aristocratic Schwarzenbergs who moved the plant into the castle and rebuilt it, complete with its own maltings. Since the Velvet Revolution the brewery has been

Ivan Dufek now owns the Regent Brewery following the fall of communism.

privatized and an injection of money has allowed the brewhouse to be refurbished. It was a dank and dismal place when I first knew it in the 1980s, but now every copper vessel gleams and head brewer Ivan Dufek is fired with optimism. The brewing process is painstaking: mashing and boiling last for twelve hours, followed by a slow primary fermentation in open squares that takes twelve days, followed by ninety days lagering in horizontal tanks for 12 degree beers. The house yeast originates in Ceské Budejovice. Regent makes pale lagers but its classic is Dark Regent (4.8 per cent), brewed from pale, caramalt and dark malts and Zatec hops. It is ruby-red in colour and has a tempting aroma of hops and bitter chocolate, with dark malt in the mouth and a finish reminiscent of cappuccino coffee.

JAPANESE BLACK BEER

The Japanese only developed a taste for beer in the late nineteenth century. Modern Japan may be best known today for its pale

Dark lager has reached the far north; Steiger is brewed by a subsidiary of Holsten.

lagers, but visitors will also find occasional versions of Dortmunder Export, Düsseldorf Alt, Bavarian Weisse, English Stout and black lagers. The last are more in the Saxon than the Franconian style and, frustratingly, there is no known record of just how the link between Japan and eastern Germany was made.

The Black Beer (5 per cent) brewed by Sapporo is the classic of the style. It is made with pale, crystal, Munich and chocolate malts with a small amount of rice. Hops are aroma varieties, home-grown and imported. When poured, Sapporo Black Beer throws a heavy head of foam. The aroma is intense and dominated by dark malt with a roasted coffee appeal; it has dark fruit, hops and malt in the mouth, and rich hints of coffee, bitter chocolate and hops in the finish.

Kirin Black Beer (5 per cent) has a pronounced roasted coffee and liquorice palate after a gentle, grainy start. The finish is light and refreshing with some delicate hop character. Asahi Black (also 5 per cent) is less dark, with a hint of red-brown in the colour. It has a sweet palate and finish, and drinkers often blend it with lager to balance the caramel flavour. Suntory's Black Beer (yet again 5 per cent), is so dark as to be opaque. It has a pronounced chocolatey aroma and palate with soft, creamy malt and a hint of hops in the delicate malt and chocolate finish.

Bohemia Regent enjoys a slow process to produce the richest flavours.

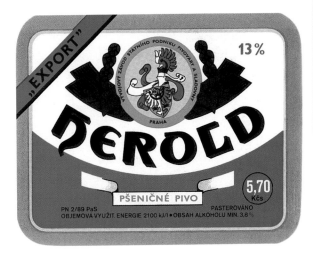

At 13 degrees Herold is a strong Czech interpretation of dark lager.

DUNKEL AND BLACK BEER STYLE

Creamy malt, roasted grain, chocolate, licorice and aromatic hops give great depth and complexity to dark lager.

There is no record of black lager being exported to Japan but all the major breweries there, including Sapporo (left) produce versions of the style from Saxony.

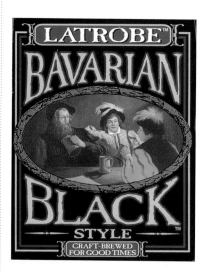

In the United States, Latrobe of Pennsylvania makes a beer in the Bavarian dark fashion.

DUNKEL AND BLACK BEER BREWERS

GERMANY
Altstadthof
18 Berg-strasse, 8500 Nuremberg

EKU Erste Kulmbacher Actien Brauerei AG
EKU-strasse 1, Kulmbach

Münchshof Braugaststätte
Hofe-strasse 20, Kulmbach

Neuzeller Klosterbräu
Brauhausplatz 1, 15898 Neuzelle

Schlossbräuerei Kaltenberg
8 Schloss-strasse, 8085 Geltendorf

Köstritzer Schwarzbierbrauerei
Heinrich Schütz-strasse, Bad Köstritz, 6514 Thüringen

CZECH REPUBLIC
Regent
Trocnovské ná, 379 13 Trébon

U Fleku
1 Kremencova, Prague 1

JAPAN
Asahi Breweries
23–1 Azumabashi 1-chome, Sumida-ku, Tokyo 130

Kirin Brewery Company
26–1, Jingumae 6-chome, Shibuya-ku, Tokyo 150

Sapporo Breweries
7–10–1 Ginza, Chuo-ku, Tokyo 104

Suntory Brewery
1–2–3 Motoakasaka, Minato-ku, Tokyo 107

MARZEN AND OKTOBERFEST

A Munich beer tent with painted scenery, a bandstand and hordes of thirsty drinkers.

Oktoberfest beer is served by women who carry an astonishing number of foaming tankards.

The annual Munich Oktoberfest is the world's best-known and best attended beer festival, but the special style of beer brewed for this great jamboree is in danger of disappearing. Märzen means 'March beer': in the time before refrigeration, the Munich brewers would make a strong beer in March, the last to be brewed before the summer, which was stored or lagered in ice-filled caves. The casks were then ceremonially broached on the opening day of the beer festival. The beer that refreshes the vast crowds that swarm into the tents every autumn, with the first cask tapped by the city's mayor, is now more often a golden Oktoberfest lager rather than an amber Märzen. The reason has nothing to do with a lack of demand for genuine

March beer from the people of Munich, but has everything to do with the international character of the beer festival. Inside the great beer tents, you are as likely to hear American, Australian, English and New Zealand accents as Bavarian ones. As the brewers consider this polyglot audience will have little appreciation of the finer points of beer styles, they consider Oktoberfest beer will suffice. It is certainly a better beer than the mainstream lagers found in most anglophone countries.

When I last visited the Löwenbräu Brewery in Munich, I was invited to sample the company's entire range. Only one was missing. When I asked for a Märzen, I was told none was available as it was brewed in one small batch every year. When I inquired about it a couple of years later, I was told it had been stopped completely. The other Munich brewers are more reticent. Spaten still makes a genuine March beer but confuses the issue with a separate Oktoberfestbier.

Spaten's Ur-Märzen is a vital and now tenuous link with the earliest days of commercial lager brewing in Munich. When Gabriel Sedlmayr embarked on his development of cold fermentation at the Spaten Brewery, he collaborated closely with the renowned Viennese brewer Anton Dreher. Dreher's beer had a red-bronze colour due to the use of 'Vienna red' malt, a well-cured malt similar to English mild ale malt. While Gabriel Sedlmayr's first commercial

Hacker-Pschorr hedges its bets with a beer called Märzen and Oktoberfest.

Löwenbräu brews only an Oktoberfest beer and has phased out its March version.

lagers were dark or Dunkel, his brother Josef brewed a Vienna-style beer at his Franziskaner Brewery. It was this amber version of a March beer that became the benchmark for the new lagers offered every year at the Oktoberfest. The two breweries merged in the 1920s, but the Ur-Märzen brewed today at Spaten is based strictly on the original Franziskaner recipe. It is 5.6 per cent alcohol by volume and has 32 colour units and 21 bitterness units. It is a malt-accented beer but it is clean and quenching, the long storage removing any tendency towards cloying sweetness. It is balanced by a gentle but firm hoppiness, and the finish is bitter-sweet with chewy malt and a hint of nuts from the amber malt.

The state-owned Hofbräuhaus, the former royal court brewhouse in Munich, is a vast, cavernous building with wooden tables and Bavarian high-backed settles. The Hofbräu's 5.7 per cent Märzen is russet-coloured with a creamy malt aroma, a refreshing palate and a bitter-sweet finish that becomes dry.

Mexico has a long brewing tradition dating from the sixteenth century. From the nineteenth century, Germanic influences encouraged a switch to cold fermentation. The influence of Anton Dreher crossed the Atlantic. His amber lagers may be forgotten in his own country but they remain popular in Latin America. They are produced by Mexico's two giants, Moctezuma and

Full Sail of Portland, Oregon brews a rich and rounded October beer for its bar and restaurant.

Modelo, best known but best forgotten for their bland and briefly fashionable pale lagers Sol and Corona. Moctezuma of Monterrey dates from 1894 and includes in its portfolio Dos Equis (Two Crosses), a 4.8 per cent amber beer with a dark fruit and chocolate aroma and palate, with more chocolate and light hops in the finish. Modelo in Mexico City brews Negra Modelo (Black Modelo), 5.3 per cent, with a chocolatey aroma and some hop character, sweet dark malt in the mouth, and a long finish with a hint of spices, roast malt, chocolate and hops.

In the United States, craft brewers ensure that Märzen and Oktoberfest beers have found a new home, the former usually offered as amber beer to avoid troubling Americans with a difficult German name. Sea Dog Brewing of Bangor, Maine, started life as a brew-pub but has developed into a fully-fledged commercial company. Its 5.2 per cent Oktoberfest has won a gold medal at the Great American Beer Festival for its rich, rounded, malty-hoppy palate and finish. F.X. Matt of Utica, New York, in the foothills of the Adirondack Mountains, was founded by Francis Xavier Matt from the German Black Forest. His descendants have maintained the German tradition with a Saranac Chocolate Amber (5.8 per cent), a cross between a Munich Dark and a Vienna Red, with a smooth, rounded malt and chocolate character balanced by spicy hops.

In Pittsburgh, Pennsylvania, the Penn Brewery is owned by Tom Pastorius who learnt his brewing skills in Germany. He

In Boston, with owner Jim Koch's German origins, Samuel Adams is a fine amber-bronze interpretation of the style.

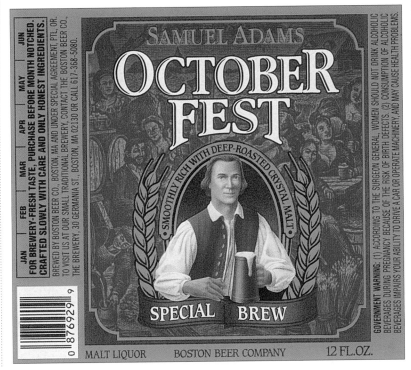

222

MARZEN AND OKTOBERFEST STYLE

Clean and quenching, with a firm hoppiness, chewy malt, some vinous notes and hints of chocolate and nuts in darker versions, these beers offer a rich and rewarding drinking experience.

Great Lakes of Cleveland stresses the Bavarian roots of the style with a traditional beer jug on the label.

ferments in traditional horizontal lagering tanks to make both a 5 per cent Dark based on the Munich Dunkel style and a 5.6 per cent Märzen, malty, nutty and bitter-sweet.

In Denver, Colorado, the Tabernash Brewing Co. produces a clutch of cold-fermented beers perfected by brewer Eric Warner, who has a diploma from the Weihenstephan brewing faculty in Munich. His Tabernash Oktoberfest is tapped every September after a lengthy lagering and emerges with a powerful 6 per cent alcohol by volume. It has a rich and slightly toasted malt aroma and palate with a big, slightly fruity and perfumy note from the hops.

MARZEN AND OKTOBERFEST BREWERS

GERMANY
Staatliches Hofbräuhaus in München
Hofbräuallee 1, 81829 Munich 8

Spaten-Franziskaner-Brau
Mars-strasse 46, 80335 Munich

Löwenbräu AG
Nymphenburge-strasse 4, Munich 2

MEXICO
Cerverceria Moctezuma
Avenida Alfonso Reyes 2202, Nte, Monterrey NL 64442

Cerverceria Modelo
156 Lago Alberto, Mexico City 11320

UNITED STATES
F.X. Matt Brewing
811 Edward Street, Utica, New York 13502

Penn Brewery
800 Vinial Street, Pittsburgh, Pennsylvania 15212

Sea Dog Brewing
26 Front Street, Bangor, Maine 04401

Tabernash Brewing
205 Denargo Market, Denver, Colorado 80216

GREAT LAKES
BREWING CO.

Oktoberfest
A Handcrafted Märzen Style Beer
From Cleveland, Ohio
12 fl. oz.

Our traditional Oktoberfest style beer is brewed in the same way it was for the first Oktoberfest in 1810 which celebrated the betrothal of the Crown Prince of Bavaria. It is medium-strong and malty flavored – just the thing for any celebration!
In keeping with the Bavarian Purity Law of 1516, this beer is traditionally brewed from all-natural ingredients: hops, malted barley, yeast and water. No preservatives or chemicals are used.
Since this hand-crafted brew is unpastuerized, it must be kept refrigerated. For the freshest taste, drink before:

Glass Recycles

Brewed & bottled by:
The Great Lakes®
Brewing Co.
2516 Market St.
Cleveland, OH 44113
(216) 771-4404

Photo: Beth Segal

BOCK

In Germany the name Bock indicates a strong lager (not less than 6.4 per cent alcohol by law) usually drunk at special times of the year. A Maibock will be consumed in May to celebrate the arrival of summer, while the strongest form of the beer, Doppel Bock or Double Bock, is associated with the Lenten period when monks traditionally refreshed and nourished themselves with a beer they called 'liquid bread'. Above all, Bock is a beer style considered to have powerful roots in Munich and Bavaria. Yet its origins lie in the north of Germany and its name stems from the wide differences in dialect in that vast country.

As you approach the town of Einbeck in Lower Saxony you will see road signs announcing 'Beer City'. Einbeck was an important member of the medieval Hanseatic League of trading towns and cities. It vied with Hamburg as a major producer of beer, and as well as refreshing its own citizens it exported to the Low Countries and Scandinavia. The beers of Einbeck acquired fame and notoriety in the sixteenth century when Martin Luther, leader of the Protestant revolution, sustained himself with beer from the town as he awaited the sessions of the Diet of Worms in 1521, where he was excommunicated for heresy. A commercial brewery was established in Einbeck in 1794 and has been rebuilt several times. The present site, finished in 1975, is called the Einbecker Brauhaus and bears the legend 'Ohne Einbeck gäb's kein Bockbier' ('Without Einbeck there would be no Bock beer'). To emphasize the point, the brewery's products are all labelled Ur-Bock or Original Bock. The company uses soft spring water, barley malt from the Brunswick region, and Hersbrucker, Northern Brewer and Perle hops from Bavaria. Hopping is more emphatic than in Bavaria: the pale Hell (6.9 per cent alcohol)

Thrown out in style. . .Martin Luther is reputed to have refreshed himself with Einbeck beer while on trial for heresy.

has 38 units of bitterness, a toasted malt aroma and palate and a big hoppy finish. Dunkel, with the same strength and bitterness rating, has an aroma and palate rich in dark fruit and coffee with a late burst of hops in the spicy, chocolatey finish. Maibock, again 6.9 per cent, is sold between March and mid-May, has 36 IBUs and a clean and quenching palate. The beers enjoy between six and ten weeks' lagering.

The style went south in the seventeenth century when a Duke of Brunswick in Lower Saxony married the daughter of a Bavarian aristocrat. The wedding was held in Munich and the duke brought a master brewer with him to make Einbecker beer to aid the celebrations. The Bavarians took to the strong, rich beer style and a century later their broad dialect had turned the name into 'Oanbocker'. Bock was plucked from the term as a jocular nickname, for Bock is the German for billy-goat, a symbol of

Einbecker labels carry the tag 'Ur-Bock', meaning it is the original version of the style.

224

virility and strength. Today many labels for Bock beer include the image of a billy-goat.

Bavarians dismiss any suggestion that Bock's origins lie elsewhere. For them it is a south German style, locked into the traditions of the region. They underscore the point with the diversity of Bock beers on offer: Maibocks for spring and summer, winter Bocks to ward off the cold, Doppelbocks (also known as Starkbier, meaning strong beer) for Lent. Bock is synonymous with festivals. On May Day the Hofbräuhaus in Munich heralds the arrival of summer with its 7.2 Helles Bock, an amber beer with a dense head of foam, a nutty malt aroma balanced by floral hops, a toasted malt palate and a long finish packed with malt, hops and fruit. The first cask is ritually tapped by the mayor of Munich, who performs the same ceremonies at the Oktoberfest and the Starkbierfest.

The most famous of all German Doppelbocks comes from the Paulaner

Ayinger near Munich produces an aromatic Bock for drinking in spring time.

Brewery in Munich and is the benchmark for the style. Paulaner was founded in 1634 by monks who were followers of St Francis of Paula from Calabria in what is now Italy. They built a small brewery in their monastery and brewed a strong beer to sustain them during Lent. The monks started to sell beer commercially from the late

eighteenth century. A century later, the brewery was secularized and its new owner, Franz-Xaver Zacherl, vigorously developed Doppelbock under the name of Salvator, which means Holy Father Beer. Its success prompted other brewers to make imitations, and Paulaner was forced to take legal action to protect its title. As a result, its competitors changed the names of their Doppelbocks but all added 'or' at the end to stress the style and pay homage to the original. Hofbräu makes Delicator, Augustiner Maximator, Spaten Optimator and Hacker-Pschorr Animator.

Paulaner Salvator Doppelbock is 7.5 per cent alcohol, is russet brown and has a malt loaf aroma, a yeasty and bready palate and a complex finish rich in fruit, malt and hops: liquid bread indeed. It is made from three malts and is hopped with Hallertauer varieties. Löwenbräu's Triumphator is 7 per cent and is a magnificent beer with an aroma and palate of roasted malt, spices and chocolate and a long fruity and malt loaf finish.

The monastic brewery at Münnerstadt brews a firmly traditional 'double' bock, its label adorned by billy-goats.

Munich's Paulaner Brewery makes the city's classic Doppelbock based on ancient recipes used by monks to make Lent beers.

Outside Munich, Ayinger's Fortunator (7.5 per cent) has a fruit cake aroma and flavour followed by a rich and warming finish while Prince Luitpold's 6.8 per cent Dunkel Ritterbock from Kaltenberg (Dark Knight's Bock) has a big coffee and spices aroma, a good hop presence in the mouth and a dry finish with a dark malt character. While a Bavarian Doppelbock is not twice as strong as an ordinary Bock, law and convention stipulate that it must be not less than 6.9 per cent alcohol.

The Bock tradition travelled to and survived in countries close to Germany. As long ago as the seventh century, an Irish Benedictine monk named St Gall built an abbey with a brewery in the German-speaking canton of Switzerland that took his name. He brought learning and Christianity as well as the knowledge of brewing to the region. The town where his abbey stood is named St Gallen in his honour. Not surprisingly, the cantons of northeast Switzerland, with their close proximity to Germany, have the most powerful brewing traditions.

Hürlimann of Zürich brews a Bock-style beer called Samichlaus that, at 14 per cent alcohol, is registered as the strongest beer in the world. From time to time other brewers attempt to steal Hürlimann's crown with beers of even greater strength, but the Zürich company's reason for making Samichlaus was based not

Oss in the Netherlands makes a wide range of organic beers including a Bock that makes even billy-goats pie-eyed.

Feldschlössen's impressive plant is the new home for Hürlimann following the closure of the Zürich brewery.

on a desire to grace the pages of the *Guinness Book of Records* but on a scientific analysis of brewer's yeast. The brewery was founded in 1865 by Albert Hürlimann just as beer making in central Europe was converting to cold fermentation. His scientists' dedicated research into the temperatures at which yeast will ferment malt sugars was an important footnote to the pioneering work of Dreher and Sedlmayr. Unlike a wine or Champagne yeast, which can produce high levels of alcohol, brewer's yeast gives up or 'goes to sleep' at around 12 per cent alcohol by volume, overwhelmed by the alcohol it has produced. The Hürlimann researchers worked for decades to culture a strain of brewer's yeast that would continue to work above 12 per cent. In 1979 they used the new culture to make an experimental Christmas beer. The interest this created encouraged the brewery to make the beer as a regular Christmas

226

one with the name of Samichlaus, German for Santa Claus. To avoid the cloying sweetness associated with some strong lagers of the 'Special Brew' variety, Samichlaus enjoys a full year in the lager cellar. It is mashed every year on 6 December and is released on the same day 12 months later. During that long period of secondary fermentation and maturation, the beer is occasionally roused by pumping it from one tank to another to ensure the yeast does not go to sleep. The chestnut-coloured beer has a blend of pale and three dark malts from France, Germany and Moravia and enjoys a double decoction mashing regime. The wort is hopped three times during the copper boil with Hallertauer, Hersbrucker and Styrian Goldings varieties with some Stammheimer hops grown near Zürich. The hops create 30 units of bitterness. The beer that emerges from the long maturation process has an aroma of port wine, dark fruit and spicy hops, with coffee, bitter chocolate, nuts and malt in the mouth and a finish reminiscent of Cognac.

Scandinavians have a long tradition of brewing German-style beers, and there are several interpretations that include references to Bavaria and Munich in their names. The Norwegian independent Aass in the harbour town of Drammen near Oslo built its fame on the quality of its Bock. Aass (pronounced 'oss') is Norway's oldest brewery,

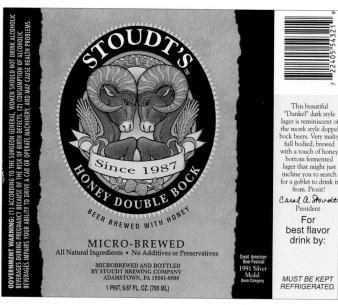

Carol Stoudt is an American brewster who trained in Germany to perfect her Double Bock and other lagers.

founded in 1834 as a 'pot beer house' supplying customers who brought jugs to the door. Poul Lauritz Aass took control in 1860 and busily developed the brewery into a

In Seattle Thomas Kemper's Mai-Bock uses a Bavarian yeast strain to obtain the right balance of flavours.

full-scale commercial enterprise. Today the company makes more than a dozen brands, including a popular pale lager broadly in the Pilsner style, an amber Münchner and a Bayer (Bavarian) Dunkel. Aass Bok is the export name; for the home market it is known as Bokkøl. The 6.5 per cent beer is lagered for six months and is dark, rich and creamy with a hint of fennel on the aroma and palate.

Mack of Tromso is one of the most northerly and coldest breweries in the world, 300 kilometres (187 miles) inside the Arctic Circle. As well as Arctic Beer, it also makes a 6.5 per cent Bokkøl that is chestnut coloured with a good balance of malt and hops. It is lagered for ten weeks.

Carlsberg's premium beer from Copenhagen is Elephant (7.5 per cent), named after the Elephant Gates entrance to the brewery, and is firmly in the Bock tradition. It is brewed from pale malt and brewing sugar while Hallertauer hops produce 38 units of bitterness. It is big bodied, malty and smooth and easy drinking, with delicious hints of honey sweetness balanced by tart hops.

Bock is a popular style in the Netherlands, so popular that one new and innovative brewery makes no fewer than four versions. Maasland was founded in the north Brabant town of Oss in 1989 and quickly established a name for itself with warm fermented, bottle-conditioned beers made from organic

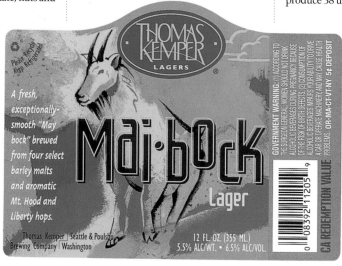

Saxon in Oregon brews three bocks. Its Golden Helles version has a strikingly traditional label.

The Boston Beer Company matures its Triple Bock, finished with a Champagne yeast, in Bourbon whiskey casks.

materials, and promoted with the aid of eye-catching labels. Its main beer is d'n Schele Os, meaning the Dizzy Ox, while its Bocks include Volkoren, copper coloured with a rich balance of dark malt and hops, pale and dark Meibocks and Ossebock. All the beers are 6.5 per cent and are neither filtered nor pasteurized. The hop varieties used are Brewers Gold, Hallertauer and Challenger.

Brand, part of Heineken, produces a 6.5 per cent Imperator, a cold fermented Bock in the Bavarian style. It is an all-malt beer made from pale, chocolate and Munich varieties with Hallertauer, Hersbrucker and Perle hops. A 7.5 per cent winter Dubbelbock has a deep, almost purple russet colour and is fruity and malty, while Meibock (7 per cent) has a spicy aroma, a tart fruity palate and more spice in the finish. Several Dutch Bocks (often spelt Bok) are warm fermented and include Drie

228 Ringen's 6.6 per cent Bokbier and 6.5 Meibok, both fruity with gentle hops, and Drie Horne's Bokbier (7 per cent), dry and fruity with peppery hops and conditioned in the bottle. Grolsche has added a 6.5 per cent Bok and a 6 per cent Mei Bok to its portfolio, the former dark, sweet and smoothly drinkable, the latter amber coloured and dry on the palate, with a good balance of fruit and hops.

The United States was once awash with Bock beer thanks to the influence of German immigrants. The style disappeared during Prohibition but they are being revived as part of the beer renaissance led by craft brewers. In the Pacific North-west, Thomas Kemper of Seattle, part of the Pyramid Ales group, has a 6.6 per cent Mai-bock, fermented with a Bavarian yeast strain. It is brewed in the spring and has a big perfumy hop, sweet malt aroma and palate with a lingering malt-and-hops finish. In Boston, Samuel Adams Double Bock (8.5 per cent) is a superb rendition of the Bavarian style,

Billy Goat Gruff…an old Spaten label for Bock has a scarey version of the traditional goat.

BOCK BEER STYLE

Bocks offer a massive perfumy 'noble' hop aroma and flavour balanced by a rich vinous alcohol with raisin and sultana fruit, with chocolate notes when darker malt is used.

brewed in the spring (making it a Maibock) with a perfumy hop and juicy malt character with hints of chocolate from darker malt. Saxer of Lake Oswego, Oregon, brews three bocks, a pale Helles, a Dark and winter Jack Frost doppelbock. They are lagered for between six and eight weeks, use two-row pale, Vienna caramunich and caramel malts and are hopped with the rare Ahtanun hop along with Cascades and Hersbrucker.

BOCK BEER BREWERS

GERMANY
Augustiner Brauerei,
Neuhauser-strasse 16, 8000 Munich 1

Ayinger Brauerei Inselkammer
1 Zornedinger-strasse, 8011 Aying

Einbecker Brauhaus
4-7 Papen-strasse, 3352 Einbeck

Hacker-Pschorr Bräu GmbH
Schwanthalerstrasse 113, 8000 Munich 2

Löwenbräu AG
Nympenburger-strasse 4, 8000 Munich 2

Paulaner-Salvator-Thomasbräu
Hoch-strasse 75, 8000 Munich 9

Spaten-Franziskaner-Bräu KGA
Mars-strasse 46-48, 8000 Munich 2

Staatliches Hofbräuhaus in München
Hobräuallee 1, 8000 Munich 8

NETHERLANDS
Koninklijke Brand Bierborouwerij BV
Brouwerijstraat 2, Postbus 1, 6300 AA Wijlre

De Drie Horne Bierbrouwerij
Berndijksestraat 63, 5171 BB Kaatsheuvel

Maaslandbrouwerij
Kantsingel 14, 5349 AJ Oss

DENMARK
Carlsberg Brewery
100 Vesterfaelldvej DK, 1799, Copenhagen

NORWAY
P Lauritz Aass
PO Box 1107, Drammen 3001

Macks Olbryggeri
9005 Tromso

UNITED STATES
Boston Beer Company
30 Germania Street, Boston, Massachusetts 02130

Thomas Kemper Lagers
1201 1st Avenue South, Seattle, Washington 98134

Oldenberg Brewing
400 Buttermilk Pike, Fort Mitchell, Kentucky 41017

Saxer Brewing Company
5875 SW Lakeview Blvd, Lake Oswego, Oregon 97035

RARE BEERS

There are several rare beers around the world that are worthy of some discussion here, including steam beers from California, along with smoked beers and ice bocks from Bavaria.

SAN FRANCISCO STEAM BEER

There are several steam beer breweries in the world and a number of German plants use the term 'dampfbierbrauerei'. But the steam they are referring to is the energy created by steam engines when they were installed in breweries during the Industrial Revolution. In San Francisco it means something quite different – a beer inextricably linked with the city's history and its transformation from a small and mainly Mexican town into a major city.

Steam Beer was created as a result of the California Gold Rush of the 1890s. When gold prospectors poured into the town they found a Mexican population which drank wine as the beverage of preference. But the prospectors wanted beer and they wanted the cold lagers they were used to drinking

on the east coast of the United States. The handful of small brewers in San Francisco at the time made ale and they had no access to refrigerators or ice-filled caves in which to store beer, so they began to improvize brilliantly. They acquired supplies of bottom-fermenting yeast and used it to

Fritz Maytag turned a forgotten San Francisco style into an American classic.

Anchor Steam Beer is based on a style that is a crossover between ale and lager with such a high levels of carbonation that casks when tapped were said to steam.

The impressive copper brewhouse at Anchor was built by Germans to Maytag's exacting design.

make a hybrid beer. Brewing was carried out at ale temperatures but fermentation took place in large, shallow copper trays measuring 0.6 metres (2 feet) in depth, compared to the 1.8 metres (6 feet) of conventional vessels. The trays allowed a larger surface area of the fermenting beer to be open to the atmosphere and would thus cool more quickly. Fermentation continued in wooden casks and the beer had such a high level of carbonation that when the casks were broached in bars there was a hiss of escaping gas as the beer was poured. It was this effervescence and the sound it made that gave these beers their nickname of 'steam'.

The sole brewer of steam beer in San Francisco today is the Anchor Brewery owned by Fritz Maytag. It is an all-malt beer, a blend of pale and crystal. The hops are Northern Brewer, added three times in the kettle. The beer is 4 per cent alcohol by weight/5 per cent volume. After mashing

An old plaque for Steam Beer in the Anchor Brewery's reception area.

and boiling in conventional copper vessels, the hopped wort is pumped into 0.6 metres (2 feet)-deep fermentation trays, inoculated with lager yeast and fermented at a warm temperature of 16–21°C (61–70°F). Following primary fermentation, the green or unfinished beer is warm conditioned in tanks for three weeks and is then kräusened by having some sugar-rich unfermented wort added to encourage a second fermentation. The beer that emerges from this complex system is bronze coloured and has a malty and nutty aroma, more malt and light fruit in the mouth, and a long finish in which the hops slowly dominate. It has 30–35 units of bitterness and is a fascinating beer to drink, with the thirst-quenching character of a lager and the fruitiness of an ale.

SMOKED BEER

Once all beers would have had a smoky character as a result of brown malt being cured over wood fires. The style still survives in the Bamberg area of Franconia. This striking town with its mix of Romanesque, Gothic and Baroque buildings is an important malting as well as brewing centre. The maltsters' kilns are fired with beechwood gathered from the surrounding forests, and the finished malt is then supplied to the town's brewers. In some cases, however, the brewers have their own maltings. The classic Rauchbier (smoked beer) is brewed by Heller-Trum. Its origins lie in the Schlenkerla Tavern in Bamberg which dates from 1678. The brewery yard is piled high with beechwood logs, and

inside there is a smokehouse where the barley malt is spread on a wire mesh above a beechwood fire.

Brewing takes place in copper vessels with fermentation in open containers, followed by two months' lagering. The principal beer is Aecht Schlenkerla Rauchbier, 5 per cent alcohol with 29–32 units of bitterness. It is a deep copper colour and has an intense smoked malt aroma, palate and finish. The name is a combination of a Franconian dialect word, *Aecht*, meaning Old, while *Schlenkerla* is a rude description of a former brewer in the tavern who had long arms and an ape-like walk. Heller-Trum also makes an autumn Bock, a Helles and a Märzen, all with smoked malt. Also in Bamberg, the Christian Merz Spezial

Brewery is housed in a brew-pub founded in 1536. Malt is still kilned in a courtyard at the back of the pub. The Rauchbier is known simply as Lagerbier (4.9 per cent). It has a pale brown colour, a smoky and malty aroma and palate, and a dry finish with a hint of burnt toffee. The Bürgerbräu Kaiserdom Brewery specializes in a 4.8 per cent Rauchbier that has an appealing amber colour with a smoky and malty aroma and palate followed by a dry finish.

ICE BOCK

This is another Bavarian speciality. It inspired the short-lived Canadian ice beers but should not be confused with them. The Bavarian beers have finesse, the Canadians just hype. The true ice beers come from Kulmbach and enjoy such a long lagering at low temperatures that ice forms in the vessels. The leading ice beer is brewed by Kulmbacher Reichelbräu: it is known as Eisbock with the tag line *Bayrisch G'frorns*, which means 'Bavarian frozen'. The beer is 10 per cent alcohol and is made from five malts, including a dark variety and one that has a deliberate sour and lactic character to avoid such a strong beer ending with a cloying character. It has 27 units of bitterness from Brewers Gold, Hersbrucker, Perle and Tettnanger varieties.

After primary fermentation the beer is frozen for two weeks. Water freezes at a higher temperature than alcohol and forms ice crystals in the brew. The ice is removed, thus concentrating the alcohol. The beer is then kräusened to start a strong second fermentation. The finished beer has warming alcohol, is aromatic with hops and is rich and fruity in the mouth followed by a long

The Schlenkerla Tavern in Bamberg dates from 1678 and brews the classic version of smoked beer.

EKU is one of the strongest beers in the world. Ice forms in the lagering tank towards the end of the nine-month storage period.

finish with a pronounced coffee taste from the dark malt. The beer is brewed in August and September and stored until the last Saturday in March when a frozen cask is tapped at the Eisbock Festival in the Rathaus or town hall.

The world's best known Double Bock also comes from Kulmbach. EKU 28 is not marketed as an Ice Bock but ice does form during the nine-month lagering period. EKU 28's fame rests on its formidable strength of 13.5 per cent alcohol, which made it the world's strongest beer until beaten to the punch by Hürlimann's Samichlaus in Switzerland. EKU stands for *Erste Kulmbacher Unionbrauerei* and means the First Union Brewery of Kulmbach: it was created by the merger of two smaller concerns in 1872. The brewery uses mountain spring water, Franconian malt and Hersbrucker, Perle and Tettnanger hops. It makes a conventional 7.5 per cent Kulminator Double Bock with a claret colour, a rich malt aroma and palate, with hops and dark fruit in the finish. The mash kettles are then charged with even more malt to make Kulminator 28: the 28 comes from an old German method of declaring strength. It is brewed from just pale malt but some caramelization of the malt sugars gives it an amber colour. Towards the end of the long lagering period, ice forms in the tanks: the brewery says the level of ice does not concentrate the alcohol and therefore does not claim it to be a true Ice Bock. EKU 28 emerges with ripe malt on the aroma balanced by tart hops, light citric fruit on the palate, and a long and warming finish with great malt, hops and fruit character.

RARE BEER BREWERS

Anchor Brewing Co.
1705 Mariposa Street, San Francisco, California 94107

EKU Erste Kulmbacher Actien Brauerei AG
EKU-strasse 1, Kulmbach

Heller-Trum Schlenkerla
6 Dominikaner-strasse, 8600 Bamberg

Kulmbacher Reichelbräu GmbH
Hofe-strasse 20, Kulmbach

America

There are now 1300 breweries in the United States. The country vies with reunited Germany as the biggest brewing nation in the world. Charles Finkel, who owns the Pike Brewery in Seattle and brews acclaimed East India Pale Ale, Porter and Barley Wine, says America is undergoing a beer renaissance, returning to the brewing shoots nurtured by the Founding Fathers, with their English ale culture, and the second wave of immigrants from central Europe who brought the new techniques of lagering with them.

The US has rediscovered its brewing soul. A challenging movement led by the craft brewers has shaken a deeply conservative and complacent industry to its roots. Only a handful of brewers survived Prohibition, and their number fell as a result of the great economic depression of the 1930s. It seemed that Americans were destined to drink for ever only ice-cold, bland and pallid beers, unaware of both great European beer styles and their own once-revered ales, porters, stouts, stock ales, lagers, wheat beers and bocks.

The revolution that began fitfully in the 1960s and 1970s gathered pace in the 1980s. An army of dedicated home brewers gathered under the banner of the American Home Brewers' Association and started to tease out recipes for great brewing styles. Many of them went the extra mile, built small craft breweries and started to sell their beers commercially. It was a difficult route to go down. Under American law, brewers cannot own pubs; the British 'tied house' system is illegal. With most of the national delivery companies either directly owned or controlled by the brewing giants, the craft brewers either stayed local, selling their beers to a handful of bars or organized cooperatives to deliver beer more widely. Even

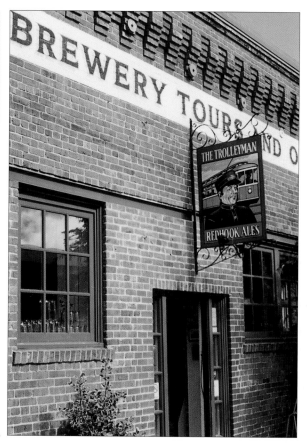

The Redhook Brewery in Seattle is one of the major North American craft breweries. Its original site is based in an old street car trolley shed.

Anheuser-Busch, the biggest brewer in the US, has taken a substantial share in Redhook and there are fears that some leading craft breweries could be swallowed by the giant breweries.

brew-pubs were (and still are) illegal in some states, and brewers with just enough cash to build a small brewery and sell their beer in an attached bar and restaurant have had to challenge the law in their states. It was only in 1997 that the state of New Jersey, for example, capitulated and agreed to permit brew-pubs to exist.

The craft brewing movement now seems unstoppable. In total it accounts for only two per cent of the beer made and sold in the US, but that proportion is much higher in California and the Pacific North-west. It is easier to find an Anchor Steam Beer than a Budweiser in San Francisco, while Portland, Oregon, and Seattle burst with an abundance of choice. The East Coast, especially in New York State and New

Bert Grant of Yakima Brewing in Washington State, produces a number of fine beers including India Pale Ale, Imperial Stout, Amber Ale, Perfect Porter, Scottish Ale and Hefe Weizen

Sierra Nevada in Chico, California brews several fine interpretations of English warm-fermented beer styles.

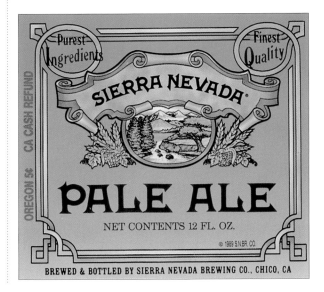

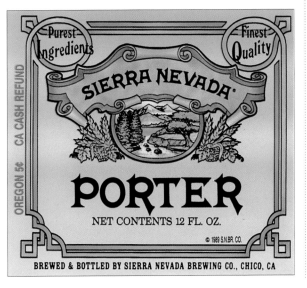

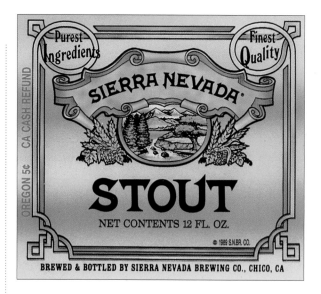

England, challenges the West Coast for choice and the number of small breweries. Chicago is a demi-paradise for beer lovers while Denver, Colorado, high in the Rockies, grows brew-pubs like mushrooms. The craft brewers' market share is expected to rise to ten per cent and will make them a major presence on the American beer scene.

Founded in 1981, Sierra Nevada has grown its sales by 50 per cent a year and now brews 200,000 barrels of ale and lager annually.

Anheuser-Busch, owners of Budweiser, and Miller have set up speciality brewing divisions to challenge the craft brewers. A-B uses the names Michelob and Elk Mountain for its own craft beers while Miller flies under the flag of American Specialty & Craft Beer Co. With amber ales, honey porters and bocks flowing from A-B and Miller, it is clear that the craft brewers have had an impact beyond mere sales. They have created a consumer backlash and a demand for beers with taste. The giants

Sierra Nevada carefully keeps ale and lager yeasts apart to avoid any cross-fertilization of its ales and lagers.

have had to respond to that demand or lose out in an important niche market. The worry for craft brewers is that A-B and Miller, with their vast marketing resources, can force smaller brewers out of business.

The craft brewers owe their existence to the pioneering work of Fritz Maytag, owner of the Anchor Brewing Company in San

Francisco. Maytag, a member of the wealthy washing-machine dynasty, enjoyed a local style called Steam Beer when he was a student at Stanford University. In 1965 he heard the brewery, the last producer of San Francisco Steam, was about to close. He cashed in some of his shares in the family business and bought the brewery. It was so run-down that it was using baker's yeast to ferment the beer. It took Maytag ten years to turn the company round. During that time he immersed himself in the skills of brewing, toured breweries in Britain and Europe and eventually built a brand-new plant in San Francisco with German vessels made to his demanding specifications. No one else can brew a San Francisco Steam Beer, for that is Maytag's copyright, but a legion of home brewers have been encouraged to go commercial as a result of his other brands, including the immensely hoppy Liberty Ale, a creamy Porter and a superb Old Foghorn barley wine.

The other pioneering influence is Bert Grant of Yakima Brewing in Washington state. His determination to make beers that burst with malt and hop character — a Scottish Ale, a Celtic Ale, India Pale Ale, Porter and Imperial Stout — has revolutionized brewing in the Pacific North-west. On the other side of the Cascade Mountains, Charles Finkel in Seattle moved from a wine merchant to a cult figure with his Pike Brewery where he brews with an impressive dedication to style, importing floor-malted Maris Otter malt and East Kent Goldings hops to give authenticity to his East India Pale Ale and Porter. Also in Seattle, Pyramid Brewing and Thomas Kemper Lagers, two jointly owned companies, have aggressively grown market share due to beautifully crafted ales, wheat beers and genuine lagers.

In California's university town of Chico,

Pete Slosberg upset some traditionalists with his heavily hyped ales and lagers and faux-naif labels but he has grown his Palo Alto business into one the major craft breweries in the United States.

238

the Sierra Nevada Brewing Co. has established a countrywide reputation for its ales and lagers. Founded in 1981 by Ken Grossman and Paul Camusi, the company has grown by fifty per cent a year, installed new brewing plant in 1987 and a decade later output reached 200,000 barrels a year. Its pale ale, porter and brilliant Big Foot barley wine have set the highest standards for craft brewing. In Palo Alto, Pete Slosberg has set the beer world alight with his range of Wicked Ales. His super-hype promotions have not pleased all beer lovers but he has overcome the criticism by the sheer brilliance of his Wicked Ale, Lager, Amber, Honey Wheat and Winter and Summer brews. The size of his operation – he is now arguably the biggest craft brewer in the US – has forced him to have his beers brewed under licence by the large brewing group Stroh. It is a tactic disliked by some small brewers but has been used with great success by Jim Koch, owner of the Boston Brewing Company in Boston, Massachusetts. Harvard-educated Koch, a descendant of immigrant Bavarian brewers, gave up a business career to start brewing in 1985. He sold his Samuel Adams Boston Lager bar-to-bar until he was sufficiently established to take on brewing and sales staff. He brews his lager, Boston Ale, Cream Stout and Wheat Beer in the former Haffenreffer Brewery in Boston and also under licence in plants carefully based throughout the country.

Elsewhere in New England, David Geary was one of the early pioneers of craft brewing with his Geary Brewing in Portland, Maine and superb Pale Ale. Geary learnt his skills in Britain, and his first plant was installed by Peter Austin, father of the British micro-brewing revolution. Geary worked for a time with Alan Pugsley, an English brewer and pupil of Peter Austin.

Alan Pugsley (left) learnt his brewing skills in England and joined forces with Fred Forsley to create Shipyard Brewing in Portland, Maine.

Shipyard has a full range of ales, including Old Thumper, based on a beer Pugsley first brewed in Hampshire in England.

Pugsley has since moved to become co-owner with Fred Forsley of the Shipyard Brewing Co., also in Portland, whose ales include pale ale, export ale, Longfellow Winter Ale and Old Thumper, a premium pale ale first brewed in England by Peter Austin's Ringwood Brewery.

The growth of brew-pubs continues apace. American entreprenuer John Hickenlooper, owner of the Wynkoop brew-pub in Denver, close to the railroad station, has joined forces with David Bruce, founder of the Firkin chain of brew-pubs in England. The Wynkoop, which includes cask-conditioned beers in its portfolio, is the biggest brew-pub in the US, and Hickenlooper and Bruce have pooled their resources to expand the operation throughout the country. The latest brew-pub opened in Jersey City late in 1997 while one at Niagara Falls has the aim of refreshing both Americans and Canadians.

In North Carolina Daniel Bradford's Top of the Hill brewery and restaurant bridges the gap between England and the US with an India Pale Ale, Pale Ale, Golden Ale, Extra Special Bitter, Porter and Stout. It is a gap Bradford is ideally placed to fill as his forebears came to North America on the *Mayflower*. For good measure Bradford (who is also the publisher of the influential *All About Beer* magazine) employs a British brewer, John Withey, former head brewer with Shepherd Neame in Kent.

The pace of the American brewing revolution is now so fast and its practitioners sufficiently mature that many are now embracing British cask-conditioned ales. In 1996 and 1997 the Craft Beer Institute in Chicago staged two festivals of American-brewed cask ales. The festivals have been packed with brewers determined to make the apotheosis of ale, the version that matures naturally in its own container.

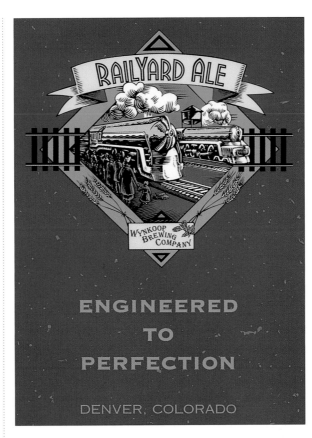

Railyard of Denver recalls the great days of the train. It is brewed by Wynkoop, a few yards from Denver Railroad station. John Hickenlooper of Wynkoop has joined forces with David Bruce from Britain, who founded the Firkin home brew-pub chain, to expand brew-pubs across the US.

AMERICAN BREWERS

Anchor Brewing Company
1705 Mariposa Street,
San Francisco CA 94107

Anheuser-Busch Inc
1 Busch Place,
St Louis MO 63118-1852

Boston Beer Company
30 Germania Street, Boston MA 02130

D.L. Geary Brewing Company
38 Evergreen Drive, Portland ME 04103

Grant's Yakima Brewing Company
1803 Presson Place, Yakima WA 98902

Miller Brewing Company
3939 W Highland Blvd, Milwaukee
WI 53208-2816

Pete's Wicked Brewing Company
514 High Street, Palo Alto CA 94301

Pike Brewing
1432 Western Avenue,
Seattle WA 622-1880

Pyramid Ales
91 S Royal Brougham Way,
Seattle WA 98134

Sierra Nevada Brewing Company
1075 East 20th Street,
Chico CA 95928

Top of the Hill
100 East Franklin Street,
Chapel Hill NC 27514

Wynkoop Pub and Brewery
1634 18th Street,
Denver CO 80202

Shipyard Brewing Company,
86 Newbury Street,
Portland ME 04101

4

THE PLEASURE OF BEER

THE WATCHWORD for this section is a simple one: think before you eat. It is all too easy to reach for the wine bottle, say 'red with meat, white with fish' and assume you have the best companions for food. But long before the beer-drinking nations of the world became obsessed with wine, beer was the natural drink at the dining-table or with rustic food served in country cottage or field. When the British were at war with the French (and there have been long periods of history when the British were constantly at war with the French), even the aristocracy abandoned claret in favour of home-produced ale or cider, served from the finest cut-glass tumblers.

FOOD

First, an aperitif – we need to get the gastric juices moving, the taste-buds set up to appreciate food. This is not too easy to find these days, but the nutty sweetness of an English mild ale is a fine way to cleanse the palate. A Belgian 'white' or wheat beer, such as the famous Hoegaarden, spicy, aromatic and only lightly hopped, is a good alternative. For those who like something tarter, who prefer a gin and tonic to a sherry, the stunningly hoppy Jever from northern Germany, with its almost quinine-like finish, should prove highly acceptable. Champagne drinkers would approve of a framboise, the raspberry version of Belgian lambic. For those who prefer a Scotch whisky, a smoked German Rauchbier or a French or Austrian lager made from peated malt will fit the bill.

While wine is notoriously difficult to match with soup, beer hits the spot: perhaps a robust Belgian Trappist ale or a well-hopped British pale ale. A Belgian kriek (cherry) beer, dry and shockingly sour, would be ideal for beetroot soup.

Meat dishes cry out for beers that are packed with aroma and flavour. Pale ale has already been mentioned. Other contenders would be the new-wave pale ales of North America, the hoppy ales of Belgium and the powerful, vinous Trappist ales from the same country. Sweeter meats – pork or lamb – are well balanced by dark lagers, such as Munich Dunkel, a Vienna 'red' or a Mexican interpretation of the Viennese style, exemplified by Dos Equis or Negra Modelo. Sausage is synonymous with German beer: Müncheners drink wheat beer with white sausage and a strong Bock or an Alt ale from Düsseldorf would go well with darker versions.

Smoked fish needs the balance of smoked beers, which is where the German Rauchbiers come into play again. White fish

Whichever way you slice it, beer makes a brilliant companion for all food styles. A dark mild, stout or German Bock goes well with the rich fruitiness of cake.

should not be overwhelmed by beery flavours, and a genuine Czech Pilsner, malty, toffeeish but with a perfumy hop character, is a superb companion – though the natives would think it better suited to pork and dumplings. At Christmas time, both Czechs and Bavarians drink dark lager with carp.

Ale goes very well with cheese. Jan de Bruyn, who runs the splendid beer café in Bruges, 't Brugs Beertje, will happily marry a Belgian ale with every variety of cheese made in the country. As the Trappist monks of Belgium also make cheese for sale, it goes without saying that Chimay, Rochefort or Orval ales are the perfect match for their soft creamy cheeses. In England, the harder and more robust styles of cheese, such as

Cheddar and Stilton, demand hoppy and aromatic pale ales.

For puddings, we need beers with less hop attack and more sweetness. Darker beers, such as German Bocks, Vienna lagers or English and Irish stouts that use dark or chocolate malts, bring out the best in dishes in which chocolate itself is used. Belgian fruit beers, using cherries, raspberries, peaches and banana, come into their own when they accompany dishes using the same fruits.

And finally, a digestif. A rich and warming Thomas Hardy's Ale, a Belgian Trappist, a German Bock or strong dark wheat beer such as Schneider's Aventinus will see you happily off to bed.

BREWERS' BREAKFAST

rewers throughout the world start work ealy in the morning. In Britain a 6 o'clock start is common and by eight o'clock the smells of mashing malt and boiling hops will have got the brewers' gastric juices working and ready for the feast that follows two hours of hard early morning work. I was an invited guest at a brewers' breakfast at the Mansfield Brewery in the eponymous Nottinghamshire town where the eight o'clock feast has not altered since Victorian times. It amounts to a massive fry-up, a great burst of carbohydrate to keep the brewing staff going until they finish their shift in the late afternoon. The groaning plates were made up of grilled

tomatoes, fried eggs, mushrooms, locally cured bacon and Southwell Minster pie with hop sausages and hop bread, both flavoured with Deakin's Wild Boar Ale and seasoned with crushed hops; vegetarian sausages were also available. Gallons of tea were consumed but before we sat down to eat we were given cups of hot wort straight from the mash tuns. This is the sweet sugary extract that is the result of mashing the malt with pure hot water. It is malty and biscuity, wonderfully reviving and, most important, proves that the first stage of brewing is progressing well. The hot wort came fortified with an optional raw egg. Beer was available for those hardy souls who could face

it that early in the morning: it came in the shape of Deakin's Wild Boar and Riding Mild. It is the tradition for brewers to have a small glass of Guinness stout with their breakfast.

Early riser. . .Mansfield head brewer Richard Westwood gets a raw egg in a glass of his sweet wort.

RECIPES

Beer goes so well with so many foods and it is also a versatile ingredient in the kitchen. The following are a selection of recipes which demonstrate just that – be sure to accompany the dishes with the same beer used in the cooking.

KENTISH BEER SOUP

This recipe was inspired by a similar dish in the book *Cooking with Beer*. It calls for Bishop's Finger Strong pale ale, brewed by Shepherd Neame of Faversham in the heart of the Kent hop fields. If this is unavailable, substitute any well-hopped pale ale.

Serves 4
1 onion, chopped
1 garlic clove, crushed
50g/2oz butter
3 small apples, preferably Cox's, peeled and chopped
500g/1lb potatoes, scrubbed and chopped
500ml (15 fl oz) Bishop's Finger
700ml/1pint chicken or vegetable stock
½ teaspoon allspice
Pinch of sugar
Salt and freshly ground black pepper
Small handful each finely chopped fresh parsley and chives, for serving

Melt the butter in a large casserole. Add the onion and garlic and cook, over low heat, until just softened. Stir in the apples and potatoes and cook for a further 2-3 minutes. Season to taste with salt and pepper. Raise the heat and add the pale ale, stock, allspice and sugar. Bring to the boil, skim off any foam that rises to the top, then reduce the heat to low and simmer, covered, until the potatoes are tender, about 30 minutes. Liquidize the soup, then check the seasoning. Before serving, stir in the finely chopped parsley and chives.

CREME DE CHICONS A LA BIERE BLANCHE

This dish (Cream of Chicory Soup with Wheat Beer) hails from Belgium, a country of both fine beer and fine cuisine. This recipe was taken from the *Belgo Cookbook* by Denis Blais and André Plisnier, which celebrates Belgian gastronomy.

Serves 4
4 heads of chicory
50g/2oz butter
1 small onion, thinly sliced
4 large potatoes, quartered
50g/2oz brown sugar
1 bouquet garni
300ml/½ pint wheat beer
1 litre/1¾ pints chicken stock or water
Pinch of grated nutmeg
Salt and freshly ground black pepper
250ml/8 fl oz double cream

Cut the chicory in half lengthways and cut out the cores. Slice thinly. Melt the butter in a saucepan, add the onion and cook for 1 minute. Add the chicory, potatoes, sugar and bouquet garni and cook over a low heat for 15 minutes. Add the beer, stock or water, nutmeg and season to taste. Simmer gently for about 1 hour. Remove the bouquet garni and liquidize in a blender or pass through a food mill. Return the soup to the saucepan, add the cream and bring back to the boil. Taste for seasoning and serve hot.

MUSSELS WITH BEER

This is a classic Belgian dish, so try it with a Trappist ale, a Belgian pale ale such as De Koninck or Palm or a hoppy lager such as Cristal Alken.

Serves 2
1 bottle of beer
2 sticks of celery, finely chopped
1 onion, finely chopped
1 clove garlic, crushed
1kg/2.2lb live mussels, cleaned
Salt and freshly ground black pepper
Small handful finely chopped fresh parsley
Crusty French bread, for serving

Put the celery, onion, and garlic in a large saucepan. Add the mussels, then pour over the beer. Turn the heat on high and bring to the boil. Cook only for a few minutes, just until the mussels begin to open. You can remove the mussels as they open, leaving the others to steam a bit longer, until the shells open. Do not overcook or the mussels will be rubbery; discard any mussels that do not open. Ladle the mussels and cooking juices into shallow soup bowls, season to taste and sprinkle with the chopped parsley. Serve with plenty of bread.

VEGETARIAN MUSHROOM CREOLE WITH BARLEY WINE

This is an English recipe: a strong fruity ale or a German Bock can replace the barley wine.

Serves 4

500g/1lb button mushrooms
3 medium onions, sliced
1 each red, green and yellow peppers, cored, seeded and sliced
1 large tin chopped plum tomatoes
1 teaspoon chopped fresh rosemary
1 teaspoon ground cinnamon
1 teaspoon mixed spice
1 small tin pineapple chunks in juice
1 teaspoon caster sugar
50g/2oz creamed and grated coconut
Salt and freshly ground black pepper
3 tablespoons sunflower oil
700ml/1pint barley wine
2-3 tbsp double cream (optional)

Heat the oil in a heavy-bottomed casserole. Add the onions and cook over low heat until softened. Add all other ingredients except the mushrooms and diced peppers. Simmer gently for about 15 minutes. Add the mushrooms and peppers and cook for a further 10 minutes. Season to taste. Stir in the cream if using. Serve immediately, with plain boiled rice.

CARBONNADE FLAMANDE

This is a classic dish from the Flanders region and is popular throughout Belgium. The recipe is just a blueprint and is essentially a good excuse to experiment with beer in cooking. Try it with a Belgian brown ale such as Liefman's Goudenband, a Trappist or Abbey ale, an English brown or pale ale, an Irish dry stout, an American pale ale, brown ale or Scotch ale, a chocolatey Belgian ale such as Gouden Carolus or a German Dunkel or Bock – to name a few.

Serves 4

2 tbsp vegetable oil
1 tbsp butter
1kg/2lb chuck steak, trimmed and cut into large cubes
1 onion, chopped
1 tbsp flour
1 tbsp tomato purée
700ml/1 pint beer, plus beef or vegetable stock (optional)
Salt and freshly ground black pepper
2 teaspoons brown sugar
1 bay leaf
Few sprigs fresh thyme or 1 teaspoon dried

Heat the oil and butter in a large heavy-bottomed casserole. Add the meat and brown on all sides. Remove the meat with a slotted spoon and transfer to a plate. Add the onion and cook until just golden, then stir in the flour and mix well. Add the tomato purée and the browned meat and stir well. Season to taste. Pour in the beer, adding some stock or water if necessary to completely cover the meat. Stir in the sugar and herbs. Bring to the boil, skim off any foam that rises to the top, then simmer gently until the meat is very tender, about 1½ hours. The flavour will improve if allowed to stand, in the refrigerator, overnight. Reheat before serving.

RYBA NA CERNO (FISH IN BLACK SAUCE)

This is a traditional Czech dish so use a good Budweiser, Pilsner or Prague beer, pale or dark.

Serves 4

2 teaspoons pickling spice
1 teaspoon dried thyme
2 bay leaves
2 garlic cloves, crushed
700ml/1 pint water
150ml/5 fl oz white wine vinegar
2 small onions, thinly sliced
1 stalk celery, diced
12 prunes, sliced
4 carp, or other white fish, fillets
2 teaspoons salt
1 teaspoon ground ginger
8 crushed gingersnaps
700ml/1 pint beer
2 tablespoons lemon juice
2 tablespoons brown sugar
50g/2oz seedless raisins
2oz/50g sliced almonds

Place the pickling spice, thyme, bay leaves and garlic in a small square of muslin cloth and tie to enclose the spices. Place in a deep saucepan with the water, vinegar, onions and celery. Bring to the boil, then simmer gently for 30 minutes. Meanwhile, in a small saucepan, cook the prunes in boiling water for 20 minutes. Add the fish to the spiced water and stir in the salt and ginger. Cook over a low heat for 30 minutes. While the fish is cooking, soak the gingersnaps in the beer. Discard the bag of spices, then add the gingersnaps and beer, along with the lemon juice, sugar, raisins, almonds and prunes (undrained). Cook for a further 10 minutes before serving.

BLAZING SADDLES STEW

From the American midwest, this is a hearty beer-based chilli worthy of cowboys and ranch hands after a long day in the saddle. Use an American brown ale or steam beer for the cooking, and the serving. A vegetarian alternative can be made by adding another tin of beans and some quarterd mushrooms in place of the meat. If you have a recipe for American corn bread, it would make a nice accompaniment.

Serves 4–6
500g/1lb chuck steak, thinly sliced
3 tbsp vegetable oil
1 large onion, sliced
2 stalks celery, sliced
1 red pepper, sliced
3 garlic cloves, crushed
Salt and freshly ground black pepper
1 teaspoon crushed chillis, or to taste
2 teaspoons ground cumin
2 teaspoons dried oregano
1 bay leaf
2 tbsp molasses, or dark brown sugar
700ml/1 pint beer
1 small tin chopped Italian tomatoes
2 tins red kidney beans, drained

Heat the oil in a large heavy-bottomed casserole and add the meat, onions, celery and red pepper. Cook, stirring often, until the meat is browned and the vegetables begin to soften. Add the garlic, season to taste and cook for 1 minute. Stir in the remaining ingredients, adding more water (or beer) as necessary to cover. Bring to the boil, then lower the heat, cover and simmer gently for 30 minutes. Remove the lid and continue simmering for a further 15 minutes, or until some of the excess liquid evaporates. Do not allow the stew to become too dry. Taste for seasoning and remove the bay leaf before serving.

COUCOU DE MALINES A LA MOINETTE

Also known as Poussin with Beer, Cream and Mustard Sauce, this dish is exceptionally delicious and delicate, and demonstrates that beer can be a very refined addition in the kitchen. Pan-fried salmon steaks are a tasty alternative to the poussin. This recipe was also taken from the *Belgo Cookbook* by Denis Blais and André Plisnier.

Serves 2
1 poussin, about 1kg/2.2lb
Salt and freshly ground black pepper
Softened unsalted butter
200ml/7 fl oz Moinette beer
250 ml/8 fl oz double cream
2 teaspoons Dijon mustard
Celeriac purée
½ celeriac, peeled and cubed
25g/1oz butter

Preheat the oven to 190°C/375°F/Gas Mark 5. Rub the poussin all over with butter, season inside and out and roast for about 45 minutes, or until cooked through. Meanwhile make the pureé. Bring a large saucepan of water to the boil, add celeriac and cook until just tender, 15–20 minutes. Drain and set aside. For the sauce, mix half the beer with half the cream and the mustard; set aside. When the poussin is cooked, remove from the oven and leave to rest while you finish the dish. Purée or mash the celeriac and reheat gently with the butter, taste for seasoning; set aside. Pour remaining beer into the roasting pan set over medium heat and stir, scraping to loosen the juices. Bring to the boil, add the remaining cream and simmer gently for 2 minutes. Remove from the heat and whisk in the mustard mixture. Cut the poussin in half down the middle and put each half on a serving plate, with the celeriac purée and the sauce poured over.

RASPBERRY BEER SORBET

This recipe calls for raspberry beer and raspberry purée, but you can make as many sorbets as there are flavours of fruit beer. Cherry and peach are particularly successful. To make raspberry purée, simply blend some fresh or defrosted frozen raspberries and pass through a fine sive to remove the seeds. This recipe was also taken from the *Belgo Cookbook* by Denis Blais and André Plisnier.

Serves 4
200g/7oz caster sugar
85ml/3 fl oz raspberry kriek
100ml/3½ fl oz raspberry purée
Sprigs of fresh mint, for serving

Put the sugar in a saucepan with 200g/7 fl oz water and bring to the boil. Boil for 2 minutes, then remove from the heat and leave to cool. Mix the cooled syrup with the beer and fruit purée and freeze in an ice-cream maker according to manufacturer's instructions. When the sorbet is firm, transfer to a freezer container and freeze until needed. Serve with sprigs of fresh mint.

CHOCOLATE AND STOUT CAKE

This recipe was devised by top British chef Gary Rhodes with Tate & Lyle, who supply many breweries with specialist brewing sugars. The recipe is used with the kind permission of Tate & Lyle.

Serves 8–10
300g/9oz plain flour
1 teaspoon baking powder
1 tablespoon bicarbonate of soda
250g/8oz unsalted butter
500g/1lb Tate & Lyle light brown soft cane sugar
4 eggs
400ml/14 fl oz stout
100g/4oz cocoa powder, sifted

For the icing:
100g/4oz plain chocolate, finely chopped
2 tablespoons strong coffee
100g/4oz unsalted butter

Preheat the oven to 180°C/350°F/Gas Mark 4. Butter and line the base of a 20cm/8inch cake tin with greaseproof paper. Sift together the flour, baking soda and bicarbonate of soda. Cream the butter and sugar until light and fluffy. Add the eggs one at a time, beating well between each addition. Whisk the stout and cocoa together and beat one-third of this mixture into the butter, followed by a third of the flour mixture. Continue alternating the mixes until thoroughly blended and a soft consistency is formed. Pour into the tin and bake for 30-35 minutes, or until cooked through. Cool before turning out. For the icing, melt the chocolate and coffee together in a bowl set over a pan of simmering water. Remove from heat and beat until smooth, then add the butter. Beat well until glossy and a good spreading consistency is achieved. Spread the icing on top of the cooled cake and serve.

Ushers of Trowbridge, Wiltshire, has produced three ales specifically designed to complement food.

PREPARING A BEER TASTING

One fascinating and fulfilling way to appreciate beer, its styles and its flavours to the full is to organize a tasting in your home with a group of friends and beer-lovers. You may decide to stick to one style, such as pale ale or Pilsner lager, or you may decide to taste a variety of styles.

Preparation is vital to the success of the event. You will need sufficient beer to satisfy all the tasters, who may wish to go back and taste a beer they had earlier in the event. If you buy beer in half pint/300ml bottles you should get sufficient from each bottle for three small tastings. If your guests want a full half-pint of each beer, then you will need more stocks.

If you buy all the beer from one stockist, they may loan you beer glasses for the event. Over the course of years of beer appreciation, you will probably have built up a stock of glasses. You can easily buy small plastic cups, which I often use for public beer tastings, but they are less appealing than glasses. Although a traditional straight Pilsner glass, an English pint or a large, fluted wheat beer glass adds to the appreciation of beer, whatever is to hand will do as well. My own preference is for a large red wine glass, ideal both for holding a good measure of beer and to allow you to swirl the beer to release the aroma. A stemmed glass is always best for beer tasting and appreciation: the greatest enemy of good beer is the human hand. Clasped round a glass, the warmth of the hand is transferred to the beer. What the British call 'a jug' – a beer glass with a handle – is better than a glass without a handle.

The temperature of beer is critical to the success of a tasting. All beer should be served cool: the myth of 'warm' British beer is just that – myth. The only beers that should be served at room temperature are

Glass and bottle must be held at the right level to create a good collar of foam.

strong barley wines and old ales which, as a result of their spicy and vinous aromas and flavours, should be served '*chambré*'. All other beers should be stored in a refrigerator. The length of time will depend on individual fridges, and you will have to experiment to see how long it takes for ales and lagers to reach the desired levels.

The ideal serving temperature for ales is 11–12°C (52–54°F), while for lager it should be 6–8°C (46–48°F). Ales will need about two hours in a fridge before serving, lagers four hours and, ideally, overnight. Beer is a robust product but it should be chilled slowly rather than placed in the freezer compartment for half an hour. Most beers can either be laid flat or stood up in the fridge, but bottle-conditioned ales must stand upright to avoid disturbing the sediment of yeast. Only remove the beers from the fridge as you need them, as they will warm up quickly. If you have too many beers to get into a fridge, you will have to place the

All beer should be kept and served cool; 'warm' ale is a myth.

bottles in buckets of ice. In cold weather, I find that keeping beer in an unheated conservatory keeps it at a good cool temperature.

When opening bottle-conditioned ales or wheat beers, it is a good idea to remove the caps carefully a few minutes before serving to allow some of the natural carbon dioxide to vent off. When pouring, hold glass and bottle at eye level, with the mouth

A large wine glass allows the beer to be swirled to release the aroma.

should note the name of the beer and then allow the tasters to give marks out of ten for appearance (clarity), aroma, palate and finish. The marks should be totalled at the foot of each sheet. If you are tasting a specific style, say porter and stout, you may wish to add an additional mark for 'colour'. A tasting with marking works only if you are drinking beers within one style: you cannot compare or mark such disparate styles as stout and Pilsner. The aim of a semi-professional tasting is to determine which beer within a certain style is considered the best.

Clean the palate between different beers with plain bread and cheese. If you provide crisps (potato chips) for your guests, use only the unflavoured variety – pickled onion or salt-and-vinegar crisps will not help discerning drinkers appreciate the more delicate flavours of beer. Cheese is a brilliant companion for beer, the biscuity nature of malt and the acidity of hops in the beer blending well with and cutting the creamy, milky, tart and pungent flavours of different varieties of cheese.

of the bottle close to or resting on the rim of the angled glass. As beer and foam run into the glass, slowly reduce the angle of the glass to the vertical: this will ensure the beer doesn't foam too much and you will get all the beer into the glass. If a beer has sediment, stop pouring when you see the yeasty deposit approaching the neck of the bottle. The traditional Bavarian method of serving a yeasty wheat beer is to rotate the bottle while lowering the glass to the vertical and then finally tipping the deposit into the beer. Unless you demand a perfectly clear beer, the deposit will do you no harm as it is full of minerals and proteins.

When the tasting begins, encourage the participants to sniff the aroma before drinking. You will detect, depending on the style, malt and hoppy aromas with a fruitiness generated by fermentation and implanted by the yeast. As the beer warms up, hop character will develop and so will the fruitiness of an ale. Let the beer pass slowly over the tongue as different parts of this most sensitive of organs detect sweetness, saltiness and bitterness. Finally, allow the

beer to slip down the back of the tongue to appreciate the aftertaste or 'finish'. This is an important stage of a tasting because a beer that begins hoppy on the aroma may end with more malt character on the finish, or vice versa.

If you run a tasting in a fully professional way, you will need tasting sheets. Each sheet

The tongue detects sweetness, saltiness and bitterness as the beer passes over this most sensitive of organs.

THE LANGUAGE OF BEER

Abbey: commercial Belgian beer styled to resemble a Trappist Ale, often licensed by a non-brewing monastery.

Adjuncts: materials used to augment barley malt, such as rice, maize (corn), torrefied grains and wheat. Many British and Belgian brewers also use forms of brewing sugar.

Alcohol by Volume (ABV): the standard measurement used in most countries to measure the strength of beer. In the US, the measurement used is Alcohol by Weight, though brewers are not required to declare strength. Both ABV and ABW are given for American beers.

Ale: a beer made by warm fermentation.

Alt: German for 'old', a beer from Düsseldorf, member of the ale family.

Attenuation: the extent to which the brewing sugars turn to alcohol during the fermentation process.

Beer: generic name for all types of alcohol made from cereals.

Bière de Garde: French ale, meaning 'keeping beer', origins in rural farmhouse ales.

Bitter: British term for well-hopped and usually copper-coloured draught ales.

Bock or Bok: strong beer style of Germany and the Netherlands, either cold or warm fermented. Extra strong versions are known as Dobbelbock.

Bottle-conditioned: beer that undergoes a secondary fermentation in the bottle.

Bottom-fermentation: inaccurate but widely used term to describe lager fermentation.

Burtonise: addition of salts (mainly gypsum and Epsom) to harden brewing liquor and replicate the waters of Burton-on-Trent.

Campaign for Real Ale (Camra): British consumer organization that campaigns for traditional draught (cask-conditioned) ale.

Cask-conditioned: beer that undergoes a secondary fermentation in the cask. Identified principally with British ales and popularly known as 'real ale'.

Copper: vessel, also known as a brew kettle, where the sugary extract or wort is boiled with hops.

Decoction mash: system used mainly in European lager brewing to deal with poorer quality and less modified barley malts. Parts of the mash are heated at a higher temperature and then returned to the original vessel. Method allows saccharification to take place to turn starch into sugar.

Dry-hopping: mainly British practice of addition of a handful of hops to casks of finished beer to improve aroma and bitterness.

Dunkel: German dark lager.

EBC: European Beer Convention that indicates colour of malts.

Ester: flavour compounds produced by the action of yeast turning sugars into alcohol and carbon dioxide. Esters may be fruity or spicy and are found predominantly in ales and some strong lagers of the Bok style.

Fining: substance that clarifies beer, usually made from the swim bladder of the sturgeon (isinglass) or Irish moss (carageen).

Framboise/frambozen: a raspberry-flavoured lambic beer.

Grist: coarse powder, the result of milling or 'cracking' grain in a mill in the brewery prior to mashing.

Gueuze: blended Belgian lambic beer.

Helles/Hell: pale Bavarian lager or wheat beer.

IBU: International Units of Bitterness, a scale that measures the bitterness of beer.

Infusion: method of mashing grain, principally used in ale brewing: grains of malt and other cereals are left to soak in hot pure water while enzymes convert starch to sugar.

Kölsch: ale-type golden beer brewed only in Cologne, Germany.

Kräusen: the addition of partially fermented or unfermented sugary wort to a lager tank to encourage a second fermentation.

Kriek: cherry-flavoured lambic beer.

Lager: German word meaning 'storage': the cold-conditioning of beer to encourage yeast to settle out and increase carbonation.

Lambic: Belgian beer made by wild or spontaneous fermentation.

Lauter tun: vessel with slotted base used to separate spent cereal grains from the sugary extract.

Liquor: brewers' term for pure water used for mashing.

Malt: barley and wheat that have been partially germinated and then heated to allow starches to be converted into fermentable sugars.

Mash: first stage of brewing process where malt is mixed with hot water or 'liquor' to extract sugars. Mashing takes place in mash tun or mash kettle.

Märzen: March beer, traditionally brewed in Munich and stored (lagered) until the Oktoberfest.

Mild: dark brown (occasionally pale) English and Welsh beer, lightly hopped. Known as 'light' in Scotland.

Milk Stout: stout made with the addition of unfermentable lactose.

Pilsner: beer originally brewed in Pilsen, Bohemia, Czech Republic: the first golden lager. Elsewhere spelt Pilsener or shortened to Pils.

Porter: dark ale first brewed in London and known as entire or entire butt, name changed as a result of popularity with street porters.

Priming: addition of sugar to cask or bottle to encourage a second fermentation.

Reinheitsgebot: Bavarian 'Pure Beer Law' of 1516 that stipulates that only malt, hops, yeast and water can be used to brew beer.

Saison: warm-fermented beer style associated with rural French-speaking areas of Belgium: similar to French bière de garde.

Schwarzbier: literally Black Beer, a dark lager associated with Franconia and Thuringia in Germany.

Scotch Ale: strong warm-fermented ale associated with Scotland, popular in Belgium and frequently brewed by American craft brewers.

Shilling: ancient method of invoicing beer in Scotland based on strength: hence 60 Shilling, 70 Shilling ales and so on.

Sparging: sprinkling or spraying wort in the mash tun or lauter tun to flush out remaining malt sugars. From French *esparger*, meaning to sprinkle.

Square: traditional open fermenting vessel.

Steam Beer: hybrid ale-cum-lager associated with San Francisco.

Stout: the strongest form of porter.

Top fermentation: inaccurate but widely used term to describe ale fermentation.

Trappist: ales brewed by Trappist monks in Belgium and Netherlands.

Union: wooden casks linked or 'held in union' in which ale ferments. Associated with Burton-on-Trent.

Ur or Urtyp: German for 'original', used to define a beer that is either typical of a brewery's style or its original brand. 'Urquell', as in Pilsner Urquell, means original source or original spring.

Weizen/weisse: German term for wheat or white beer. Wit in Flemish.

Wort: sugary extract produced by the mashing system.

SOURCES

T.R Gourvish and R.G. Wilson, *The British Brewing Industry 1830–1980* (Cambridge, 1994).

H.S. Corran, *A History of Brewing* (Newton Abbot, 1975).

Graham Lees, *Camra Good Beer Guide to Munich & Bavaria* (St Albans, 1994).

Michael Jackson, *Michael Jackson's Beer Companion* (London, 1993 & 1997).

Michael Jackson, *The Great Beers of Belgium* (Antwerp, 1991 & 1997).

Tim Webb, *Camra Good Beer Guide to Belgium & Holland* (St Albans, 1995).

Graham Wheeler, *Home Brewing, the Camra Guide* (St Albans, 1993).

INDEX

PHOTO CREDITS
Page 240 Brueghel: A
Peasant Wedding/Bridgeman
Art Libray, London;
Nicholas Redman; the
Whitbread Archive; the
Guinness Archive; the
Bass Museum; Tuckers'
Maltings; Steve Sharples
(barley; Rupert Ponsonby
(hops); Anthony Lambert
(river scene); Ted Bruning
(Bass Museum micro-
brewery); Mike Benner
(studio shots); Cressida
Feiler (beer tasting). All
other photographers are
taken by the author or
supplied by breweries.